15

29200

*The Duty of Discontent*

# The Duty of Discontent

## ESSAYS FOR
## DOROTHY THOMPSON

---

EDITED BY

OWEN ASHTON, ROBERT FYSON
AND STEPHEN ROBERTS

MANSELL

First published 1995 by
Mansell Publishing Limited, *A Cassell imprint*
Wellington House, 125 Strand, London WC2R 0BB, England
215 Park Avenue South, New York, New York 10003, USA

**British Library Cataloguing in Publication Data**
A catalgue record for this book is available from the British Library

**Library of Congress Cataloging-in-Publication Data**
The duty of discontent : essays for Dorothy Thompson / edited by Owen
Ashton, Robert Fyson, and Stephen Roberts.
    p.   cm.
    Includes bibliographical references (p.     ) and index.
    ISBN 0–7201–2201–5
    1. Chartism   2. Women—Great Britain—History.   3. Thompson,
Dorothy, 1923–   .   I. Thompson, Dorothy, 1923–   .   II. Ashton,
Owen R.   III. Fyson, Robert.   IV. Roberts, Stephen, 1950–   .
HD8396.D87   1996
301—dc20                                                    95–12596
                                                                CIP

Frontispiece photograph by Hopcraft of Worcester

Printed and bound in Great Britain by Biddles Ltd,
Guildford and King's Lynn
Typeset by Chapter One (London)

# Contents

# CONTENTS

# Notes on Contributors

OWEN ASHTON is a Principal Lecturer in the Division of History, School of Arts, at Staffordshire University. He is the author of various articles on Chartism and of *W.E. Adams: Chartist, Radical and Journalist (1832–1906)* (1991); and co-editor of *The Chartist Movement: A New Annotated Bibliography* (1995).

CLIVE BEHAGG teaches History at the Chichester Institute of Higher Education, where he holds a Personal Chair. His publications include *Politics and Production in the Early Nineteenth Century* (1990), and *Labour and Reform: Working Class Movements 1815–1914* (1991).

JOHN BELCHEM is Reader in History at the University of Liverpool and is currently Secretary of the Society for the Study of Labour History. He is the author of *'Orator' Hunt: Henry Hunt and English Working-Class Radicalism* (1985), *Industrialization and the Working Class: The English Experience, 1750–1900* (1990), and *Popular Radicalism in the Nineteenth Century* (1995).

CARL CHINN gained his Ph.D. at the University of Birmingham in 1986. Now Community Historian and Lecturer in Modern History at the University of Birmingham, a post part-funded by Birmingham City Council, he is author of *They Worked All Their Lives: Women of the Urban Poor in England 1880–1939* (1988), *Better Betting with a Decent Feller: Bookmakers, Betting and the British Working Class 1750–1990* (1991), and *Birmingham: The Great Working City* (1994).

JAMES EPSTEIN teaches History at Vanderbilt University, Nashville, Tennessee. He is the author of *The Lion of Freedom: Feargus O'Connor and the Chartist Movement, 1832–1842* (1982) and co-editor of *The Chartist Experience: Studies in Working-Class Radicalism and Culture, 1830–1860* (1982). He has recently published *Radical Expression: Political Language, Ritual, and Symbol in England, 1790–1850* (1994).

ROBERT FYSON, formerly Senior Lecturer in History, is now an Honorary Research Associate in the School of Arts at Staffordshire University. He contributed to *The Chartist Experience: Studies in Working-Class Radicalism and Culture, 1830–1860* (1982) and *British Trade Unionism 1750–1850: The Formative Years* (1988); and he is co-editor of *The Chartist Movement: A New Annotated Bibliography* (1995).

ANGELA V. JOHN is Professor of History at the University of Greenwich. She is the author of a number of books and articles, including *By The Sweat of Their Brow: Women Workers at Victorian Coal Mines*, (1980 and 1984), *Unequal Opportunities: Women's Employment in England 1800–1918* (1986), and *Elizabeth Robins: Staging A Life* (1995). She is Chairperson of *Llafur*, the Society for Welsh Labour History. Her decision in the late 1960s to pursue postgraduate study was largely prompted by having been taught by Dorothy Thompson at the University of Birmingham.

NEVILLE KIRK is Reader in Economic and Social History at Manchester Metropolitan University. In 1987 he was Visiting Associate Professor at Yale. He studied at Birmingham, Warwick and Pittsburgh Universities, gaining his Ph.D. at the latter in 1974. He has published two books: *The Growth of Working Class Reformism in Mid-Victorian England* (1985) and *Labour and Society in Britain and the USA 1780–1939* (1994).

GLEN MATTHEWS is a Lecturer at Evesham College, a Visiting Lecturer at Worcester College of Higher Education and a part-time tutor with the Open University.

STEPHEN ROBERTS was taught, as both an undergraduate and postgraduate, by Dorothy Thompson at the University of Birmingham. He is a Fellow of the Institute for Advanced Research in the Humanities in the University of Birmingham, and also teaches History and Law at Hagley R.C. High School. He is the author of various articles on Chartism and of *Radical Politicians and Poets in Early Victorian England: The Voices of Six Chartist*

*Leaders* (1993) and co-editor of *The Chartist Movement: A New Annotated Bibliography* (1995).

L.D. SMITH has spent most of his professional career as a mental health social worker. He gained his Ph.D. in 1982, and subsequently published two books on the Kidderminster carpet weavers in the industrial revolution. His more recent research has focused on psychiatry and the asylum in eighteenth- and nineteenth-century England, on which he has published a number of articles. A Fellow of the Institute for Advanced Research in the Humanities in the University of Birmingham, he was awarded in 1994–5 a Research Fellowship by the Wellcome Trust.

KATE TILLER began her research career at the University of Birmingham where, supervised by Dorothy Thompson, she completed her Ph.D. on working-class politics in the post-Chartist period. Since 1979 she has been in charge of extramural courses in local and social history at Oxford University Department for Continuing Education, where she is University Lecturer in Local History. She has pioneered part-time degree work in Oxford and is Senior Tutor of Kellogg College, Oxford's newest college. Her publications include work on Chartism and nineteenth-century religious dissent. Her *English Local History: An Introduction* was published in 1992 and she was editor of *The Local Historian* from 1983 to 1988.

# *Preface*

'The Duty of Discontent', the title of a lecture given by the
Chartist-poet Thomas Cooper in 1853,[1] seemed to us to be an
appropriate title for this volume of essays in honour of Dorothy
Thompson. Dorothy's historical writings, as well as her campaigning political activities on the left and in the peace movement, have always been informed by a passionate radicalism,
sympathy for the underdog, and a critical approach to conventional orthodoxies, of the Victorian age as of her own lifetime.
This general stance has underlain her position as the leading
historian of Chartism, and her contributions to Irish and
women's history, including a notably irreverent study of Queen
Victoria. Her major historical concerns, like the essays offered
here, have indeed been with 'Outsiders'. In her treatment of, for
example, class, gender and nation, she has, sometimes at vari-
ance with current intellectual fashions, resolutely pursued her
own independent paths of enquiry.

The contributors to this collection are all either former research
students whose work was supervised by Dorothy at the University of Birmingham, or scholars who have benefited from her
advice and encouragement. As a teacher and supervisor, her
interest in her students was genuine and unforced. The warm
hospitality, ready sharing of information and suggestions for
lines of approach by both Dorothy and Edward Thompson, at
what Dorothy has referred to as the 'Thompson academic
factory' at Wick Episcopi, have been a solace and inspiration for
her students, friends and fellow-historians for many years.

This collection is offered in recognition and appreciation
of Dorothy Thompson's work, influence and friendship. We
should add that Professor David J.V. Jones, Department of

History, University College, Swansea, had intended to contribute to this volume: his untimely death in October 1994
deprived not only us, but also the world of social history, of an
important scholar and friend.

## NOTE

1    Stoke-on-Trent, Hanley Reference Library, Thomas Cooper Papers,
     Lecture, 6 February 1853.

# Setting the Standard:
# Dorothy Thompson, the Discipline of
# History and the Study of Chartism

NEVILLE KIRK

Increased sensitivity and attention to the thoughts and actions of the Other—especially the feminine, ethnic and black Others long deemed by those in the academic mainstream to be 'the incidental, the inessential as opposed to the essential'—have been marked features of transatlantic history writing and social and cultural theory during the past.[1] This enhanced focus and awareness has issued from the convergence of a host of social and cultural factors. Prominent among the latter have been the following: post-1950s feminism; the growth of multi-cultural and multi-ethnic societies; the unstinting efforts of advocates of anti-sexist and anti-racist educational provision; the massive expansion of higher education and its culturally and socially heterogeneous constituencies; and the mounting importance within academia of post-structuralist and post-modernist concerns with the key significance of a plurality of shifting linguistic, subjective and meaning-centred constructions of the world.[2] Given the traditional neglect of the Other in much mainstream British historiography (attention to ethnicity, black history and racism has figured more prominently in the work of historians of North America), growing concern with the thoughts and actions of those people living beyond the confines of the males of the upper and middle classes is to be warmly welcomed.

In extending this welcome we must, however, simultaneously be aware of both the dangers of marginalizing or rendering invisible important and longstanding 'alternative' histori-ographical traditions, as well as the pitfalls attendant upon the false invention of a 'new' tradition. For example, while generally of little concern to the traditionally mainstream preoccupations of narrative British political and constitutional history, the structured experiences and powers of agency of class, ethnic and gender-based Others—such as male and female workers, peasants and poor Catholic immigrants—have long constituted important subjects of study within British labour and economic and social history. Thus the Hammonds, the Webbs, G.D.H. Cole and members of the Communist Party Historians' Group established serious left historical traditions in this country which had at their cores the study of the working-class Other or Outsider—and this long before the appearance of the post-structuralist 'linguistic turn(s)' and 'post-modernist' politics of identity.[3]

A key purpose of the second part of this essay is to demonstrate, with reference to the work of Dorothy Thompson on class, gender and ethnicity within the Chartist movement, the enduring importance of an alternative historiographical tradition's attention to the Other. But the reader's attention will first of all be drawn to the tough-minded empirical historical practice of Thompson, and then to a consideration of those influences which attracted her to the study of Chartism. The essay maintains that, as demonstrated in her deeply researched and finely crafted writings—in, for example, *The Chartists*[4] and *Outsiders*[5]—Thompson has shown herself to be the foremost historian of Chartism whose work merits full recognition in its own right.

## THE HISTORIAN'S CRAFT

Before proceeding to an examination of Thompson's substantive work on aspects of Chartism, we can first of all usefully consider the 'rules of method' and 'the disciplined historical discourse of the proof' (to borrow E.P. Thompson's phrase) which have informed her historical practice.

To the best of my knowledge, Dorothy Thompson has not written extensively and in a purely self-contained and highly abstract manner upon the methodologies of history in general and the assumptions, norms and values underpinning her own practice. There are various references in *Outsiders* to theories of and approaches to history as disciplines and processes, and class, gender and ethnicity which will be taken up below. And there is little doubt that Dorothy Thompson fully endorsed her husband's withering onslaught in *The Poverty of Theory* against the theoreticism of Althusser and the scepticism of Popper, and his defence of history as the pursuit of objective, if provisional and limited, truths.[6] Indeed, it is not theory *per se* but rather *theoreticism*—theory as fetish, as frozen structure, as a discrete, self-referential, internally consistent and sufficient body of 'truth', and as divorced from a dialogue of correspondence with the empirical world—which has met with full Thompsonian ire. Resistant to being 'theorized' by Althusserian and other theoreticists who often display little familiarity with the procedures, rules and practices of history as an acquired discipline of craft, the Thompsons have nevertheless been steeped in the theory of history—as the inextricable process of engagement between theory and practice; between higher and lower levels of abstraction; and as, to quote E.H. Carr, 'a continuous process of interaction between the historian and his (*sic*) facts, an unending dialogue between the present and the past'.[7]

More precisely, for Dorothy, as for Edward Thompson, it has been the enduring dialogue between concept and evidence, between hypothesis and empirical research, closely interwoven in the historical text, which lies at the heart of the historian's practice. Far-reaching methodological procedures and substantive issues both emanate from and are developed out of this core. First, if concepts cannot adequately withstand their rigorous questioning by the evidence then they must be modified or jettisoned in the search for historical truth. This hard-headed, unsentimental realism is clearly at work in Dorothy Thompson's approach to class. In *Outsiders* Thompson thus observes:

If earlier definitions of class can now be seen to have been over-simplified and inadequate to describe all kinds of social tension, *then we need different definitions*. Gender, regional and national loyalties, religious and ethnic divisions have been neglected as divisive factors, just as monarchism, an over-arching 'British' form of patriotism and a generalized adhesion to Christian principles have been under-estimated as forces of national cohesion. The hidden or overt teleologies of class, nation and gender have often led us to ignore or suppress movements or occasions in history which don't fit in. (p. 17) (emphasis added)

This example of unambiguous, open-minded commitment to the fact-theory dialogue and attentive caution to the adequacy of concepts also acts as an effective response to those critics who continue to accuse left historians of manipulating the facts to fit preconceived theories. Thompsonian 'commitment' is, at least in terms of academic practice, above all a commitment to historical accuracy and adequacy.[8]

Second, the process of engagement between concept and evidence further involves the careful framing of relevant, if provisional, questions and analytical frameworks, due attention to theoretical rigour and consistency, and the exploration of the available evidence in all its richness and complexity. This demanding, ambitious and exciting approach to historical study necessitates the careful probing of wide-ranging kinds of evidence (literally, quantitative, primary and secondary, as respectively required by the particular topic and framework of reference adopted), and different levels of thought and action.

Third, in its exploration of what people say, think and do, Dorothy Thompson's practice has embodied the 'realist' viewpoint that society exists both in consciousness and in structures or 'experiences'. The latter can take place in unintended and unrecognized ways: but Thompsonian emphasis has rested upon the claim that 'experience' is not permanently hidden from human cognition and influence. What we have here is an interactive notion of social behaviour and a humanistic epistemology: of the 'inseparable and mutually dependent character' of culture and social structure, of discourse and the material world; and the abilities of people, as the subjects or agents of history, to modify and transform their inherited and largely unwilled conditions of existence.[9] Dorothy Thompson's work on Chartism has thus consistently embraced both the languages and ideas of the movement (well in advance of the recent 'linguistic turn'), and its material, political and cultural underpinnings and characteristics. In sum, the dialogue between social consciousness and social being, between agency and conditioning, has centrally informed Thompson's historical project.

Fourth, Thompson has explored, in complex and nuanced as opposed to simplistic and reductionist ways, the links and contradictions between, and the respective limits and pressures (determinations) exerted by, the various political, economic, ideological, social and cultural structures and practices which constitute the social world. And long-term investigation of Chartism, and of wider historical study and personal observation and experience, has led to a rejection of the view that it is the economic factor which has mattered most in shaping the direction of history (either as a matter of course or in the 'last instance').

Rather Thompson has arrived at a more eclectic, contingent and pluralist conclusion than Marx and Engels: in terms of both history in general and the Chartist movement in particular undoubtedly significant material influences have often been accompanied by non-material forces of equal or greater importance. For example, Thompson writes in relation to the Chartists, 'Theirs was a political movement which did not, as Stedman Jones has pointed out, for the most part see the oppression of the working people as beginning in the productive process'. Furthermore,

the underlying teleology of a Marxist interpretation of history suggests that class consciousness, once achieved, becomes the driving force of popular politics ... Historians have therefore tended to become concerned to account for the apparent retreat in the post-Chartist period. They have ... looked for economic or socio-economic explanations. It has usually been acknowledged that the late 1840s and early 1850s saw an improvement in trade and the rapid decline of a few of the most distressed trades ... combined with a considerable emigration from the manufacturing districts. This, together with the natural exhaustion after ten years of energetic involvement, is sufficient to account for the decline of Chartism after the end of 1848 ... It does not, however, account for the lack of a political revival during the next period of distress in the mid-1850s.[10]

And more generally in terms of teleologies,

There are many other places in which changes in the contemporary world or in my own circumstances have led me to reconsider my version of the past. This is part of the experience of all scholars who are not simply antiquarians. Our awareness of the fragility of the physical environment has made us look again at one of history's major teleological assumptions—the measurement of 'progress' in terms of economic growth and the exploitation of natural resources. That other teleology which saw history as the inevitable and predictable movement from one mode of production to another in which each produced greater material wealth and increasingly egalitarian liberating social formations made possible by greater material resources, whilst not identical with the first, nevertheless underlay much social and historical theory which was by no means Marxist in origin. Various versions of enlightenment thought which envisaged the gradual replacement of superstition, bigotry and prejudice by tolerance, scepticism and free enquiry have received heavy punishment in an age which has seen the revival of nationalism and passionate adhesion to religions and sects which have over-ridden loyalties to class, gender or other assumed trans-national loyalities.[11]

If the long and twisting passages of historical time, historical enquiry and personal experience have thus induced a growing scepticism and pluralism on Thompson's part, they have not, however, diminished the significance of the discipline of history's lasting pursuit of the truth. And in terms of the latter, two observations merit special note.

First, Thompson argues cogently that, notwithstanding the marked limitations of a purely 'social' interpretation of Chartism, a long tradition of historical scholarship has rightly placed class at the very heart of the movement. Indeed, as we will observe in more detail in due course, Thompson clearly demonstrates the ways in which class strongly developed *within* the politics, cultures, households and ideologies of the Chartists as well as in the sphere of social production.

Second, and far more generally, neither the imperfections of the evidence nor the subjective bias of the historian should stand as insuperable obstacles to the pursuit of truth. As E.P. Thompson has noted, the historian must abide by the 'logic' or procedures of the discipline—due attentiveness to the fullness, complexities and independent, determinate properties of the evidence, the latter's close and rigorous engagement with competing hypotheses, theoretical clarity and precision, the accurate presentation and balanced evaluation of different points of view, and the elimination of inadequately supported hypotheses—in order to arrive at the truth. The latter, necessarily involving indirect representations of the past, subjectivity, selectivity and incomplete and provisional (bounded by the existing paradigms, the questions posed and the available evidence) is not absolute (new evidence and new paradigms will unearth new truths). But within its disciplinary terms of reference and 'rules of logic', history has and will continue to produce 'truths' and good and bad examples of practice. The discipline's court of appeal thus lies not in the procedures of exact science, but in the continuous dialogue between concept and evidence.[12]

Introduction to, growing familiarity with, and supervised practice in the disciplinary 'rules of method' or 'logic' outlined above constitute one's apprenticeship to the craft of history. Brief reference to personal experience may usefully amplify this general point.

My own apprenticeship began in 1967 during a second-year undergraduate course at Birmingham University on the theme of religion in fourteenth-century England. The bishops' visitation returns consulted in this course provided fascinating insights into the tensions which were afflicting English society, and especially peasant grievances, conditions and mentalities. Contrary to the intention of the tutor to demonstrate the superiority of religious to economic factors, the visitation returns clearly showed (at least to my sophomoric mind) the key importance of the 'social' to village life and the grievances which reached a climax in the Peasants' Revolt of 1381.[13] Having enjoyed the engagements with theoretical debate and primary source material and the sudden realization that Rodney Hilton and other scholars were writing the history of medieval society 'from below', I eagerly looked around for a course which addressed itself to the history of the 'popular classes' in the modern period.

Fortunately, Dorothy Thompson's special subject on Chartism was about to be offered and I enrolled on this course with great anticipation. I was not to be disappointed. Dorothy was an inspirational teacher, both democratic and rigorous in her practice, generous with her knowledge, and demanding of her students. Very late in my undergraduate career, history assumed unprecedented excitement and relevance.

I come from a family with strong cotton, mining and building trades connections in rural Cheshire (my paternal grandfather was a coalminer turned coal merchant, my maternal grandfather a farm worker and council worker, my father a carpenter and my mother a winder in a Bollington cotton mill for some fifteen years before marriage), with links to weaving ancestors in Ireland, and with strong and divided socialist and Conservative political allegiances. Given such a background, I related immediately to the writings and speeches of James Leach, Richard Pilling, Feargus O'Connor and other Chartists and to

7

the debates about Chartism and class, the nature and popular influence of Toryism, the decline of Chartism and the movement from Chartism to Liberalism which were among the topics covered in the course. (The very nature of these topics shows that recent and current concerns with the language(s) of radicalism, political and other continuities and discontinuities, and the nature and influences of class and the 'social' are far from new.)

In addressing such topics students were required, as a matter of standard historical practice, continually to engage and question the nature and adequacy of concepts and evidence and to be attentive to, and satisfactorily to accommodate, evidence which ran counter to one's initial hunches or ideological preferences. We were also expected to attend to the contradictory and many-sided nature of reality, to unintended as well as intended effects of thought and action, to express ourselves clearly and concisely and offer reasoned conclusions based upon a considered reading of the evidence.

In sum, this was the Dorothy Thompson school for expert, disciplined and exacting instruction in the 'mysteries of the craft'. Of course, most of us aspired towards rather than attained the ideal set. But of the benefits of such rigorous training there was (and continues to be) no doubt. On a personal level, induction into the craft of the historian at Birmingham enabled me to continue my apprenticeship at Warwick and Pittsburgh. On a more general and topical level, we must urgently reaffirm the great virtues of Dorothy Thompson's 'traditional' approach to learning—wrestling with the evidence, developing the capacity for independent thought and study under expert guidance and presenting and publishing considered research findings—in the face of current fads both for immediate, and often superficial and second-hand 'packages of knowledge', neatly wrapped and attractively presented to largely passive 'clients', and for the market-based 'rule' of 'publish or perish'.

## THE FOCUS ON CHARTISM

Having identified the general 'rules of method' which underpin Thompson's historical practice, we can proceed to a more particular concern. Why did a general interest in history lead

Thompson to develop a lasting interest in nineteenth-century popular radicalism, its specific manifestation in Chartism and especially the class, gender and ethnic characteristics of the movement?

The introduction to *Outsiders* contains many important pointers to the crucial influences of family, school, college and politics upon Thompson's growing fascination with the history of working-class movements and women. Dorothy hails from a musical family with artisanal roots. Within the family there were unusually strong commitments both to education and equality of opportunity. In *Outsiders*, Thompson writes 'As the only girl among the four children, I can remember no occasion on which it was suggested that I was less likely to have a career or should receive inferior education to that of my brothers' (p. 2).

Dorothy first attended a small private school in Bromley, Kent, travelling eight miles by bus from the family home in the village of Keston. Academically bright, artistically talented, reared in 'a family of non-believers', and poorer than most of their schoolmates (Dorothy and her brothers were warned not to mention the fact that their father was 'in trade' to any of the other children at school), the children developed an early sense of being 'apart'. And the latter was probably most acutely experienced in relation to those elements of middle-class culture rooted in religious observance, Conservatism, studied distance from the 'mass', 'watching the pennies', smug respectability and the narrow empiricism of immediate experience. Thompson's observations are instructive:

Perhaps attending a suburban school while living in a country village gave me an interest in *outsiders* very early in life. My brothers and I had very little in common with the children at our first school, and I remember thinking then, as I still do, that the villagers and the gypsies on the common were more interesting and lively than the people at school and their parents. (p. 3) (emphasis added)

Dorothy went on to the local Girls' County. There she was taught by 'powerful, impressive women' of high academic ability (but 'almost all unmarried and childless') who were 'actively concerned to establish a female presence in public life'. Students were encouraged both to study the history of feminist movements and actively to advance the interests of women. Thompson thus records:

Women like Maud Royden presented the prizes and addressed us on speech day. We were given *A Room of One's Own* as essential reading in the sixth form and the history of the women's suffrage movement and the struggles for the admission of women to higher education and the professions was taught in the classroom and illustrated by visiting speakers . . . (pp. 3, 4)

An interest in the history of women was accompanied while at school by a growing fascination with what was to become her 'first interest', Chartism. Both interests were carried over into Thompson's undergraduate career in history at Cambridge. Conscripted after two years, Dorothy became the first draughts-woman ever employed by a subsidiary of Royal Dutch Shell.

By the end of the war left-wing political activism and life with Edward Thompson (they met at Cambridge) had been firmly added to the earlier influences of family life and school. She writes,

By the time we first began to live together—in 1945—both Edward and I were already strongly committed to political action. We were both members of the British Communist Party. I was already involved in socialist and communist seminars concerned with working-class history . . . (p. 6)

Not wishing to work inside the 'academic establishment', the Thompsons set up home in Halifax, Yorkshire and worked within adult education for seventeen years. Bearing and raising three children and having extensive political commitments did not leave space for full-time paid work for the female partner in the household. Dorothy did, however, obtain part-time tutoring and other part-time work for university departments, and continued her active involvement in the work of the Commun-ist Party Historians' Group (until her departure from the party in 1956).

The experiences of work in the adult education, communist and peace movements and the mass radicalizing effects of wartime meshed with the earlier influences of family and education to produce a life-long commitment to the study of the 'people'. As Thompson writes:

In the CP we were encouraged to study the history of earlier socialist movements—albeit often by way of the immensely condescending judgements of Marx and Engels. In the peace movement the experience of 'single-issue' campaigning and its ability to draw together energy and aspirations from many sources illuminated the power of a slogan or a prophecy to release bursts of energy and commitment far exceeding those usually involved in party political campaigning. (p. 14)

The influences which would find full expression in *The Chartists* had thus been set in place by the 1950s.

## CHARTISM: CLASS, GENDER AND ETHNICITY

Having identified some of the key factors which moved Dorothy Thompson to study working-class history, we can now move to a consideration of her contribution to, and her place in, the historiography of Chartism. As indicated early in this essay, attention will be concentrated upon those aspects of Chartism relating to class, gender and ethnicity.

### *Class*

'Until very recently,' observes Thompson in *Outsiders*, 'few writers have questioned the definition of Chartism as a class movement.' On the same page (p. 21) the author states, 'The language of class is to be found in all three of the main kinds of historical writing about Chartism . . . accounts by participants . . . by mainstream historians and . . . by historians and publicists involved in the labour movement'. The truth of these claims can be demonstrated by means of representative, if brief, references to the observations of contemporaries and historians. There was little doubt among contemporaries of various shades of opinion that Chartism represented a significant leap in working-class consciousness, as expressed in a growing identity of interests and opposition to other social classes. Some, such as Thomas Carlyle, Dickens, Eliot, Gaskell and Kingsley, articulated the view that social distress largely underpinned the rise of the movement. Marx and Engels also emphasized the social factor. Engels thus wrote in *The Condition of the Working Class in England*:

Chartism is of an essentially social nature, a class movement. The 'Six Points', which for the Radical bourgeois are the beginning and end of the matter . . . are, for the proletarian, a mere means to further ends. 'Political power our means, social happiness our end,' is now the clearly formulated war-cry of the Chartists . . .[14]

It is, however, important to note, especially in view of Gareth Stedman Jones's characterization of Chartist historiography as offering a predominantly 'social' interpretation of the movement, that many contemporaries, participants and historians did not neatly compartmentalize their views into the 'social' and the 'political'.[15] Disraeli, Gammage (who was both a participant in and the first historian of Chartism), and O'Connor, James Leach, Peter Murray McDouall, Bronterre O'Brien and many other leaders saw Chartism as rooted in all manner of political, cultural, social and economic experiences, campaigns, struggles and perceptions, often of a class-based kind. 'We had no wealthy men amongst us,' recorded Ben Wilson of Halifax Chartism. The latter was perceived as far too politically and socially extreme to meet with the approval of the vast majority of Halifax's middle class—a view which could be applied, with the exception of a few notable sympathizers such as the radical mill owner John Fielden, across the manufacturing districts of the country.[16]

Gammage, whose history was issued originally in serial form in 1854, and who expressed few sympathies with O'Connor and 'physical force' methods, nevertheless clearly assumed the central importance of multi-faceted class experience and political independence to the Chartists. For a start, the middle classes had, since the Reform Act of 1832, practised *political* deception on a grand scale. As the following observation makes clear, they could, for the most part, no longer be trusted:

The new middle class constituency gave to the reformers an immense majority in the Commons, and on that majority the hopes of the people were fixed. But a short time, however, elapsed before all their magnificent castles evaporated into that air in which they had been erected . . . it became evident that the reformed House of Commons was powerful only for the perpetuation of evil. Such was the Parliament to which the deluded people had looked forward with such sanguine hope.[17]

Second, Gammage provided numerous examples and criticisms of middle-class examples of 'social tyranny' which had mushroomed alongside acts of political betrayal. There was, for example, the attempt of the members of the Anti-Corn Law League to divert the Chartists from the primary goal of manhood suffrage. This had been thwarted in large measure by the operatives' 'outraged feelings' towards and 'detestation of the social tyranny' of League manufacturers. Political reforms were 'certainly valued because of their abstract justice', but 'they were also looked upon as a means of securing a better social position for the humbler classes'. 'The masses look on the enfranchised classes, whom they behold reposing on the couch of opulence,' observed Gammage, 'and contrast that opulence with the misery of their own condition.' And, 'Abolish ... Monarchy to-morrow, and leave the fundamental relations between capital and labour on their present footing, and you will have accomplished virtually nothing'.[18]

In truth, and notwithstanding Gammage's contention that exploitation and misery issued primarily from political exclusion, the middle class had now joined the aristocracy in the common political *and* socio-economic oppression of the 'people'. According to Gammage, 'the great power that now leagued with the Aristocracy against the millions, and which was more powerful than its brother in the cause of political proscription, was the middle class'. Similarly,

it ought to be known that whatever the middle class might promise the people, Lord John Russell and his aristocratic friends never made a profession of attachment to Democracy. It is true that they interlarded their speeches with general remarks upon popular rights and constitutional liberty, which might mean anything that occasion required, and which, with them, never meant more than liberty for the middle class to share with the Aristocracy *their despotism over the labouring millions*. (emphasis added)

In effect, as argued by Bronterre O'Brien, the House of Commons represented 'the fellows who live by profits, who live by usury ... It represented men who had no interest in the welfare of the country'.[19]

Finally, suffering from widespread oppression, it was in the interests of the 'people', the 'labouring millions', the 'masses' or the 'working class' to unite. 'In pursuing the path of political and social elevation,' counselled Gammage, the 'people' must 'place reliance only on themselves'. Concrete experience, centrally located in the politics, economics and cultures of class, demanded that Chartists maintain their independence in the face of middle-class advances.[20]

Much in the manner of Gammage, the early twentieth-century histories of Chartism—by Mark Hovell in 1918 and Julius West in 1920—treated wide-ranging class grievances and demands as being at the very heart of Chartism. Hovell saw Chartism as 'an effort towards democracy and social equality', a 'strong protest' against 'the autocracy both of the landlord and of the capitalist', and the means to 'the social and economic regeneration of society'. Chartism further marked

a real new departure in our social and political history. It was the first movement of modern times that was engineered and controlled by working men. . . . It was the first genuinely democratic movement for social reform in modern history.[21]

For West class divisions and anti-middle-class feelings were essential, if largely unwelcome, aspects of Chartism.[22]

More recent accounts of the movement—as reflected in the works of Cole, Briggs, Ward, David Jones and Royle—have also highlighted the centrality of Chartist attempts to draw upon the undoubted and developing, if far from totally 'made', class consciousness of working men (apart from Jones, these authors have not paid detailed attention to the feelings of working-class women). On the first page of *Chartist Portraits* (1965), Cole thus wrote:

Hunger and hatred—these were the forces that made Chartism a mass movement of the British working class. Hunger gnawed at the hearts of the people, and seemed to gnaw the more fiercely as, under the spur of the new industrialism, the means of producing wealth increased . . . Even the 'good' employer was compelled to grind the faces of the poor . . . The bad, ruthless employer was in a position to drive him out of business if he did not conform. And ruthless employers were many, and well assured of being justified in what they did.

In *Chartist Studies* (1959) the editor, Asa Briggs, noted that 'A main theme in Chartist history was the attempt to create a sense of class unity', and that within Chartism,

All the groups talked the language of 'class' in a frank and uninhibited manner. 'If they whose interests are (so) identified', the L.W.M.A. had stated, 'do not investigate the causes of the evils that oppress them, how can they expect others to do it for them?' This conception of mutual self help was associated with the view that 'union of sentiment is essential to the prosecution of any great object'. The 'division of classes', treated by the *Northern Star* as a law of nature and history, made it essential, it was claimed, for the working classes to preserve and develop an intense feeling of emotional identification.[23]

The detailed local studies undertaken in *Chartist Studies* illustrated Briggs's national observations. For example, in explaining the rise of Chartism in Manchester, Donald Read saw as 'paramount' the local 'class issue' and 'class division', 'aggravated usually by economic distress'.[24]

Edward Royle's *Chartism* (1980) extended, in important ways, the notion of class consciousness into the areas of leisure and cultural norms and values:

Chartism embodied the values of the working-class world, carried over from the place of work . . . and from the place of leisure. It nurtured hostility to those outside—the fancy shopkeepers and rich capitalists who considered themselves above the common herd . . . It was class-conscious more in the sense of 'us' and 'them' than in any more precise way: the two were separated as much by attitude as by economics, which is why a sense of 'working class' is always easier to feel than define. This was the common bond which brought educational Chartists like Lovett to the support of the O'Connorites against the Complete Suffragists in 1842: a sense of worthiness, self-respect, and independence based on natural rights, education and mutuality.[25]

Similarly, part of David Jones's *Chartism and the Chartists* (1975) had earlier explored the cultural dimensions of class with respect to Chartist attitudes towards religion, education and temperance. Jones, too, had seen Chartism as an intensely class-conscious movement which had 'looked forward to a time . . . when kings, aristocracies and money-grabbing capitalists would be of interest only to antiquarians'.[26]

It is finally worth noting that J.T. Ward's *Chartism* (1973), while less sympathetic to aspects of Chartism than some of the more recent works already quoted, did nevertheless recognize that 'class-consciousness was undoubtedly spreading' (p.86). But whereas for Briggs in *Chartist Studies* the Chartist attempt to create class unity was 'never completely successful' (p. 4), for Ward 'the chimera of proletarian unity remained as elusive as ever (p. 86).

This, then, is the longstanding historiographical tradition strongly disposed towards the class-based nature of Chartism in which Dorothy Thompson's work on Chartism and class must be situated. Thompson has made two highly significant and distinctive contributions to this tradition.

First, Thompson has clearly demonstrated that during the Chartist years sources of working-class unity generally outweighed sources of division and fragmentation. 'I find it difficult to believe,' writes Thompson in *Outsiders*,

> that anyone who has worked in the archives and has studied the published and unpublished language of the Chartists can fail to see that the idea that above all united them into a nation-wide movement was the belief that there was a profound unity of interest between working people of all kinds. What is astonishing, in the light of later developments, is the extent to which the movement was able to incorporate people of different regional and ethnic origins, different genders and different occupations into a national campaign involving millions. The unifying factors were primarily a sense of class, a unifying leadership and a nationally distributed journal.[27]

It should be recorded that this demonstration of working-class unity has emerged out of the most profound, considered, and extended academic study of Chartism so far undertaken.

Second, Thompson has added both depth and breadth to the insights offered by Gammage, Briggs, Jones, Royle and others to provide us with a uniquely comprehensive, sophisticated and acute picture and understanding of the political, cultural and *linguistic* dimensions of class within Chartism. Eschewing, on the basis of considered historical practice, an identification of class purely and simply with the 'economic', and especially the 'economic' as relating to social production, Thompson has in many ways pioneered and greatly illuminated our understanding of the many-sided character of class in Chartism.

For example, and contrary to the 'populist' claims of Stedman Jones and Patrick Joyce, Thompson has clearly shown that political experience was highly productive of class-based understanding and language. Thus:

> The advocacy of suffrage extension to non-property-owners was, after 1832, almost entirely confined to politicians and political journalists who looked to a working-class constituency for support. Apart from the short and rather lonely excursion into complete suffrage by Joseph

Sturge and a few associates in 1842, the middle and upper classes held firmly aloof.[28]

To the middle and upper classes the Chartists 'represented a threat to far more than their political exclusiveness'. 'There were,' notes Thompson,

very many people who agreed with Macaulay's statement in the House of Commons that universal suffrage was 'incompatible with the very existence of civilisation'. What they feared was the lack of respect for property, the lack of respect for authority, and the lack of dignified behaviour which they perceived in these Chartist demonstrations, as well as their avowed purposes. There were, indeed, a certain number of radicals among the middle classes who supported in principle the idea of manhood suffrage. But these middle-class politicians never made common cause with the Chartists for more than a fleeting moment.[29]

Chartism was, after all, a movement whose language 'at all levels was class language', and in which 'the concepts of universal suffrage, the rights of man and of equality of citizenship were only held by the lower orders, the working class or classes'.[30]

Class also centrally informed leisure and culture. Thus, 'The middle classes certainly believed themselves to be superior in every way to the classes above and below them in morality, knowledge and understanding'. And, 'Class domination was not confined to the work-place. All aspects of social life— dwelling-places, shops, drinking-places, recreational and in-structional institutions, churches and chapel seating—were segregated on class lines'.[31]

As fully substantiated by the historiographical tradition out-lined above and in Thompson's *The Chartists* (particularly Chapters 6 and 11), the accelerated pace of capitalist transform-ation of the workplace and workplace relations ensured that class was at the heart of questions concerning independence, control, skill, living standards, and 'due acknowledgement, reward and protection' for workers. There is no need to rehearse the established picture. But it is instructive to note, and should be required reading for anyone interested in the multi-faceted nature of language and meanings, that class in its economic form did not assume single and uniform expression and meaning within Chartism. As Thompson declares, 'Chartist speakers and writers did not use the term 'class' in the same way on all occasions. Sometimes it meant only waged workers, sometimes it included "good" employers'.[32] We must, therefore, be attentive in our linguistic endeavours to the Chartist complexities of usage of, and to the contextualized engagement between, flexible and often interchangeable terms such as the 'people', the 'useful classes' and the 'working class'.

It is a measure of the strength of the class-based historiography of Chartism, complete with its attention to the constituencies, identities and independent manifestations of class, that competing approaches have traditionally exercised far less academic appeal. It can further be noted that, notwithstanding their recent popularity, the 'linguistic' interpretations of Stedman Jones and Joyce, emphasizing the superior claims of the extra-class based notion of the 'people' to the notion of class in mid-nineteenth-century popular consciousness, also largely fail to pass the test of the 'disciplined historical discourse of the proof'. As Thompson herself has noted, Stedman Jones's work operates with an unduly narrow Marxist definition and standard ('true' test) of class, is based on a very narrow range of evidence (which in turn is susceptible to an alternative, class-based reading), and is insufficiently alive to the importance of context in 'setting' and changing the meanings of long-standing words and demands. For example,

The appeal for manhood suffrage and an open, constantly-renewed Parliament elected by citizens whose votes were protected by the ballot . . . may have been similar to the programme of the Association Movement, of Major Cartwright and of the London Corresponding society. But the context in which it was proposed was very different. In still another context it was exactly the same programme which was put forward in 1791 by the United Irishmen and which led them directly into participation in the biggest rising against the British Government since the seventeenth century. This too was part of the context in which the Chartists put forward their arguments.[33]

In his undue haste to claim the primacy of non-class-based continuities of political language to Chartism (of the 'people' and the political origins of exploitation), Stedman Jones provides too literal an approach to the study of language and ideas, effectively misses the centrality of class to the movement, underestimates the role of the 'social', and mistakenly portrays the movement from Chartism to Liberalism in far too easy, untroubled and narrowly political terms.[34]

We may add that Patrick Joyce's case, as presented in *Visions of the People* (1991), is extremely weak. Joyce not only adopts Stedman Jones's unsatisfactory definition of class but also, and far more damagingly, rests his 'populist' case, as applied to the cotton districts of north-west England, upon exceedingly slight empirical evidence. In effect, Joyce simply fails adequately to engage with the vast mass of evidence unearthed by a long line of historians in support of the class-based nature of north-west Chartism. Rather, sweeping and extremely partial (one might even suggest preconceived) 'populist' conclusions are constructed upon an unduly literal reading of language, and the languages and meanings of the 'people' are not taken into contextualized engagement with languages of class. Furthermore, in his great underestimation of the issue of class-based independence to the Chartists of Ashton-under-Lyne and elsewhere, Joyce also presents a highly idealized, consensual and misleading account of the relations between Chartists and Liberals in south-east Lancashire and north-east Cheshire.[35]

## Gender

If Dorothy Thompson has greatly extended and deepened our understanding of Chartism and class—setting a standard and an agenda which future historians will ignore at their peril—then her work on gender and women in Chartism has been truly pioneering.

Unlike the subject of class, the issues of gender and women's roles in Chartism have traditionally been of marginal importance to historians of the movement. As Thompson herself has noted, 'none of the various ways of writing the history of Chartism have so far included the women'. Historical definitions of class and community 'have too often been so dominantly male that they have failed to see the women'. And for many early historians of Chartism, the presence of women within 'a serious political movement was an embarrassment'. They were 'either a decoration or a trivialization, when they were there a meeting became a fair or a tea party'.[36] To be sure, one can find positive references to women's participation in Chartism in the early accounts of Gammage and Ben Wilson. For example, the former wrote that 'The women, all honour to their public spirit, were not behind in the march towards Democracy', while the latter proudly recalled that in his West Riding village of Skircoat Green women had long been involved in radical politics.[37] Julius West did provide a very brief sketch of post-1818 women's political radicalism, Mark Hovell drew attention to infant Chartism's support for women's suffrage, and more recently David Jones and Edward Royle have noted the involvement of women in Chartism, albeit primarily as the supporters of 'the political ambitions of their husbands and brothers'.[37] But in truth, with the notable exception of David Jones's article, 'Women and Chartism' in *History* (February 1983), none of the histories and historians noted above devoted significant amounts of time and space to the subject of women and Chartism. Even more striking is the omission of any references to women's involvement in the movement in Marx and Engels' *On Britain*, and in the indexes of Briggs's *Chartist Studies* and Ward's *Chartism*. Women and gender have, of course, been subjects of intensive feminist investigation, but, as Thompson observes,

Women's historians of the modern variety have shown little interest in Chartism because it was a movement for manhood suffrage. The fact that many women took part was not seen as significant, since they took part in a movement whose agenda was written by men, and since they never combined as women for specifically women's issues.[39]

Historians such as Thomis and Grimmett and Martin,[40] concerned less with the history of Chartism as a whole and more with specifically female aspects of popular protest, have provided useful foundations upon which Thompson could build. But apart from the work of these historians, Thompson has more or less single-handedly constructed the history of women in Chartism. In the process Chartist women have been rescued from virtual historical invisibility.

Thompson's findings, presented most compactly in Chapter 7 of *The Chartists* and in her essay 'Women and nineteenth-century radical politics: a lost dimension' (reprinted in *Outsiders*), conclusively establish the 'active participation' of women in Chartism. Drawing upon significant traditions of involvement in forms of protest relating to the cost of living, political and industrial radicalism, and the defence and advancement of the interests of their families and communities, Chartist women formed female radical associations ('well over a hundred' having been recorded 'in the first few years of the movement'), were active in demonstrations and processions and took out membership cards of the National Charter Association.

Thompson also observes that support for women's suffrage 'was always widespread amongst the Chartists', especially between 1838 and 1843, although it was taken as axiomatic that the vote should be extended to 'unmarried and widowed women only'. Male Chartists did recognize the worth of married women's labours, whether in the home or outside, and rigid and extensive working-class applications of the notion of a 'woman's place', the male as sole breadwinner and associated male superiority and female inferiority were not widespread before the mid-Victorian period. Earlier traditions of the relatively flexible sexual division of labour associated with household production, and the continuation, in Lancashire, Yorkshire and some centres of 'artisan' production, of family employment and paid work for women meant that in many centres of Chartist strength mutuality between the sexes, women's involvement in community life and in some cases women's independence, were marked.[41] As Anna Clark has observed,

working-class women had long been out in public, laboring for wages and drinking in public houses. Women rioted, organized, struck, demonstrated ... Chartists ... provided a political role for women in the larger community. But women also acted independently.

Developing what Clark calls a 'militant domesticity', Chartist women justified 'their actions in stepping outside the home by defining the responsibilities of motherhood, not just as nurturing children in the home, but laboring to feed them and organizing to better their lives'. Women's involvement in campaigns against the new Poor Law, in favour of factory legislation, in Chartism, against poverty, hunger, 'unnatural' male unemployment in the midst of paid work for women, and for control over their children against the centralizing and controlling designs of the state was thus conducted in defence of female domesticity. But, as emphasized by Clark, this was a notion of domesticity very different from the 'separate spheres' approach of the middle classes.[42]

As Thompson and Clark both demonstrate, notions of mutuality and partnership between working-class men and women and spheres of women's independence did not, however, generally signify either equality between the sexes or Chartist women's commitment to specifically feminist causes. Initial Chartist support for the formal endorsement of votes for women did not carry over into the six points of the Charter. As Thompson writes in *The Chartists*,

The question of the vote for women was not only of less importance to the Chartists than the vote for working men; in some ways it could be seen as standing in the way of the working-class franchise. If women had been granted the vote on the same terms as men, the voting strength of the propertied classes would have been strengthened.[43]

In truth the Chartists adhered to the general patriarchal principle that husbands and wives were 'as one', with the husband largely speaking and acting on behalf of the wife. As a corollary, and notwithstanding important examples of women's independent political behaviour, it appears to be the case that the vast majority of Chartist women generally played a supporting role to their menfolk and accepted the primacy of family-, community- and class-based issues over those relating to the specific needs of women. Thompson thus shows that the main speakers and leaders of the movement were usually male; while

The women at this stage did not see their interests as being in opposition to those of their husbands—or if they did, they did not see any solution to such conflict in political action. Chartist women seem for the most part to have worked together with their husbands, sons and brothers in a joint opposition to oppression perceived as coming from employers and administrators. Those Owenites who attacked marriage and the family met with little response among working women.[44]

Finally, the mid–late 1840s saw the growth of more structured, formal, male-dominated and increasingly workplace-based kinds of popular protest in which women, as 'guardians of hearth and home', were to be further marginalized.[45]

## Ethnicity

The leading authority on the subject of women and Chartism, Thompson has also figured prominently in relatively recent debates concerning Chartism and ethnicity, especially the relations between the movement, Irish nationalists and Irish immigrant and the place of Feargus O'Connor in the history of Chartism.[46] What follows below is a necessarily brief summary of the key historiographical and substantive issues involved.

While mentioned in some of the earlier histories of the movement and studies of the working class, the issues of Irish immigrant relations with Chartism and the interactions of class and ethnicity have become subjects of detailed and extended debate mainly since the 1960s. Among the earlier historians Gammage and West provided a few references to an Irish immigrant presence in Chartism, mainly on the part of the Irish Confederates in 1848. But neither of these historians offered any systematic treatment or considered analysis of the subject. Marx and Engels and Hovell were even more neglectful. All three authors were quick to argue that Irish immigration had adversely affected the living conditions, habits, customs and unity of the working class in England, but none of them investigated the issue of the Irish and Chartism.[47]

Uneven levels of coverage and sharply differing conclusions in relation to ethnicity and class have often characterized both general histories of Chartism and more specialist treatments of the Irish since the Second World War. For example, Royle's *Chartism* (1981), while duly recognizing the weak presence of Chartism within Ireland and the divisive and debilitating effects of O'Connell's opposition to Chartism from the late 1830s onwards, nevertheless concluded in 1981 that 'the Irish in England contributed an important element to Chartism at all levels'. Briggs's *Chartist Studies* had, some two decades earlier, contained brief references to both conflicts between the O'Connellite Irish and the Chartists and to the period of short-lived unity between the Chartists and Irish repealers in 1848.[48] Sandwiched chronologically between the works of Briggs and Royle, Ward had expressed, in 1973, what was becoming the conventional wisdom among many historians:

O'Connor ... maintained his efforts to recruit proletarian Irish support. This inevitably involved detaching immigrants from the spell of his old enemy, O'Connell, 'the dictator to the Whig Cabinet, the base, bloody and brutal traitor'. Progress was slow: most Irishmen stood by 'the Liberator' . . . O'Connell's advice to avoid 'the insane or dishonest Radicals of England, who instead of appealing to common sense, declared their reliance on arms' was thus followed . . . Certainly, many more Irishmen rallied to the repeal movement than to Chartism. The Roman Catholic priesthood was heavily involved and there was clerical talk of refusing the sacraments to Chartists.[49]

Ward's conclusion echoed that expressed by J.H. Treble in the same year in what was to become an influential article. Contrary to the views of O'Higgins, Treble strongly argued that the official opposition of the Catholic church and the massively popular O'Connell to Chartism ensured that the vast mass of immigrants were not favourably disposed towards or involved in Chartism before 1848.[50] It is within this context of historiographical debate that Thompson's work has developed.

Drawing upon her own research, her considerable knowledge of Irish history (unusual among British labour historians) and the work of scholars such as O'Higgins, Belchem, Epstein and Kaijage,[51] Thompson has presented a fundamental and convincing critique of the 'orthodoxy' of Ward and Treble. Thompson has, for example, pointed out that Treble relied excessively upon 'official' sources and the pronouncements of leaders of the Catholic Church and Irish organizations, and that the allegedly adverse effects of such pronouncements upon Irish immigrant involvement in Chartism had not been adequately established. The Chartists 'always expressed common cause with the Irish repealers', especially those rooted in the tradition of the United Irishmen. And instances of ethnic conflict during the Chartist period had been inflated and the forces making for working-class unity understated. Thus Thompson:

Hostility to the Irish on ethnic and religious grounds certainly existed among the common people, but among the Chartists a feeling of community based on common work experience and a joint feeling of oppression was always very much stronger, and in many cases seems to have produced the opposite effect—that is, a great admiration for Irish nationalism.

And:

In conclusion, whilst not denying that there were divisive factors in national and ethnic differences during the Chartist period, I find a much greater cohesion in the consciousness of exclusion from the constitution of both Irish and English workmen, in a sense of being under attack from government and employers, and of being misunderstood and rejected by those with political power . . .

In sum, 'there was a very considerable Irish presence in the Chartist movement' and for a time at least class solidarity and ethnic identity were perfectly compatible companions.[52]

Thompson has also offered the related, and highly original and challenging thesis, that the failure to construct an effective and durable alliance between the Chartists and the nationalists before 1848 'foundered more on the Irish rejection of a democratic programme than on the "racist" or "imperialist" attitudes of the English, Scottish and Welsh Chartists, or on the personal disagreements between Feargus O'Connor and Daniel O'Connell'.[53] Taking to task 'most twentieth-century labour historians' for their 'monolithic' as well as 'unproblematical' views of Irish nationalist politics and the immigrants as an undifferentiated out-group, Thompson has skilfully traced the differences between the republican, democratic and revolutionary nationalism derived from the Jacobinism of the United Irishmen and the more moderate, 'moral force', anti-trade union, socially hierarchical, and Catholic-related nationalism of O'Connell which 'believed in the continued rule of Ireland by the British Crown'. Indeed it was the control exercised by O'Connell over the pre-1848 nationalist movement in Ireland and on the British mainland and the 'suppression or extinction of the Jacobin tradition in Ireland itself' which underlay the failure of Chartists and nationalists to make common cause.

Finally, we must note the importance of O'Connor, both to general assessments of Chartism and ethnicity and more specifically as a subject upon which Thompson has written with authority and passion. It is only when one returns to the historiography of Chartism that one remembers the full extent of the condemnation and ridicule which has traditionally been heaped upon the head of the main leader of the movement. There are occasional positive evaluations and appreciations in the literature. One can cite in this context Asa Briggs's and Edward Royle's respective views that O'Connor 'did most to "nationalise" discontent in 1838', and that 'it was O'Connor who succeeded in transforming a pressure group into a truly national movement'.[54]

But against such views we must set a barrage of criticism. For example, G.D.H. Cole, while recognizing that O'Connor was a 'tremendous popular force', nevertheless contrasted O'Connor's alleged irrationality and anti-industrialism with Lovett's supposed rational and progressive views. Cole offered the following unflattering picture of the leader of Chartism:

O'Connor was, in fact, a great mob-orator, with a large fund of sympathy for the people, a great deal of egoism . . . and a very small stock of ideas. He wanted to be boss; but he had no clear policy, especially at moments of crisis, when he said first one thing and then another, and always came down in the end on what he felt likeliest to be the winning side. *He was, in truth, a disastrous leader*; but it is necessary to bear in mind that it is doubtful whether any leadership could have enabled the Chartist movement to succeed. (emphasis added)[55]

Cole was following a well-worn path. Gammage had seen O'Connor, 'the idol of the operatives in the manufacturing districts', as possessing great oratorical and intellectual skills which were unfortunately more than offset by self-centredness, empty boastfulness, erratic behaviour and lack of reflection and steadiness. Hovell and West were to offer less qualified verdicts. The former saw O'Connor as 'the only leading Chartist who was devoid alike of idealism and of statesmanship', and as 'the blustering, egotistical, blarneying, managing, but intellectually and morally very unreliable Irishman, who probably had never done an honest day's work in his life'. To the latter O'Connor was the 'Dictator' who had 'most of the qualities of a great demagogue, and all the defects of the lower-grade politician'. And in the recent past Ward has accused O'Connor of spouting 'heated verbiage', of 'rousing radical enthusiasm without committing himself', and of being 'the great menace to Lovett's vision'.[56]

It is a remarkable fact of Chartist historiography that, notwithstanding this formidable wall of adverse criticism, Dorothy Thompson and James Epstein have done a great deal to restore proper historical accuracy, balance and respect to O'Connor's role in Chartism. Both in Epstein's biography of O'Connor, *The Lion of Freedom*, and in Thompson's *The Chartists* and *Outsiders* O'Connor is rescued from historical ridicule and hatred. Above all, Thompson and Epstein convincingly demonstrate that

O'Connor forged a national movement and, by means of the *Northern Star* and his leadership and political skills, held the movement together for some ten years. This was an unprecedented feat in terms of early nineteenth-century popular radical movements and should not be forgotten. Ethnic, regional, local, personality, skill, income and many other differences and divisions threatened the national unity of Chartism, and many of these differences had prevented the development of a durable national popular radical movement in the past. O'Connor, with his overriding and single-minded commitments to universal manhood suffrage, working-class independence and hostility to all oppressors of the 'people', not only exerted massive popular appeal which transcended differences within the working class, but also prevented Chartism from splintering into all manner of 'isms' and tendencies. 'Remove him and his newspaper from the picture,' writes Thompson, 'and the movement fragments, localises and loses its continuity.' In moving to the primacy of 'knowledge Chartism' over the struggle for the vote Lovett did abandon the centre-ground of the Chartist cause and accordingly lost appeal and support. In addition to his shrewd and capable political and leadership qualities, O'Connor was in all probability far less egotistical and boastful than usually portrayed. The final word rests with Thompson:

In his personal relationships, he evinced charm, good humour, energy and a total commitment to the movements with which he was associated. Had O'Connor been the brutal braggadocio, self-important figure that so many historians have presented, he could not possibly have maintained his leadership of the Chartists for ten years, years in which it was never seriously questioned or challenged.[57]

As seen in this essay, Dorothy Thompson's historical method and her work on class, gender and ethnicity in relation to Chartism have set standards of excellence and rigour which constitute indispensable points of reference for all students of Chartism and modern British working-class history. Attention to the Other has been accompanied in Thompson's work with fierce opposition to intellectual 'closure' and frozen orthodoxies. Thompson's concern with the complexities, contradictions, ambiguities and nuances of life demonstrate that, contrary to many current claims, attention to many-sidedness and diversity has not been the sole preserve, or indeed invention, of postmodernism. Furthermore, in her detection of patterned processes in the midst of the seeming chaos of history, Thompson has exposed the fallacy of the current 'wisdom' that history cannot constitute a search for truth. And in her pursuit of truth Thompson has displayed an independence and toughness of mind and practice which has not permitted her work to be enclosed within either of the Marxist or Fabian traditions which have constituted the dominant modes of interpretation of Chartism. We would be well advised to carry Thompson's legacy of accurate, detailed, well-researched and considered historical work, rooted in the unending dialogue between concept and evidence, into the twenty-first century.

## NOTES

I am grateful to Stephen Roberts for his helpful comments and suggestions concerning my essay.

1   The quoted phrase is taken from Simone de Beauvoir's *The Second Sex* (Harmondsworth, 1975), p. 16. De Beauvoir used the phrase with reference to the way in which woman is defined as the Other in relation to man. I am grateful to Katherine Kirk for this reference. See also D. Roediger, 'Race and the working-class past in the United States: multiple identities and the future of labor history', *International Review of Social History*, supplement 1,38 (1993), 127–43; S.O. Rose, 'Gender and labor history: the nineteenth-century legacy', in ibid., 145–62; J.W. Scott, *Gender and the Politics of History* (New York, 1988); C. Hall, *White Male and Middle Class: Explorations in Feminism and History* (London, 1992); P. Gilroy, *There Ain't No Black in the Union Jack: The Cultural Politics of Race and Nation* (London, 1987); A. Sivanandan, *Communities of Resistance: Writings on Black Struggles for Socialism* (London,1990).

2   See the illuminating book by Joyce Appleby, Lynn Hunt and Margaret Jacob, *Telling the Truth about History* (New York, 1994); A. Easthope, *British Post-Structuralism Since 1968* (London, 1991).

3   See, for example, R. Johnson, G. McLennan, B. Schwarz and D. Sutton (eds), *Making Histories: Studies in History-Writing and Politics* (London, 1982); J. Clarke, C. Critcher and R. Johnson (eds), *Working-Class Culture: Studies in History and Theory* (London, 1979); H.J. Kaye, *The Education of Desire: Marxists and the Writing of History* (London, 1992); H.J. Kaye and K. McClelland (eds), *E.P. Thompson: Critical Perspectives* (Cambridge, 1990); H.J. Kaye, *The British Marxist Historians: An Introductory Analysis* (Oxford,1984).

4   D. Thompson, *The Chartists: Popular Politics in the Industrial Revolution* (Aldershot, 1984).

5   D. Thompson, *Outsiders: Class, Gender and Nation* (London, 1993).

6   E.P. Thompson, *The Poverty of Theory and Other Essays* (London, 1978), pp. 229–42.

7   E.H. Carr, *What is History?* (Harmondsworth, 1967), p. 30; C. Parker, *The English Historical Tradition Since 1850* (Edinburgh, 1990), Ch. VIII and pp. 223–9.

8   N. Kirk, 'Commonsense, commitment and objectivity: themes in the recent historiography of Peterloo', *Manchester Region History Review*, **III**, I (1989), 61–6.

9   E.P. Thompson, 'The politics of theory', in R. Samuel (ed.), *Peoples History and Socialist Theory* (London, 1971); M. Savage and A. Miles, *The Remaking of the British Working Class 1840–1940* (London, 1994), p. 18.

10  D. Thompson, *Outsiders*, pp. 37–8 and 39–40

11  Ibid., p. 15.

12  Thompson, *Poverty of Theory*, pp. 219, 230–2; G. Himmelfarb, 'Telling it as you like it: post-modernist history and the flight from fact', *Times Literary Supplement*, 16 October 1992, 12–15.

13  R.H. Hilton, *Bond Men Made Free: Medieval Peasant Movements and the English Rising of 1381* (London, 1973).

14  K. Marx and F. Engels, *On Britain* (Moscow, 1953), p. 270; Thompson, *Outsiders*, pp. 22–3.

15  G.S. Jones, 'The language of Chartism', in J. Epstein and D. Thompson (eds), *The Chartist Experience: Studies in Working-Class Radicalism and Culture 1830–1860* (London, 1982); 'Rethinking Chartism' in his *Languages of Class: Studies in English Working-Class History 1832–1982* (London, 1983).

16  B. Wilson, *The Struggles of an Old Chartist* (Halifax, 1887), reprinted in D. Vincent (ed.), *Testaments of Radicalism: Memoirs of Working-Class Politicians 1790–1885* (London, 1977), pp. 207, 223; K. Tiller, 'Late Chartism: Halifax, 1847–58' and R. Sykes, 'Early Chartism and trade unionism in south-east Lancashire', in Epstein and Thompson (eds), *Chartist Experience*; N. Kirk, 'In defence of class', *International Review of Social History*, **XXXII** (1987); S.A. Weaver, *John Fielden and the Politics of Popular Radicalism 1832–1847* (Oxford, 1987).

17  R.G. Gammage, *History of the Chartist Movement 1837–1854* (London, 1969), pp. 4–5.

18  Ibid., pp. 9, 25, 102–3.

19  Ibid., pp. 33, 38, 119.

20  Ibid., pp. 7, 25.

21  M. Hovell, *The Chartist Movement* (Manchester, 1918), pp. 7, 307, 311.

22    J. West, *A History of the Chartist Movement* (New York, 1968),
      pp. 63–7, 72, 173–81. West's own sentiments were fiercely anti-
      O'Connor, pro-Lovett and in favour of an alliance between the
      Chartists and middle-class radicals such as Joseph Sturge.

23    A. Briggs (ed.), *Chartist Studies* (London, 1959), pp. 4, 294.

24    D. Read, 'Chartism in Manchester' and J.F.C. Harrison, 'Chartism
      in Leicester', in Briggs, *Chartist Studies*, pp. 33, 41, 139.

25    E. Royle, *Chartism* (Harlow, 1980), p. 80.

26    D. Jones, *Chartism and the Chartists* (London, 1975), p. 11.

27    Thompson, *Outsiders*, p. 36.

28    Ibid., p. 29.

29    D. Thompson, *The Chartists*, p. 237.

30    D. Thompson, 'The languages of class', *Society for the Study of
      Labour History Bulletin*, **52**, I (1987), 57.

31    Thompson, *Chartists*, pp. 240, 253.

32    Thompson, *Outsiders*, p. 37.

33    Thompson, 'The languages of class', *Society for the Study of Labour
      History Bulletin*, **52**, I (1987), 55.

34    Thompson, 'The languages of class', 54–7; Kirk, 'In defence of
      class'. The central importance of context is also highlighted in
      Savage and Miles, *The Remaking*. As these authors rightly note, in
      some contexts class is largely taken for granted and does not
      require formal linguistic articulation. Thus:

      > To judge popular culture purely in terms of the formal structure of its
      > discourse is actually to intellectualise it, and to subject it to fundamentally
      > academic ways of thinking. Much of the meaning which specific texts
      > possess depends on the contexts in which they are created and under-
      > stood. If texts are used within environments powerfully structured by
      > class there may be little point in establishing class as a salient divide
      > discursively—it may be so obvious to people that it needs no reference in a
      > particular text. (p. 18)

35    The core of Joyce's case against the class-based nature of (mainly
      north-west) Chartism is contained in eleven pages (pp. 33–7, 94–9)
      of his *Visions of the People: Industrial England and the Question of
      Class 1848–1914* (Cambridge, 1991). His case relies far too heavily
      upon the speeches and writings of J.R. Stephens (who was not a
      Chartist), William Aitken of Ashton (who is read selectively in
      relation to acute class divisions in 1830s and 1840s Ashton), and
      Benjamin Grime's observations on Oldham radicalism. Joyce fails
      to attend to the centrality of class in the languages of such promi-
      nent north-west Chartists as Leach, Pilling and McDouall. *Visions
      of the People* also lacks detailed and rigorous engagement with the
      work of those historians—including that of Dorothy Thompson—
      which convincingly presents the case in favour of the class-based

character of Chartism. Much closer attention to the findings of Robert Sykes, John Cole, Peter Taylor, John Foster and Kirk—which strongly suggest the centrality of class and independence to Chartism in the cotton districts—would have been particularly welcome. See, for example, R.A. Sykes, 'Popular politics and trade unionism in south-east Lancashire, 1829–1842' (unpublished D.Phil. dissertation, University of Manchester, 1982); P.F Taylor, 'Popular politics and labour–capital relations in Bolton, 1825–1850' (unpublished D.Phil. dissertation, University of Lancaster, 1991); J. Cole, *Rochdale Revisited: A Town and Its People* (Littleborough, 1990); J. Foster, *Class Struggle and the Industrial Revolution* (London, 1974); Kirk, 'In defence of class'. The most recent work on Ashton-under-Lyne reaffirms the militant class-based and independent nature of local Chartism and the far from easy and untroubled nature of the movement into Liberalism. See R.G. Hall, 'Work, class and politics in Ashton-under-Lyne, 1830–1860' (unpublished D.Phil. dissertation, Vanderbilt University, 1991).

36  Thompson, *Outsiders*, pp. 42 and 18.

37  Gammage, *History*, pp. 28, 77–8; Wilson, *The Struggles*, pp. 195, 197.

38  West, *Chartist Movement*, pp. 36, 37, 83, 156–7; Hovell, *Chartist Movement*, pp. 70, 207; Jones, *Chartism*, pp. 24, 49, 182; Royle, *Chartism*, pp. 82, 107.

39  Thompson, *Outsiders*, p. 41.

40  M.I. Thomis and J. Grimmett, *Women in Protest* (London, 1982); C.E. Martin, 'Female Chartism: a study in politics' (unpublished M.A. dissertation, University of Wales (Swansea), 1973).

41  N. Kirk, *Labour and Society in Britain and the USA*, Vol. I, *Capitalism, Custom and Protest, 1780–1850* (Aldershot, 1994), pp. 39–40, 46–50, 128–31; W. Seccombe, 'Patriarchy stabilized: the construction of the male bread-winner wage norm in nineteenth-century Britain', *Social History*, **21** (1986); E. Gordon, *Women and the Labour Movement in Scotland 1850–1914* (Oxford, 1991), pp. 17–39, 73–101; S.O. Rose, *Limited Livelihoods: Class and Gender in Nineteenth-Century England* (London, 1992), Introduction.

42  A. Clark, 'The rhetoric of Chartist domesticity: gender, language and class in the 1830s and 1840s', *Journal of British Studies*, **31**, I (1992), esp. 76–7.

43  Thompson, *Chartists*, p. 126.

44  Ibid., p. 126; J. Schwarzkopf, *Women in the Chartist Movement* (London, 1991).

45  Thompson, *Chartists*, pp. 128–32. The accelerated movement of women into the home at mid-century was, however, unevenly spread throughout the country. In some instances the opportunity to devote more time to domestic matters was seen in a very posi-

tive way by working-class women, and especially those women who had operated the 'double shift' of unpaid home work and paid work. See C.E. Morgan, 'The domestic image and factory culture: the cotton district in mid-nineteenth-century England' (unpublished MS, 1994). I am grateful to Carol Morgan for a copy of her paper.

In general terms, the 'retreat' into the working-class home at mid-century was, however, accompanied by hardened notions of a 'woman's place', male superiority and female inferiority. See D. Thompson, 'Women and nineteenth-century radical politics: a lost dimension', in *Outsiders*, esp. pp. 97–100.

46  For a summary of these debates and Thompson's contribution, see D. Thompson, 'Ireland and the Irish in English radicalism before 1850', and 'Seceding from the seceders: the decline of the Jacobin tradition in Ireland, 1790–1850', in *Outsiders; Chartists*, pp. 96–101.

47  Gammage, *History*, pp. 297–9, 332–6; West, *Chartist Movement*, pp. 79, 236, 252; Marx and Engels, *Britain*, pp. 61, 94–5, 111–12, 123–7, 504–6; Hovell, *Chartist Movement*, pp. 14, 80, 81.

48  Royle, *Chartism*, p. 67; Briggs , *Chartist Studies*, pp. 50–1, 394–5.

49  Ward, *Chartism*, pp. 145–6, 211–12.

50  J.H. Treble, 'O'Connor, O'Connell and the attitudes of Irish immigrants towards Chartism in the North of England 1838–1848', in J. Butt and I. F. Clarke (eds), *The Victorians and Social Protest: A Symposium* (Newton Abbott, 1973); R. O'Higgins, 'The Irish influence in the Chartist movement', *Past and Present* , **20** (November 1961).

51  J. Belchem, 'English working-class radicalism and the Irish, 1815–1850', in R. Swift and S. Gilley (eds), *The Irish in the Victorian City* (London, 1985); J. Epstein, *The Lion of Freedom: Feargus O'Connor and the Chartist Movement 1832–1842* (London, 1982); F.J. Kaijage, 'Labouring Barnsley, 1815–1875' (unpublished D.Phil. dissertation, University of Warwick, 1975).

52  Thompson, *Outsiders*, pp. 104, 126–8; but see K. Moore, '"This Whig and Tory Ridden Town": Popular Politics in Liverpool in the Chartist era', in J. Belchem (ed.), *Popular Politics Riot and Labour: essays in Liverpool History 1790–1940* (Liverpool, 1992), p. 50 for the 'relative lack of involvement of the Irish in local Chartism'.

53  Thompson, *Outsiders*, pp. 137, 161.

54  Briggs, *Chartist Studies*, pp. 15, 25; Royle, *Chartism*, p. 58

55  Cole, *Chartist Portraits*, Ch. XI, pp. 335–6.

56  Gammage, *History*, pp. 16, 17, 44–6; Hovell, *Chartist Movement*, pp. 67, 194; West, *Chartist Movement*, p. 84, Ch. VII; Ward, *Chartism*, pp. 116, 119, 245.

57  Thompson, *Chartists*, p. 99.

# 2

## National Chartist Leadership: Some Perspectives

### JAMES EPSTEIN

Leadership implies a relationship: a relationship between leaders and followers or leadership and led. These very terms, however, present loaded categories, suggesting a one-way process: leaders lead and followers follow. Indeed, this is the perspective that informed the early studies of the Chartist movement.[1] There is now a considerable body of scholarship that has challenged such perspectives, recognizing the complex process of reciprocity that mediated these relationships.[2] None the less, it may still be worth considering how best to conceptualize the relationship between national leaders and rank-and-file adherents and the central problems that faced the leaders of the largest and most sustained movement for democratic rights in nineteenth-century Britain.

We should first note that the image of the deluded masses following an irrational and self-serving demagogue was itself a powerfully articulated contemporary view linked to middle-class fears of working-class insurgency. It was prominently voiced, for instance, in early Victorian fiction. One need only think of Dickens' portrayal of Slackbridge, the trade-union agitator, in *Hard Times* (1854) or O'Flynn in Charles Kingsley's *Alton Locke* (1850) or the workers of Wodegate led by the unforgettable Bishop Hatton in Disraeli's *Sybil or the Two Nations* (1846). Such portrayals are particularly important for what they deny: working-class political agency. It was not that such writers were unsympathetic to the plight of labouring people, but they reflected widespread middle-class fears of the mindless multitude, along with a deep-seated distrust of the chosen leaders, slogans and movements of working people. Thus Thomas Carlyle who summoned a remarkably compelling vision of working-class discontent, wrote *Chartism* (1840) as an apocalyptic warning of what might happen if the nation's leaders failed to respond to pressing social needs. By reducing Chartism to purely social causes, however, Carlyle refused to acknowledge the movement's political core, denying the appropriateness of working people acting politically: the 'condition-of-England' was a social not a political question and one to be dealt with not by but rather on behalf of working people.[3]

In approaching the subject of radical political leadership and the relationship it implies, it is necessary therefore to start with some appreciation of the political culture that sustained, set certain limits on and, to a considerable extent, defined leadership. In discussing the problems that faced national leaders, it is important to recognize Chartism's more distinctive characteristics: namely, its national dimensions, openness to 'members unlimited', democratic practice at the local level and striking capacity in towns throughout the country to generate a leadership from *within* labouring communities themselves. The movement drew upon an experienced and articulate core of plebeian activists.[4]

There can be no satisfactory understanding of Chartist leadership outside the context of the political culture that nurtured and shaped it. Many Chartists could have echoed the words of the weaver-poet Samuel Bamford: 'I was born a radical.'[5] It was in the weaving communities and burgeoning factory towns of the North that this vibrant political culture, stretching back often to the 1790s, remained most firmly intact. In 1838 the printer Henry Vincent first travelled to the North as the missionary for the London Working Men's Association. He reported his impressions in a private letter to his brother-in-law:

Ever since 1818 Yorkshire and Lancashire people have been peacefully struggling for Universal Suffrage ... You have no idea of the intensity of radical opinions here. You have an index from the numerous public house signs—full length portraits of Hunt holding in his hands scrawls [sic] containing the words Universal Suffrage, Annual Parliaments and the Ballot. Paine and Cobbett also figure occasionally.[6]

If Chartism took its name from a document produced by London artisans, it took its early tone from the smaller, more closely knit communities of the industrial North and Midlands.

The Chartist movement did of course draw many of its most prominent national leaders from outside the working class. Feargus O'Connor was a wealthy Irish landowner, lawyer and former MP; James Bronterre O'Brien was a journalist and former law student; Ernest Jones was a lawyer; Peter McDouall was a Scottish doctor. The fact, however, that such men were drawn to the Chartist cause and thus detached from their own social backgrounds is illustrative not, as is sometimes supposed, of the movement's weakness (indicative of its dependence on non-working-class leadership) but rather of its strength. These men, 'traditional' as opposed to 'organic intellectuals' (to adopt Gramsci's analytical distinction), were co-opted on the basis of their advocacy of what after 1832 had become a predominantly working-class political programme, ideology, strategy of mass action and set of organizations.[7] Conversely those middle-class political leaders who attempted to win some measure of working-class support—men like Thomas Attwood of the revived Birmingham Political Union, Richard Cobden of the Anti-Corn Law League, Joseph Sturge of the Complete Suffrage Union, or Joseph Hume of the household suffrage or 'little' Charter move — failed in this period precisely to the extent that they refused to accept popular radicalism's programme, ideas, strategy and organizations.[8]

## II

Ever since the publication of Asa Briggs' influential *Chartist Studies* (1959), much of the research that has been done on the movement has concentrated on reconstructing Chartism at the local level. This research has provided rich insights into the character and diversity of rank-and-file political activity. Indeed, there is a sense in which the movement must be understood in terms of its local manifestations. And yet by emphasizing local differences, such an approach may obscure Chartism's national achievement and miss broader themes of political convergence crucial to the movement, its leadership and organization. Thus, for example, the antinomy between the artisans of London and the more 'proletarianized' workers of the North around which so much Chartist history has been written is largely misconceived; there was much that united metropolitan artisans, both economically and politically, with the weavers, combers and factory workers of Lancashire and Yorkshire.[10]

As both Dorothy Thompson and Gareth Stedman Jones maintain, what was truly remarkable about Chartism was its national dimensions and shared aims. However, Stedman Jones argues that Chartist language did not displace earlier versions of radical ideology with some new, more 'class-conscious mode of thought'. Chartist ideology was based rather on non-class-specific language of political exclusion. The effect of the Reform Bill was to recast the term 'the People' in the form of a nearly exclusive identity with the working class, but Chartists failed to produce a distinctively class-based theory of economic exploitation. According to Stedman Jones, Chartism's purported class character, at least as formally manifest in its language, is an optical illusion that has tricked historians distracted by the perspectives of Marx and Engels.[11]

Stedman Jones's argument is important, not least for his refusal to reduce political issues to social determinants and for his emphasis on the shaping force of language in the constitution of collective political identities.[12] Moreover, Patrick Joyce and James Vernon have more explicitly called into question the status of 'class' as the master category for interpreting nineteenth-century popular politics, underscoring the range of possible meanings encoded within radical discourse and the pervasive summoning and appeal of 'the People' as opposed to 'the working class'.[13] Here we can only briefly note how Stedman Jones's broader argument touches on the question of Chartist leadership and the defining unities of Chartism.

First, although the tone and emphases of Chartist language varied between districts, the general coherence of this discourse, particularly of its political analysis, is striking. Thus, O'Connor was able to speak to audiences in districts throughout England, Scotland and Wales with relatively little variation in his style, tone or analysis; his leadership was accepted in an extraordinary range of localities despite occasional challenges from local leaders. Similarly, O'Connor's newspaper, the *Northern Star*, rapidly became the movement's unrivalled national organ. The shared perspectives and language of Chartism fostered close reciprocity between national leaders and Chartism's rank-and-file and made possible national institutions such as the *Star* and the National Charter Association.

O'Connor associated his own leadership, however, almost exclusively with the cause of working people: those with 'fustian jackets, blistered hands and unshorn chins'— an identification expressed not only in terms of formal rhetoric but symbolically inscribed within the rituals of the mass platform.[14]

Secondly, while the emphasis on the unifying quality of Chartist language and its essential political character (as well as its contingent vulnerability to shifts in the posture of the Victorian state) is well taken, we also need to consider the social programme that for many Chartists was implicit in the demand for the suffrage. To be sure, this 'programme' was never precisely defined; indeed it was often suppressed in the interests of political unity. None the less, as Dorothy Thompson argues, for many working people the demand for democratic citizenship implied, at the very least, arresting the emergent force of industrial capitalism: regulation of factory hours, repeal of the new Poor Law, some form of state intervention to guarantee a 'fair' wage for labour, a redistribution of land, and a balance between the claims of agricultural and industrial production. Furthermore, this has bearing on discussion of the character of the movement's leadership since the rejection of prevailing notions of political economy defined a fundamental difference between Chartists and middle-class radicals like J.A. Roebuck and Hume.'[15] Chartists refused to shake loose the social from the political. Thirdly, there were strong reactions among broad sections of working people experiencing intensified social and economic subordination. Despite the uneven development of capitalist manufacture and the fact that this development did not independently define either the emergence or decline of Chartism, working people did suffer a progressive loss of independence within the process of production. A widespread desire to recapture vestiges of such independence and a lost 'golden' age reinforced national solidarities.

Finally, the question of whether Chartism was or was not a class movement may be less revealing than the question of what kind of class movement it was. There are no pure languages of class or pure class movements. Moreover, as Linda Colley argues, class and nation were 'two sides of the same historical process'.[17] Intense struggles often take place over the ways in which certain 'shared' discourses and key terms are

appropriated or accented: invoking the language of constitutionalism, the nation or 'the People' does not preclude the forging of class identities.[18] Nor is there reason to assume that the
character of a movement can be determined solely on the basis
of discourse. Chartism was composed overwhelmingly of men
and women who either worked for wages in some form or
provided labour necessary for the reproduction and maintenance of those working for wages.[19] The intense and widespread opposition of those who owned and controlled
substantial property also suggests the extent to which contemporaries saw Chartist protest in class terms.

However, even if we regard the concept of class as important
to understanding Chartism, class was by no means the only
term of identity present within Chartist language and politics.
Appeals beyond class—to the nation, the people or the Bible—
were commonly expressed from Chartist platforms and in
Chartist writing. Class understandings were neither monolithic
nor stable. Moreover, the language and practice of radical politics were highly gendered: differing constructions of key
notions such as citizenship, virtue and independence based on
gender cannot be readily subsumed under the term 'class'.
Large numbers of Chartist women were in fact able to fashion
political identities for themselves as mothers, workers and
activists. However, as Anna Clark shows, the Chartist rhetoric
of domesticity while serving to mobilize working people
against both employers and the state may have contributed in
the long run to a narrowed vision of working-class politics.[20]

## III

The actual problems that faced Chartism's leaders were complex; indeed, they were often intractable. Most fundamentally,
the Chartist dilemma remained that of forging and sustaining a
unified national movement while attempting to devise a strategy for actualizing the central demand for universal male
suffrage. What is remarkable is not that the movement failed,
but rather that it managed so successfully to maintain a mass
presence for over a decade. Yet Chartist unity was always
vulnerable. This was why the charge of engendering disunity,
of betraying the movement's central goals, national institutions
and the leadership of O'Connor, the cynosure around which so

much of the movement's energy spun, could be fatal to the status of Chartist leaders.

The problems of national unity and direction were rather differently posed in Chartism's early years than they were to be in the 1840s. Chartism came together with great speed in the summer and autumn of 1838, as thousands of men and women who had been campaigning since 1832 for a range of issues—an unstamped press, factory legislation, repeal of the new Poor Law, general unionism—united behind the Charter.[21] The leadership problems of the years 1838–40 revolved around a set of interrelated questions about the tone and direction of the movement, focusing most dramatically on the issue of what course to adopt following parliament's rejection of the National Petition. The dominant strategy of open constitutionalism offered a means of mobilization centring on the ultimate testing of the supposed contractual relationship between government and people. The rejection of the National Petition, seen as the embodiment of the people's will, would mark the severance of the contract binding government and governed: the final symbol of tyranny and the point at which the democratically elected Convention would decide what action to pursue in defence of constitutional liberty.

The Convention assembled in the role of 'anti-parliament', as the 'real' parliament of the people, and more ambiguously as a possible substitute for the corrupt assembly of the ruling élite. Delegate after delegate at the meetings at which they were elected declared allegiance to the Convention's authority. In effect, the leadership of the radical movement sought to create a situation of 'dual power'; that is, they sought to develop autonomous institutions, of which the Convention was the most prominent, capable of providing an alternative to the existing structures of state power. Most delegates at the Convention, the only point of consolidated national leadership in 1839, rejected the view that they had assembled merely as a petitioning body. The Convention's role only began with the presentation of the National Petition; it was the delegates' solemn duty to coordinate a strategy for reconstructing the basis of political power in Britain.[22]

What Chartists did in 1839 was to push the boundaries of constitutionalist action as far as they could go; they reloaded categories of political reference with ultra-radical meaning.

Thus constant allusions to the National Petition as the 'last' petition in any form that the people would present to parliament represented both a recognition of the reluctance of popular radicals to petition and a way to infuse the ancient right of parliamentary petition with revolutionary content by implying that armed resistance was the appropriate response to the rejection of the people's will. Similarly, radicals seized on the presumed right of free assembly and tested their own strength and the forbearance of the state. 'Monster' demonstrations, torchlight meetings and the call for 'simultaneous' assemblies in the summer of 1839 escalated the scale and implications of constitutionalist activity.[23]

Most crucial, however, was the decision on what form of action was dictated after the rituals and protocols of constitutionalist protest were exhausted. The repertoire of mass demonstrations, petitioning campaigns and the assembling of a convention was marvellous for generating mass support and activity providing a finely calibrated course of well-understood action. It tested the political nerve of the propertied classes and the resolve of the state, including the loyalty of the military. Its very ambiguity about future action ensured high levels of unity. However, the essential ambiguity at the heart of constitutionalist mobilization also defined its limitations. It meant that the movement was highly susceptible to fragmentation in the wake of the rejection of the Petition in the summer of 1839.

Chartist strategy was modelled on the reform movement of 1831–2 and O'Connell's campaign for Roman Catholic emancipation in which physical violence was constantly threatened but was ultimately averted through the pragmatic concessions of the governing élite. In 1839, however, the government was not inclined to retreat before the spectre of radical intimidation. They were unwilling to retreat because the equation of political concession was now different: both sides of the equation had altered. There was greater political cohesion on the part of men of substantial property—which does not mean that there were no areas of conflict between the interests of landed, commercial and industrial capital. Also the actual demand being made was more fundamentally corrosive to established political and economic power than the demands of 1829 or 1832.[24] The meaning of the demand for universal suffrage in 1839 was more revolutionary than the realization of universal male suffrage was, for example, in France in 1848 or than the popular demand for 'manhood' suffrage was in Britain in the 1860s.

The bitter disputes that surfaced among Chartist leaders during the final weeks of the Convention and in the aftermath of the abortive risings of the winter of 1839–40 should not lead us to reduce the failure of Chartist strategy in the most crucial year of the movement's history to the inadequacies of national leadership *per se*. The divisions within the leadership reflected the dilemma which faced an insurgent movement in what was essentially a non-revolutionary situation. The decisions that they faced were difficult ones. On the whole, the direction they gave, and indeed which the movement demanded, was intelligent and responsible, if not usually unanimous. The decision to retreat in 1839 was taken because men like O'Connor and O'Brien felt that if provoked they would be defeated in a violent confrontation with the forces of authority. Despite moments of panic, particularly at the level of local control, government authority was never seriously shaken. Lord John Russell, at the Home Office, and General Charles Napier, commander of the North, exhibited a high degree of confidence in their ability to act against the Chartists.[25] There seems little reason to suppose that their sense of assurance was not well founded. Moreover, during the 1840s this sense of assurance grew more secure. In his careful analysis of the configuration of British state power in 1848, John Saville has concluded that the Chartist movement faced an experienced governmental élite acting with consummate resolve and intelligence, prepared to employ the full coercive powers at their disposal, both legal and military, while maintaining broad support among the landed and middle classes.[26]

This is not to argue that Chartist leaders could not have made other choices. There was a very real possibility that the Convention would call for a 'sacred month', or 'national holiday' of the industrious classes. Had they done so, the violent outcome of such a political strike might well have altered the texture of class relations in nineteenth-century Britain. Certainly the 'national holiday' offered the key strategic link between constitutionalist mobilization and insurgent confrontation on a wide scale. Chartist failure to resolve the recurrent dilemma of radical constitutionalism led to the abortive risings of the winter of 1839–40 and in the 1840s to a retreat from the overt confrontationalism of the movement's early years.[27] Chartism never quite recaptured the widespread conviction that 'the People' were on the brink of overthrowing the rule of 'the Privileged'.

## IV

Of course the central problems of Chartist unity, direction and strategy remained, but they were reordered by a realization that the struggle for the People's Charter was to be a protracted affair. This meant that in the 1840s more emphasis was given to questions of organization and also to the movement's attitude towards issues other than the demand for universal suffrage. During the 1840s, Chartist protest was characterized by a kind of 'double vision'. While formally the answer to economic and social ills was reduced to securing the vote for working people, in practice Chartism's leaders and activists had to formulate a policy concerning the movement's orientation towards the wider concerns of the labour movement without jeopardizing the unity and political direction of Chartism.

One of the notable achievements of Chartism, of its leaders and activists, was the formation of the National Charter Association (NCA).[28] Founded in the summer of 1840, the NCA marked a qualitative advance in working-class political organization. The Association has some claim to being regarded as Europe's first working-class political party. It remained the dominant national organization for the rest of the movement's history. The establishment of the association was in large part a response to the widely held Chartist belief that the movement had suffered defeat in 1839 due to the lack of national organization and united leadership.[29] Significantly, the NCA was founded during a period in which nearly all of Chartism's national leaders and many local leaders were in prison, underscoring the initiative and maturity of rank-and-file activists.

One of the NCA's central problems was the effort to establish a more formal or what might be termed 'bureaucratized' leadership—democratically elected, paid and accountable to its members. The NCA rules provided for a national executive of five members (initially the number had been seven) who were to be full-time officials and were to be paid a regular wage (30s. per week and 40s. for the secretary) for their services.[30] The wages of the executive were to be paid from membership dues, equal portions of which went to the national association and to local branches. There was considerable ambiguity, however, about what exactly the members of the executive were to be doing and whether they should draw pay during periods when they were not out lecturing and agitating.[31] The executive set policy in the loose sense of issuing addresses and making formal statements recommending certain courses of action: for example, on how Chartists should vote at the 1841 general election or what attitude the movement should take towards the mass strikes of summer 1842. But in terms of setting policy the executive's influence was never as great as that of the *Northern Star*. The executive's own journal, launched in late 1841, lasted less than a month.[32] On the other hand, the executive's policies were usually in line with those being pushed in the *Star*'s columns. Moreover, the *Star* was the only other major national Chartist institution offering regular, paid employment for Chartism's leaders. O'Connor was fully conscious that there were, in effect, two centres of national Chartist leadership and tried to ensure, not always successfully, that they remained mutually supporting. He sought to guarantee the independence of the NCA executive by not allowing anyone in his pay through the *Star* to also hold paid office in the NCA.[33]

The issue of the payment of leaders, however, remained a delicate one, and one that is instructive for grasping something about the nature of Chartist leadership and organization. Local Chartists were often reluctant to forward funds to the NCA executive, preferring to use their limited resources to employ local or district NCA lecturers over whom they had more direct control and with whom they had more direct contact. This preference highlights a prevalent concern about the accountability of paid leaders. Local lecturers—and the NCA was often remembered primarily as a lecturing body—were selected by local Chartist associations that also paid them.[34] They were usually subject to reappointment every three months.

There also continued to be distrust of working men who 'traded in politics'. The movement was, indeed, vulnerable to the pocket-books of rival movements. O'Connor contrasted the position of former working men who hired themselves out to middle-class movements with that of the NCA executive and district leaders. Thus Henry Vincent, 'the political pedlar'— once one of Chartism's most popular speakers—had sold out to the Complete Suffrage movement for £6 a week, whereas the NCA executive members drew a mere working man's wage.[35] Such middle-class attempts to 'buy' Chartist leaders, to exploit their standing in the interests of counter-agitations, became a familiar theme for denunciation. The appointment of Chartist missionaries under the auspices of the NCA represented an attempt to establish a coherent, accountable, legitimate system of Chartist lecturers.

The notion of a 'legitimate', paid leadership clashed, however, with older notions that identified 'independence' as the guarantee of political integrity. The label 'independent' had a certain resonance within British political discourse, rooted in struggles of the seventeenth and eighteenth centuries. It implied that a politician or citizen was beholden to no one else for his political beliefs and actions; that he was incorruptibly wedded to political or religious principle. Chartist leaders often made a point of their independent status. For example, R.J. Richardson, a master joiner and one of Manchester's delegates to the 1839 Convention, told a Chartist meeting:

He was not a paid political advocate, perambulating the country to excite the people to disaffection; he was an elector of the township of Salford in the county of Lancaster, and a freeholder of the same county; and he held a station in society which enabled him to employ his time and his humble talents in endeavouring to ameliorate the condition of the people . . . [36]

In contrast, at the 1842 Chartist Convention George White, one of the *Star*'s paid reporters, answered charges that he was merely O'Connor's tool. Invoking the overlapping artisanal notion of manly independence, he denied that any man could buy his services at the cost of his principles.

It was well known that when he was employed in Yorkshire he would never be controlled in his opinions or his actions by his employer, and he should act now in a similar manner. So far as O'Connor supported the cause he would support him, whether he was called a tool or no; and if O'Connor deserted the cause he would be one of the first to oppose him.[37]

White, a wool-comber by trade, was typical of Chartism's middle-range leaders. He was a working man who had left his trade for a highly uncertain career as a political agitator. Arrested at every point of Chartist crisis, he was sentenced to prison in 1840, 1842 and 1848. He died a neglected figure in the late 1860s in a parish workhouse in Sheffield and was buried in a pauper's grave before his friends could save him from this ignominious end.[38]

O'Connor constantly defended the notion that the movement needed a regularly paid national executive, particularly if they wanted to have working men as their leaders. He wrote:

I am obstinately opposed to an unpaid Executive, and for this reason. If you have an unpaid Executive [as some Chartists had proposed], you must have a purely middle-class Executive, because you cannot elect working men as your officers, that moment every door is closed against them and at once they are marked, and if in work are dismissed.[39]

O'Connor pointed to one of the most severe problems facing working-class leaders: victimization. James Leach, a power-loom weaver who served on the executive during 1841 and 1842, afterwards found it impossible to find a job in a Lancashire mill. In 1843, when the NCA was again reorganized and its headquarters were moved from Manchester to London, O'Connor himself joined the executive as treasurer. But the NCA executive that presided nearly unchanged from 1843 to 1847 was predominantly working class in social composition. It included Philip McGrath, an East End tailor, Thomas Martin Wheeler, former baker and schoolteacher, Thomas Clark (who replaced the carpenter Henry Ross in 1844), cordwainer, and Christopher Doyle, a power-loom weaver.

Yet there was a contradiction at the heart of O'Connor's defence of the paid services of the NCA executive and its lecturers since he was the movement's great unpaid leader, the epitome of the independent gentleman. He often legitimated his own claim to leadership on the basis of his unpaid services, incorruptibility and total independence. O'Connor never drew his salary as a member of the executive. His own leadership remained unincorporated within anything so mundane or bureaucratic as the NCA's structure. In an important sense the movement's most charismatic figure was needed to impart legitimacy to newer forms of leadership emerging within the Chartist movement. In practice 'charismatic' and 'bureaucratic' forms of political leadership, to employ Weber's distinction, proved to be interactive and mutually reinforcing modes.[40]

It was not always easy, however, to get Chartists or their leaders to accept the idea that they need all join a single national organization. NCA dues were often difficult to collect and certainly there were thousands of men and women who considered themselves loyal Chartists who never took out a NCA membership card. O'Brien, who refused to join the NCA, protested that the attempt to 'bully' all Chartists to join one association promoted disunion rather than union.[41] In 1842–3, however, as the movement had to arbitrate the offer of an alliance with a narrow section of middle-class reformers, in the shape of Sturge's Complete Suffrage initiative, loyalty not only to the name 'Chartist' but to the NCA became acid tests. Middle-class radicals who wanted co-operation should accept Chartism: its name, history, leadership and organization.[42]

## V

If radicals were not always convinced of the paramount necessity of joining the NCA, they were also often attracted to other movements and causes. In conclusion, therefore, we can return to Chartism's 'double vision' and to a brief consideration of a second major concern of the 1840s: Chartism's orientation towards other reform movements and priorities.

The official Chartist view was that other reforms—free trade, abolition of the new Poor Law, the establishment of a ten-hour working day, etc.—however desirable, were not only less important than but also unobtainable without manhood suffrage. Throughout the 1840s, however, particularly at the local level, Chartists took the lead across a broad spectrum of causes; they often assumed more generally the leadership of a nascent labour movement. There was also widespread Chartist interest in projects for working-class self-improvement, whether through temperance, education, co-operative retailing and production, friendly societies or schemes for settlement on the land. Furthermore, at the local level Chartists were sometimes able to create a highly integrated 'movement culture', sustaining their own democratic chapels, temperance societies, schools for children and adults, libraries, regular lecture series and debates, co-operative stores, land-plan branches. Although Chartists did not hold that working-class 'improvement' should be a prerequisite for acquiring political rights, there was strong feeling that working people should prepare themselves as future democratic citizens. Chartist participation was itself regarded as a democratic model, prefiguring the realization of universal suffrage.[43]

At least until 1848, Chartism was usually able to contain tensions between ameliorative goals and the transfigurative promise of universal suffrage. But while Chartism's self-sustaining cultural activities were central to the flourishing of the movement in the early 1840s, this trend could also imperil the maintenance of both local and national unity. The key was not allowing these social and cultural objects to displace the political struggle for the suffrage. The balance was not always easily maintained, as evidenced by O'Connor's famous denunciation of 'Church Chartism, Teetotal Chartism, Knowledge Chartism, and Household Suffrage Chartism'. It was not that O'Connor, or other leaders, opposed efforts aimed at collective self-improvement, but rather that they feared the loss of political direction and the establishment of exclusive 'moral' criteria for membership.[44] O'Connor's own land plan was merely the most ambitious attempt to contain these tensions. The Chartist land plan offered the immediate prospect of improving the condition of working people, while holding out the vision of a society based on principles of small, independent ownership, production and exchange, and on notions of refounding an organic community. Not surprisingly, there were those who accused O'Connor of diverting the movement from its political goals.[45]

Chartism never turned in upon itself: never succumbed to sectarianism. However after 1842, and Chartism's second furious assault on the bastions of privilege, the question of how best to arbitrate the competing claims of movements campaigning for ameliorative reform was more seriously posed. What 'external' demands were to be considered parallel to or compatible with the demand for universal manhood suffrage? In 1844, in one of the clearer statements of Chartist principle, O'Connor explained why Chartists should support Ashley's Factory Bill, while standing fast against the overtures of free-traders and middle-class advocates of 'complete suffrage'.

Some very sincere and enthusiastic, but misguided Chartists, have said, 'why not oppose this policy equally as the policy of the League, the Feudalists, and the Complete Suffragists'! To that view my answer is: because the agitation of each and all of those parties is intended to *subjugate labour to capital*; WHILE LORD ASHLEY'S BILL WOULD TAKE THE VERY LARGEST RIVET OUT OF LABOUR'S FETTERS. Shall I be asked if it would be prudent to move the Charter as an amendment upon the Ten Hours Bill? . . . my answer is, that it would be equally prudent to move it as an amendment to the formation of the Colliers' Union; and yet I am rather of the opinion that such a course would be scouted by every Chartist in the land.

The test was whether demands or movements addressed a 'Labour question'.[46]

The attempt to formulate a policy of Chartist action that enabled activists to participate in agitations for immediate or sectional gains (such as the strikes of stonemasons in 1841 or of miners in 1844) without losing sight of the Charter was indicative of the 1840s. The ultimate protection for all labourers might lay in winning the franchise but by the mid-1840s it had become more difficult to hold centre stage for the Charter. O'Connor also registered a shift in Chartist discourse (one inviting further study), away from the more traditional radical critique based on the political division between the Privileged and the People, towards an emphasis on the economic division between Capital and Labour. Devising a 'social programme' to complement the franchise was a pressing issue of late Chartist policy carrying over into post-Chartist radical politics.[47]

There is a sense in which the mid-Victorian labour movement is defined by the waning of Chartism's highly politicized core of belief and action. This is not the place to discuss the reasons for Chartism's decline, although the experience of defeat and the exhaustion of the strategy of constitutionalist mobilization were perhaps as important as were concessions from the Victorian state and the 'mellowing' of élite rule both nationally and locally.[48] Mid-Victorian radicalism was reduced in scale and its political vision narrowed, as working people pursued goals that appeared more immediately realizable. Socially the movement was less diverse than early Chartism; the place of women and of unorganized and less skilled male workers—whose presence had already decreased in the 1840s due to more formal practices such as dues-paying membership to associations and the ticketing of meetings—was severely diminished.[49] However, the view that Chartism's demise marked a sharp break in working-class political history has recently been challenged by revisionist historians stressing the underlying continuities between the programmatic aims, language and ideology of popular liberalism and earlier radical movements. Thus Joyce identifies the recurrent populist tropes bridging the transitions from Chartism to popular liberalism and liberalism to late nineteenth-century socialism, and Eugenio Biagini persuasively argues that working-class liberalism is best seen not as an outcome of bourgeois hegemony but rather as the 'continuation of genuine and older popular plebeian traditions'.[50] Still, some important and obvious things had changed. The suffrage demand may have been formally similar (although the Chartist and popular liberal demands were not the same) but by the 1860s the demand no longer carried the same class inflexion nor did it appear so clearly to threaten the very basis of state power. The Chartist insistence on the whole Charter contrasts with popular liberalism's more pragmatic and gradualist approach. Moreover, much of what defined Chartism lay outside its formal programme. Chartism's style of mobilization, the commitment to the mass platform and its rhetorical tone, was always more intimidating than popular liberalism or mid-century labour-radicalism; and despite their charismatic popularity, Bright and Gladstone's identification with the labour movement was hardly the exclusive bond of a leader like O'Connor. While there were important continuities between the constituent concerns and the themes of the 1860s and Chartism, a reordering of emphases and goals took place, a further blurring of radicalism's double vision.

## NOTES

This is a revised version of a paper originally given at the Consortium on Revolutionary Europe at Charleston, South Carolina, a condensed version of which appears in *Proceedings of the Consortium on Revolutionary Europe 1989*.

1   See, for example, Mark Hovell, *The Chartist Movement* (Manchester, 1925 edn), p. 96; J.T. Ward, *Chartism* (London, 1973), for a more recent example. See more generally, 'Chartism and the historians', in Dorothy Thompson, *Outsiders: Class, Gender and Nation* (London, 1993), pp. 19–44.

2 Most notably Dorothy Thompson, *The Chartists: Popular Politics in the Industrial Revolution* (London, 1984), particularly Ch. V; David Jones, *Chartism and the Chartists* (London, 1975), Ch. II; James Epstein, *The Lion of Freedom: Feargus O'Connor and the Chartist Movement, 1832–42* (London, 1982).

3 See Raymond Williams, *Culture and Society, 1780–1950* (London, 1958), Chs IV–V; Thompson, *Chartists*, pp. 250–1, and Ch. X.

4 See David Goodway, *London Chartism, 1838–1848* (Cambridge, 1982); I.J. Prothero, 'Chartism in London', *Past and Present*, **XLIV** (1969), 76–105; John Foster, *Class Struggle and the Industrial Revolution* (London, 1974), pp. 131–60; James Epstein, 'Some organisational and cultural aspects of the Chartist movement in Nottingham', in James Epstein and Dorothy Thompson (eds), *The Chartist Experience: Studies in Working-Class Radicalism and Culture* (London, 1982), pp. 230–2; Christopher Godfrey, 'The Chartist prisoners, 1839–41', *International Review of Social History*, **XXIV** (1979), 189–236.

5 Cited in Jones, *Chartism and the Chartists*, p. 63. See E.P. Thompson, *The Making of the English Working Class* (London, 1963).

6 Vincent to Minikin, 26 Aug. 1838, London, Transport House, Vincent MSS, 1/1/10.

7 Antonio Gramsci, *Selections from the Prison Notebooks*, ed. and trans. Quintin Hoare and Geoffrey Nowell Smith (New York, 1971), pp. 5–23; cf. Harold Perkin, *The Origins of Modern English Society* (London, 1969), pp. 252–70.

8 Clive Behagg, 'An alliance with the middle class: the Birmingham Political Union and early Chartism', in *Chartist Experience*, pp. 59–86; Alexander Wilson, 'The suffrage movement', in Patricia Hollis (ed.), *Pressure from without in Early Victorian England* (London, 1974), pp. 80–104; Lucy Brown, 'The Chartists and the Anti-Corn Law League', in Asa Briggs (ed.), *Chartist Studies* (London, 1959), pp. 342–71; Alex Tyrrell, *Joseph Sturge and the Moral Radical Party in Early Victorian Britain* (London, 1987); Nicholas C. Edsall, 'A failed national movement: the Parliamentary and Financial Reform Association, 1848–54', *Bulletin of the Institute of Historical Research*, **XLIX** (1976) 108–31.

9 Briggs' chapter 'National bearings', pp. 288–303, provided an important counter-point to the volume's local emphasis.

10 See Iorwerth Prothero, *Artisans and Politics in Early Nineteenth-Century London: John Gast and His Times* (Folkestone, 1979), pp. 332–40; Robert Sykes, 'Early Chartism and trade unionism in South-East Lancashire', in *Chartist Experience*, pp. 152–93.

11 Gareth Stedman Jones, *Languages of Class: Studies in English Working Class History, 1832–1982* (Cambridge, 1983), Ch. III.

12  For the debate surrounding Stedman Jones's work, see John Foster, 'The declassing of language', *New Left Review*, **CL** (1985), 29–46; Robert Gray, 'The deconstruction of the English working class', *Social History*, **XI** (1986), 363–73; James Epstein, 'Rethinking the categories of working class history', *Labour/Le Travail*, **XVIII** (1986), 195–208; Joan W. Scott, 'On language, gender and working class history', *International Labor and Working Class History*, **XXXI** (1987), 1–13; Neville Kirk, 'In defence of class: a critique of recent revisionist writing on the nineteenth-century English working class', *International Review of Social History*, **XXXII** (1987), 2–47; John Belchem, 'Radical language and ideology in early nineteenth-century England: the challenge of the platform', *Albion*, **XX** (1988), 247–59; David Mayfield and Susan Thorne, 'Social history and its discontents: Gareth Stedman Jones and the politics of language', *Social History*, **XVII** (1992), 167–88, and responses in *Social History*.

13  Patrick Joyce, *Visions of the People: Industrial England and the Question of Class, 1848–1914* (Cambridge, 1991); James Vernon, *Politics and the People: A Study in English Political Culture*, c.1815–1867 (Cambridge, 1993).

14  Paul A. Pickering, 'Class without words; symbolic communication in the Chartist movement', *Past and Present*, **CXII** (August 1986), 144–62.

15  William Thomas, *The Philosophical Radicals: Nine Studies in Theory and Practice, 1817–41* (Oxford, 1979), Ch. V; 'The philosophical radicals', in *Pressure from Without*, pp. 52–79; Ronald K. Huch and Paul R. Ziegler, *Joseph Hume: the People's M.P.* (Philadelphia 1985), pp. 117–19 and Ch. VIII.

16  Thompson, *Making of the English Working Class*, Ch. VI; cf. William H. Sewell, Jr., 'Uneven development, the autonomy of politics, and the dockworkers of nineteenth-century Marseille', *American Historical Review*, **ICIII** (1988), particularly pp. 607–8, 637; Joyce, *Visions of the People*, pp. 2–6, 16.

17  Linda Colley, 'Whose nation? Class and national consciousness in Britain, 1750–1830', *Past and Present*, **CXIII** (November 1986), 100.

18  See James Epstein, *Radical Expression: Political Language, Ritual, and Symbol in England, 1790–1850* (New York and Oxford, 1994), Ch. I.

19  Thompson, *Chartists*, Chs VI–IX; David Jones, Tables I, IV, pp. 30–2, 134–7.

20  Anna Clark, 'The rhetoric of chartist domesticity: gender, language, and class', *Journal of British Studies*, **XXXI** (1992), 62–88; Dorothy Thompson, 'Women and nineteenth-century radical politics: a lost dimension', reprinted in *Outsiders*, pp. 77–102; Jutta Schwarzkopf, *Women in the Chartist Movement* (London, 1991).

21  Epstein, *Lion of Freedom*, Ch. III; Prothero, *Artisans and Politics*; Joel H. Wiener, *The War of the Unstamped: The Movement to Repeal the British Newspaper Tax, 1830–36* (Ithaca, NY, 1969); Patricia Hollis, *The Pauper Press: A Study of Working-Class Radicalism of the 1830s* (Oxford, 1970); N.C. Edsall, *The Anti-Poor Law Movement, 1833–44* (Manchester, 1971), Ch. VIII; John Knott, *Popular Opposition to the 1834 Poor Law* (London, 1986), Ch. VI; W.H. Oliver, 'The Consolidated Trades' Union of 1834', *Economic History Review*, **XVII** (1964), 177–95.

22  T.M. Parssinen, 'Association, convention and anti-parliament in British radical politics, 1771–1848', *English Historical Review*, **LXXXVIII** (1973), 504–33; Thompson, *Chartists*, Ch. III; Epstein, *Lion of Freedom*, Ch. VI.

23  See, for example, Robert Sykes, 'Physical-Force Chartism: the cotton district and the Chartist crisis of 1839', *International Review of Social History*, **XXX** (1985), 207–36.

24  Cf. J.C.D. Clark, *English Society 1688–1832: Ideology, Social Structure and Political Practice During the ancien régime* (Cambridge, 1985), Ch. VI.

25  See W.F.P. Napier, *The Life and Opinions of General Sir Charles Napier* (4 vols, London, 1857), Vol. II.

26  John Saville, *1848: The British State and the Chartist Movement* (Cambridge, 1987). See also Stanley H. Palmer, *Police and Protest in England and Ireland, 1780-1850* (Cambridge, 1988), Chs X–XII; F.C. Mather, 'The Government and the Chartists', in Asa Briggs (ed.), *Chartist Studies* (London, 1959), pp. 372–406.

27  See David Jones, *The Last Rising: The Newport Insurrection of 1839* (Oxford, 1985); A.J. Peacock, *Bradford Chartism 1838–40* (York, 1969), pp. 28ff.; J.L. Baxter, 'Early Chartism and labour class struggle: South Yorkshire, 1837–40', in S. Pollard and C. Holmes (eds), *Essays in the Economic and Social History of South Yorkshire* (Barnsley, 1976), pp. 146–50; John Belchem, *'Orator' Hunt: Henry Hunt and English Working-Class Radicalism* (Oxford, 1985), particularly pp. 121–32, for 'forcible intimidation' in 1819.

28  See Eileen Yeo, 'Some practices and problems of Chartist democracy', in *Chartist Experience*, pp. 345–80; Epstein, *Lion of Freedom*, pp. 220–36; Jones, *Chartism*, pp. 70–7.

29  See, for example, *McDouall's Chartist and Republican Journal*, 3 Apr. 1841, pp. 1–2; *Northern Star* (hereafter *NS*), 25 July 1840, p. 1; 1 Aug. p. 1, for NCA founding conference.

30  *NS*, 1 Aug. 1840; 27 Feb. 1841, p. 1, for the revised plan; Jones, *Chartism*, pp. 195–200.

31  For doubts about executive duties, see *NS*, 19 Nov. 1842–4 Feb. 1843; Bairstow to Cooper, 5 July 1842; White to Cooper, 27 July

1842, London, Public Record Office, Treasury Solicitor's papers, 11/601 and 11/602.

32  *Executive Journal of the National Charter Association*, 16 Oct.–6 Nov. 1841.

33  *NS*, 16 Sept. 1843, p. 6.

34  Yeo, 'Some practices and problems of Chartist democracy', pp. 355–60.

35  *NS*, 4 June 1842, p. 7; 7 January 1843, p. 1. See Brian Harrison's entry for Vincent in J.M. Bellamy and John Saville (eds), *Dictionary of Labour Biography* (London, 1972), Vol. I.

36  *NS*, 1 June 1838, p. 8.

37  Ibid., 30 April 1842, p. 6.

38  White to Ironside, 6 June 1868, Manchester, Co-operative Union Library, Holyoake Papers.

39  *NS*, 4 February 1843, p. 1.

40  *From Max Weber: Essays in Sociology* (New York, 1958 edn), ed. Hans H. Gerth and C. Wright Mill, pp. 245–50.

41  *British Statesman*, 5 November 1842, p. 1; Epstein, *Lion of Freedom*, pp. 230–3, 245–6.

42  O'Connor believed, however, that economic crisis would drive impoverished shopkeepers, the 'industrious portion' of the middle class as opposed to the 'steam lords', into a radical alliance on Chartist terms. See, for example, *NS*, 2 July, 1842, p. 4; 17 September, p. 2.

43  Epstein, 'Some organisational and cultural aspects of the Chartist movement'; Yeo, 'Some practices and problems of Chartist democracy', pp. 373–4.

44  Epstein, *Lion of Freedom*, pp. 236–45; Brian Harrison, 'Teetotal Chartism', *History*, **LVIII** (1973), 193–217.

45  John Saville, introduction to R.G. Gammage, *History of the Chartist Movement* (London, 1969 edn); Joy MacAskill, 'The Chartist Land Plan', in *Chartist Studies*, pp. 304–41; Malcolm S. Chase, 'The Land and the working classes: English agrarians, circa 1775–1851' (D. Phil. dissertation, Sussex University, 1984), Ch. VII; Epstein, *Lion of Freedom*, pp. 249–57.

46  *NS*, 6 Apr. 1844, p. 1; also see 16 Nov., p. 1, on Chartist policy toward the miners' union.

47  John Belchem, 'Chartism and the trades, 1848–1850', *English Historical Review*, **ICVIII** (1983), 261–90; Margot C. Finn, *After Chartism: Class and Nation in English Radical Politics, 1848–1874* (Cambridge, 1993), *passim*.

48  John Belchem, '1848: Feargus O'Connor and the collapse of the mass platform', in *Chartist Experience*, pp. 269–310; Stedman Jones, 'Rethinking Chartism', pp. 175–8; Thompson, *Chartists*, Ch. XIV;

Saville, *1848*, pp. 217–21; Theodore Koditschek, *Class Formation and Urban Industrial Society: Bradford, 1750–1850* (Cambridge, 1990), Ch. 18.

49  Neville Kirk, *The Growth of Working Class Reformism in Mid-Victorian England* (London, 1985); Thompson, 'Women and nineteenth-century radical politics', pp. 97–100; Vernon, *Politics and the People*, particularly Ch. 6.

50  Joyce, *Visions of the People*, Chs II—III; Eugenio F. Biagini, *Liberty, Retrenchment and Reform: Popular Liberalism and the Age of Gladstone, 1860–1880* (Cambridge, 1992), p. 7; Biagini and Alastair J. Reid (eds), *Currents of Radicalism, Organised Labour and Party Politics in Britain, 1850-1914* (Cambridge, 1991). See also T.R. Tholfsen, *Working-Class Radicalism in Mid-Victorian England* (London, 1976); Michael Winstanley, 'Oldham radicalism and the origins of popular liberalism, 1830–52', *Historical Journal*, **XXXVI** (1993), 619–43. For a balanced review, see Robert Gray, 'Class, politics and historical "revisionism"', *Social History*, **XIX** (1994), 209–20.

# 3

# *Who Wrote To The* Northern Star?

STEPHEN ROBERTS

I remember Dorothy Thompson observing, during one of her classes at Birmingham University in 1980, that it was very easy to be deflected from the task in hand when reading the *Northern Star*. There were, she explained, so many interesting sections to the newspaper, not least, on the second page, the advertisements. When I came to read the *Star* for myself, I discovered the truth of this remark. My search for information on Thomas Cooper or George White or Samuel Kydd was often broken off while I perused advertisements for Old Parr's Life Pills (as used by William Hick of the *Star* office), or read graphic accounts of murders (of which, female Plymouth Chartists complained in 1841, there were not enough), or wondered what happened to the 'Young Patriots' who carried the names of the Chartist leaders into the twentieth century.[1] But I found the greatest distraction of all was the column headed 'To Readers and Correspondents'. The *Star* received hundreds of letters each week—almost one hundred at a time by some posts in the early 1840s. 'If we were to print all the communications we receive, we should, some weeks, require six or seven *Northern Stars*,' William Hill, the paper's first editor, noted.[2] Though Feargus O'Connor employed reporters—seven of them in early 1842, including Julian Harney in Sheffield, George White in Birmingham, William Griffin in Manchester, and George Bartlett in Bath — most of the material in the *Star* was supplied by unpaid local adherents.[3] Undoubtedly there was a very close rapport between the *Star* and the Chartist rank-and-file who read the paper. What follows is based mostly on the column 'To Readers and Correspondents'. It is not therefore a full exploration of this relationship; but the column does offer one window on the role of the *Star* and its importance to working people.

Most of the communications received in the *Star* office were addresses and reports of local meetings and demonstrations. The latter were accorded a position of prominence in the paper, usually appearing on either the front page or the second page. These reports came not only from the major centres of Chartist support but also from places with small numbers of activists — like the 'democratic village' of Daisy Hill in the West Riding, or Devonport, where, in January 1841, the lecturer E.P. Mead organized the first ever Chartist meeting.[4] The optimism and determination of the Chartists are always apparent in the reports in the *Star*. Here is an account of a camp meeting on Norland Moor near Halifax in September 1844:

It was pleasing to behold the groups of earnest and devoted friends of liberty ascending the stupendous hills in all directions, accompanied by their wives and daughters. The sun shone brilliantly . . . At 2 o'clock Mr. G. White of Bradford, Ben Rushton, that staunch old veteran in the cause of Democracy, and a number of Chartists of the right sort from Halifax, climbed the hill. Mr. John Crossland of Halifax was unanimously called to the chair and delivered an appropriate address, after which 'Sons of Poverty Assemble' was sung in good style . . . The old veteran, Ben Rushton, followed . . . He dwelt on the persecution which himself and others had endured for the 'good old cause' and concluded by stating that, although seventy years had passed over his head and blanched his hairs, he was as devoted as ever to the principles of Chartism . . . Mr. George White of Bradford addressed the meeting at some length and pointed out . . . that the real curse of society was the admission of the right of one man to make a profit out of the labour of his fellow; and contended that instead of desiring a union with the profit-making class they should use their whole strength to destroy it . . . Mr. James Chippendale announced the places in the various townships where names might be enrolled in the National Charter Association and the business concluded by singing a Chartist hymn . . . The 'boys of the hills' are all right. It would teach a good lesson to some of our consumptive grumblers and snivelling fault-finders were they to witness the sort of stuff that composes a Yorkshire camp meeting.[5]

It was generally the responsibility of the secretary of the local body to submit reports to the *Star* — individuals like Anna Pepper of the Leeds Female Radical Association, Thomas Simnitt of Newark, Moses Simpson of Hanley, Edwin Polin of Paisley, and

J.H. Longmaid of Truro, who was known to brandish a copy of the *Star* in his hand when he spoke at public meetings.[6] Sometimes lecturers themselves supplied accounts of meetings they had addressed. Alternatively, at the end of a meeting, a resolution was passed to send a report to the *Star* and arrangements were then made.[7]

In addition to these reports, many poems were also sent to the *Star*. Composing poetry had, for the would-be working-class writer, an immense appeal. Unlike novel-writing, it could be done whilst at work and did not require long periods of leisure. Furthermore, the end product could be sung at meetings. At all times, but especially in 1841–2, there was a mass of readers' poetry in the *Star* office. 'The poets must excuse us,' Hill wrote during the 1841 election. 'We have received more Chartist election songs than we could count in an hour or sing in a week.'[8] The Chartists whose verse appeared most often in the *Star* up to 1842 were Philip Bevan and 'Iota' of Newport, T.B. Smith of Hull and later Leeds, L.T. Clancy of London, Benjamin Stott of Manchester, James Vernon of South Molton in Devon, John Watkins of Whitby, and E.P Mead of Birmingham. Confined to his home after an accident, Vernon in fact rivals Ernest Jones or W.J. Linton as the movement's most fecund poet. His best verse deals with his own paralysis.[9]

John Watkins was a friend of Ebenezer Elliott, whose daughter became his second wife in 1849, and lived in the upper-middle-class comfort of Aislaby Hall near Whitby.[10] His father, who died in 1842, was a friend of the Marquis of Normanby, who lived in nearby Mulgrave Castle and served as Home Secretary from 1839 to 1841. According to Watkins, 'when the Charter Agitation commenced the working men of Whitby called me to be their leader . . . I drew them up a set of rules and frequently preached and lectured to them'.[11] His espousal of the Chartist cause led to a rift with his father and, after he had read from a self-penned pamphlet at a meeting in Stockton-on-Tees in September 1839, to his own arrest and imprisonment in Durham Jail:

> I've nought to do but listen now,
> To hear the 'iron tongue of time',
> As day by day it tells how slow
> My heavy hours in prison climb.

The sunshine on the whiten'd wall,
Reflected through the massy grate,
A chequer'd shade where light should fall,
Mirrors to me my prison fate.

Harsh grating thunder through the walls,
Resounds as turns the pond'rous bars;
'All's safe! All's well' the turnkey calls,
His warning key my hearing jars . . .

The very smoke, in freedom curl'd,
As if rejoiced to get away,
Waves like a pennant just unfurl'd,
On some triumphant holiday.

No one to talk with, no one have I,
Exulting worklings keep aloof,
I speak and echo makes reply
Deep whispering round my vaulted roof . . .[12]

Watkins' arrest greatly pleased his neighbours, but charges of sedition were dropped after his father used his influence with the Marquis of Normanby. Triumphantly Watkins 'rode around Whitby to show my "friends" that their kind intentions on my behalf had not succeeded'.[13] In verse in the *Star* he bitterly attacked Normanby for not sanctioning the return of his pamphlets, and also cleverly lampooned the local élite:

A new church at Whitby! How charming the news!
A new priest and pulpit and handsome new pews!
How pleasant t'will be on a good Sabbath day,
To go to the new church to sing and to pray . . .

The rich men of Whitby who plunder the poor,
Will give them a stone — not a stone of ground flour—
And cure all the ills which they force them to bear,
By building a church and pronouncing a prayer . . .'[14]

Watkins' poetic tribute to George Shell, the young cabinet-maker killed during the Newport Rising, must have made the greatest impression on the readers of the *Star*; but amongst much other verse published in the paper was a sharp attack on the Duke of Wellington (inspired by a former soldier who lost an eye at Waterloo and was reduced to scavenging in Whitby) and some lines for the imprisoned O'Connor (which doubtless he tried to forget during his later arguments with the Chartist leader).[15]

Styling himself the 'Old Commodore' because of his earlier career as a naval lieutenant, E.P. Mead earned his living by sketching and by lecturing to Chartist audiences.[16] He charged one penny for lectures and examined such subjects as the corruptions of the state church and the laws of entail and primogeniture with 'dry, droll but cutting sarcasm'.[17] When O'Connor visited Birmingham in May 1842, 'Mr. E.P. Mead sang "The Charter", in excellent style, his own composition'.[18] However, he believed, 'My time and talent are thrown away amongst the Brums, who are the Most Jealous, Bickering, disunited men I ever saw . . . [sic]'.[19] Mead spent most of summer 1842 in the east Midlands. 'Things are progressing here,' he wrote from Nottingham in July, 'Johnny Pinchgut is at work.'[20] Though he privately condemned the local leader, James Sweet—'vain and dictatorial . . . a perfect money-grabber . . . I hate the little monkey'[21]—Mead's verse in the *Star* urged the Chartists to remain united:

> What can we hope from Bobby Peel,
> The blood stained cotton lord?
> Will he relieve our miseries?
> Yes — by ball and sword;
> What will Queen Victoria do,
> For her poor people's woes?
> Why get us royal brats
> To keep by the dozen, I suppose . . .
>
> Away with all your bickerings,
> All your minor points forgo,
> And show a bold united front,
> If you would crush the foe;
> O'Connor is at large again,
> Bronterre is in the field,
> And let us stick to them like men,
> Not an atom yield . . .
>
> My mouth is shut,
> The *Northern Star* is open to my pen,
> And through its columns,
> I entreat you acquit yourselves like men;
> Be of one heart and one mind,
> Avoid each silly jar
> That would disturb your harmony
> Brethren as you are.[22]

Alarmed by the wave of arrests which followed the strikes of 1842, Mead disappeared. From hiding, he composed a poem for the *Star*:

> Tis true our old ship has experienced a shock,
> By running her keel on the Corn-Leaguers' rock,
> And part of our crew in the bilboes are laid,
> The honest and true now their victims made;
> Brave Cooper and White! And a few worthies more!
> But they must not be lost tho' they're on a lee shore;
> My Nottingham worthies, tho' Clark and myself
> Perhaps a few weeks may be laid on the shelf
> (I needed, I own it, a little repose
> But not in the cell in the hands of our foes)
> Yet think not our glorious cause I forsake,
> No my heart and head, boys, are both wide awake;
> Refreshed from retirement, the Old Commodore
> Will soon at his post be fighting once more . . .
> I can write, I can act for our cause, tho' incog,
> And breathe the fresh air in sunshine or fog . . .
> The Old Commodore is yet what he should be,
> A lover of freedom and ne'er will he barter,
> For money or fame any point of the Charter;
> Then God bless our cause—he does bless it indeed
> And God bless you all, prays Old Commodore Mead.[23]

Inevitably most of the poetry sent to the *Star* was not published. That this was so does not really matter now. What the enormous number of rejections in the 'To Readers and Correspondents' column demonstrates is that, in the 1840s, poetry was being produced by the working class on a scale not seen in any other decade in the nineteenth century. Notoriety certainly did not guarantee that verse would be published. John Critchley Prince, for example, discovered that Hill did not admire his verse as much as the editors of the Manchester newspapers did.[24] James Duffy's verse, written in the most unpleasant surroundings of Northallerton prison and sent in by his wife, Margaret, was also rejected.[25] Of the *Star*'s editors, Hill was the most brutal in what he said about his readers' work. 'We advise him to give up writing poetry,' he told George Simmons and many others, 'It is a waste of time.'[26] When one disappointed poet protested and said that he could have earned half a crown for his work, Hill informed him that his poem was amongst rubbish that had been burnt.[27]

Correspondents were repeatedly asked to write on only one side of paper (so that material did not have to be recopied for the compositor), to use sealing wax sparingly (as Bronterre O'Brien did) and to write concisely and legibly. Nevertheless many poems were difficult to read. 'William Thom has sent us a sonnet which we are greatly anxious to admire but we cannot read it,' Hill lamented.[28] Thomas Paine Fielden was informed that he 'should have come along with his poetry to read it'.[29]

Occasionally poetry written by female Chartists arrived at the *Star* office. Hill did all he could to encourage them. If she would not object to 'a little correction',[30] he informed F.S. of West Ardley, her poem would appear in the *Star*. He offered Mary Hickson advice on writing verse and promised to publish her next poem.[31] He liked very much poems about O'Connor by 'Two Ultra Radical Ladies' of Wiltshire and requested 'further favours . . . from the same fair contributors':[32]

> He rose, the foremost of them all,
> To set the nation free;
> Cheer him, ye Chartists, one and all,
> O'Connor and Liberty . . .
>
> Now strong— in union, strong—we rise
> Triumphant; soon to see
> Our bosom's hope; and win the prize;
> O'Connor and Liberty!
>
> Follow where O'Connor leads so bold;
> And let your watchword be,
> Suffrage for every honest man,
> Our nation then is free![33]

Editorial policy changed after O'Connor dismissed Hill in July 1843. The unmarried Joshua Hobson, editor until October 1845, showed little interest in the work or feelings of aspiring female poets. 'We dare wager a trifle that she will make a pudding better than poetry,' he wrote of one correspondent in 1844, 'At all events she ought to do if she is unyoked and hopes to obtain a mate.'[34] 'Irish Peggy', refused employment at the Queen's Hotel in Manchester in 1847 because of her nationality, also found her poetic protest turned down by the *Star*.[35]

For most of its existence the *Star* offered legal advice to its readers. This was provided at first by O'Connor and, later on, by Ernest Jones. The two barristers would not interfere in disputes between husband and wife, but otherwise offered, without charge, help with all legal problems, printing their responses in the paper. 'Should any improper opposition be offered,' O'Connor informed one correspondent, 'the *Northern Star* will be at his service. He shall not be trampled on.'[36] Not surprisingly there were many requests for help, and legal queries often took up inches of column space in an issue. Readers wrote to the *Star* with questions about wills and illegitimacy, and complaints about landlords, employers, magistrates, lawyers and parsons. When the Padiham Chartists complained in 1838 that they were being denied access to a riverside path, O'Connor urged them to 'pull down every obstacle placed in their path and stand by their right of passage—the only enjoyment they can have after a hard week's work'.[37] In 1842 W.H. Turner of Deptford was assured that he might 'read the Chartist Circular in the open air to as many as will listen without fear of violating the law'.[38]

Readers knew that they could also turn to the *Star* for advice on non-legal matters, though answers were never given to queries involving wagers or emigration.[39] Thus, in 1840, R.J. of Islington received advice on how to deal with pawnbrokers; female correspondents were recommended to sign the 1842 Chartist petition on separate sheets of paper; an allottee from Lowbands learned in 1848 that partially diseased potatoes should be boiled, mashed, salted, stored and then fed to livestock; and Saddleworth Chartists were informed in 1842 that the best way to deal with a policeman who removed their posters was to 'set the women to watch him and let them catch him and they will doubtless hit upon some mode of summary justice . . .'[40]

It is perhaps too easily forgotten that the Chartists had a great deal of fun. The Irish leaders—Feargus, George White, Thomas Clark and others—were all capable of being very entertaining speakers, and horseplay at middle-class meetings or at the expense of the police was common. Certainly the *Star* was not devoid of humour. Hidden away amongst the answers to correspondents were jokes by the editors. 'Sir Robert Peel. His letter does not suit us' appeared amongst all the other notices in one issue in 1840.[41] Asked the same year about an incident in which Queen Victoria was rumoured to have upset her breakfast and slapped a lady-in-waiting, Hill replied: 'We did not breakfast with the Queen on that particular morning and therefore cannot tell . . .'[42] Joseph Bainbridge read that he was 'a ninny'[43] and O'Brien doubtless noted that his *National Reformer* somehow managed to appear in the *Star* as the 'National Deformer'.[44]

But, as well as the jokes, there were many stories of suffering and unhappiness. Working people turned to the *Star* when trying to locate missing persons. A Loughborough Chartist wrote in 1847 that Jonathan Bairstow's wife was 'in great distress . . . not having seen her husband for more than a year'.[45] Bairstow, however, was never seen again.[46] Whether John Taylor of Oldham was reunited with his wife and son, or Isaac Turton of Derby with his sons, will never be known.[47] There were numerous appeals in the *Star* for financial help to be given to impoverished Chartists or their wives and families. The elderly London Chartist, Thomas Mills, wrote in 1847 that he had no work but would be able to support himself if he could manage to get a volume of his poems printed.[48] The *Star* urged its readers to do what they could to help Mary Willis. Born in 1769 and active with her husband John in the 'war of the unstamped', she faced, in her old age, the distressing prospect of a workhouse funeral.[49] Emma Ellis, whose husband William had been transported in 1842, pleaded for help in January 1845. 'Tonight I am almost broken hearted, having scarce anything in my shop . . . I was obliged to pledge some bed clothes as my wearing apparel is gone. I have no hope unless my Chartist friends think of my situation.'[50] The imprisoned Thomas Cooper asked that all money raised for him be sent to Emma; but in May 1845 she was still forced to leave London for her father's house in the Potteries.[51]

The *Star's* readers wrote to the paper about a multitude of other subjects. Apart from poetic contributions, which after 1842 were not individually acknowledged, all letters appear to have been noted in the paper. For example, the Stroud Chartists' practice of leaving scraps of paper on church pews bearing such messages as 'Pray for O'Connor, Frost, Vincent and the 200 Chartist prisoners' was passed on.[52] Similarly, Hill printed a suggestion in 1842 from C. Westray of London that tables, with petition sheets on them, be placed on Westminster and Blackfriars Bridges in the early morning and evening when large numbers of working men passed over them.[53] Even absurd communications were acknowledged. The cricketers of Bingley were told in 1838 that 'we care not whether they be "conquerors" or not'.[54] Another correspondent suggested in 1843 that all male Chartists should grow moustaches, thus ensuring that 'the Charter be ever prominently before the eyes of all'.[55] It seems that Feargus decided that he would not supplement his impressive side whiskers.

Enquiries about the Chartist leader arrived fairly often at the *Star* office. His health was reported on—he was not well for several weeks in early 1839—but Hill declined to disclose his birthday or whether or not he was married.[56] Criticisms of O'Connor were also dealt with in the answers to correspondents. When O'Connor stated in 1841 whom he favoured to fill the vacancy of secretary of the National Charter Association, Susanna Inge, the London Chartist lecturer, made it clear that she 'very much questions the propriety or right of Mr. O'Connor to name or suggest to people . . . any person to fill any office whatever. It is not according to her ideas of democracy'.[57] Hobson told Inge that she believed in 'a queer kind of democracy',[58] but this rebuff did not put an end to her letter-writing or to that of her friend, Caroline Maria Williams of Bristol.[59] Inge's letters to the *Star* were signed, 'And I remain, my sisters, to the Chartist cause, and our own little army, a true devotee'.[60]

The *Northern Star* was not a paper commonly read in the breakfast rooms of Victorian England, though on occasions outraged aristocrats did find themselves in receipt of a free copy from the paper's office. The *Star* was a working-class paper, read in workshops, artisan coffee houses, public houses and the open air. By April 1839 the paper was claiming that it had 400,000 readers.[61] Readers closely identified with the *Star*. They felt it spoke for them. They knew as well that they could turn to it for advice on legal and other matters. In this sense, it was more than just a political journal. It also offered working people the opportunity to see their names in print. 'Should this piece meet with your satisfaction,' Samuel Whitelock of Sheffield wrote about his poem, 'I should like to see it sent forth in your widespread *Star*.'[62] Working men such as Thomas Haig of Kinross, Thomas Brown of Wakefield and 'A. Boon, Chartist,

Plymouth' must have been delighted when, once or twice, their verse appeared in the *Star*.[63] The members of the Bradford Chartist Temperance Society were so pleased to see their reports in the paper in 1840 that they passed a resolution thanking Hill.[64] Readers were, in fact, not expected to be inert. They were encouraged to write in—in 1841 the names of those who had taken the teetotal pledge, George Young of Worcester, Jonas Knipe of Mansfield, Mary Smith of Leeds and many more, were listed each week in the *Star*.[65] The paper's editors were certain that much of their correspondence was read by the authorities; broken seals led Hobson to suspect 'the process of Grahamisation'.[66] Sometimes letters—for example, from Richard Oastler and Samuel Healey in 1838 —were not published because the editor believed that prosecution for seditious libel would follow.[67] Correspondents often protested when letters were excluded. 'I claim the insertion of my letters,' wrote Richard Spurr of London in 1841.[68] He regarded the publication of his correspondence as his democratic right. He spoke for the paper's other correspondents. The *Star* was widely referred to as the people's paper. After the cheers for Feargus at the end of many Chartist meetings came the cheers for the *Star*.

## NOTES

I wish to thank John L. Halstead and Lewis Jones for their comments on a draft of this chapter. Crown copyright material in the Public Record Office is reproduced by permission of the controller of Her Majesty's Stationery Office.

1   *Northern Star* (hereafter *NS*), 17 July 1841, 10 Sept. 1842, 6 May 1843.
2   Ibid., 26 May 1838.
3   Ibid., 5 Feb., 12 Mar. 1842. The other three reporters were Thomas Martin Wheeler in London, James Williams in Sunderland and J. Sinclair in Newcastle.
4   Ibid., 6 Feb. 1841.
5   Ibid., 14 Sept. 1844.
6   Ibid., 27 Feb., 3 Apr. 1841, 16 Apr., 10 Sept. 1842.
7   Ibid., 2 Jan. (Bromsgrove), 16 Jan. (Longton), 17 Apr. (Sheffield), 11 May (Burnley) 1841.
8   Ibid., 3 July 1841.
9   Ibid., 13 Feb., 4 Dec., 18 Dec. 1841, 1 Jan., 15 Jan., 29 Jan. 1842. In 1842 Vernon left Devon for treatment at University College

London and ceased to contribute to the *Star*. Presumably Henry Dunn, another Chartist poet from South Molton, was a friend of Vernon's, ibid., 23 May 1840.

10   Ibid., 18 Apr., 2 May 1840, for references to Watkins' friendship with Elliott. After Elliott died in 1849 Watkins wrote a short account of his life; ibid., 25 June 1842, for a poem about Watkins' daughter by his first marriage. At the time of the 1841 census there were eight people living in Aislaby Hall. They were Francis and Christina Watkins (both aged 57), Thomas Watkins (aged 30), Sarah Watkins (aged 22), Mary Watkins (aged 20), and three servants.

11   Ibid., 4 Apr. 1840.

12   Ibid., 25 Apr. 1840; ibid. 22 Oct. 1842 for a poem about Watkins' father. The pamphlet was called *The Five Cardinal Points of the People's Charter*. Watkins did not suffer as badly as many Chartist prisoners; he had a fire, wore his own clothes and was allowed to read and write.

13   Ibid., 2 May 1840.

14   Ibid., 24 Oct. 1840; 20 June, 25 July, 1 Aug., 12 Sept. 1840.

15   Ibid., 19 Sept., 26 Sept., 17 Oct. 1840. Watkins died in 1850 at the age of 39. Some of his poetry is still worth reading. The same, perhaps, cannot be said about his 'Address to the Women of England' in the *English Chartist Circular*, no. 13 (1841).

16   *NS*, 12 Mar. 1842 for a reference to Mead formerly being a naval lieutenant. However, I have been unable to trace him in the *Navy List* for the early decades of the nineteenth century. Ibid., 9 July 1842, refers to Mead's thirty years as an active radical.

17   *NS*, 2 July 1842.

18   Ibid., 21 May 1842; 14 May, 28 May 1842.

19   E.P. Mead to Thomas Cooper, 25 May 1842, Public Record Office (P.R.O.), TS 11/601. Also see TS 11/601, Mead to Cooper 18 June, 28 July 1842; the former includes a hymn by Mead.

20   *NS*, 16 July 1842. For Mead's activities in Cornwall during the previous year see ibid., 6 Feb., 27 Feb., 3 Apr., 10 Apr. 1841.

21   P.R.O., TS 11/601, Mead to Cooper, 30 July 1842.

22   *NS*, 16 Oct. 1841.

23   Ibid., 17 Sept. 1842. For Mead's later verse see ibid., 11 Feb. 1843, 6 Jan. 1844.

24   Ibid., 14 July 1838.

25   Ibid., 21 Nov. 1840; ibid., 1 June 1839 for rejection of poetry by John Watkins; 14 Nov. 1840 for rejection of a letter by Jane Peddie.

26   Ibid., 1 Feb. 1840, 6 Jan., 17 Mar. 1838, 11 May 1844 , 10 Apr. 1847.

27   Ibid., 22 Dec. 1838.

28   Ibid., 17 Apr. 1841.

29  Ibid., 28 Mar. 1840.

30  Ibid., 3 Mar. 1838.

31  Ibid., 9 Mar. 1839.

32  Ibid., 6 July 1839.

33  Ibid., 13 July 1839. Also see ibid., 18 May 1839 for a poem about J.R. Stephens by 'E.H., a Factory Girl of Stalybridge'.

34  Ibid., 21 Dec. 1844.

35  Ibid., 15 May 1847.

36  Ibid., 26 May 1838.

37  Ibid., 4 Aug. 1838.

38  Ibid., 6 Aug. 1842.

39  Ibid., 4 June, 9 July, 10 Sept. 1842, 25 Jan., 19 Apr. 1845, 29 Jan. 1848, 10 Feb. 1849.

40  Ibid., 15 Aug. 1840, 27 Nov. 1841, 4 June 1842, 26 Aug., 2 Sept. 1848. Ibid., 10 June 1848, for a policeman removing one of Jeremiah Yates' posters in Shelton and observing 'that I, as well as the bill published, was a nuisance and the sooner I was removed the better'.

41  Ibid., 24 Oct. 1840.

42  Ibid., 5 June 1840.

43  Ibid., 12 Sept. 1840.

44  Ibid., 18 Oct. 1845.

45  Ibid., 4 Sept. 1847; 19 June 1847.

46  Thomas Cooper, *Life of Thomas Cooper. Written by Himself* (London, 1872), p.250.

47  *NS*, 28 Nov. 1840, 17 Sept. 1842. However, ibid., 3 Mar. 1838 mentions that a missing dog was restored to its owner.

48  Ibid., 8 May 1847; ibid., 24 Apr. 1841 for case of John Rose, dismissed from his employment for attending a Chartist meeting. Rose fled to Hamburg with his family in 1848 after being involved in plans for an insurrection in London.

49  Ibid., 30 Nov. 1844.

50  Ibid., 11 Jan. 1845. Ibid., 12 Jan., 2 Feb., 9 Feb., 23 Mar. 1850 for the case of Anne McDouall.

51  Ibid., 17 May, 24 May 1845.

52  Ibid., 17 Oct. 1840.

53  Ibid., 5 Feb. 1842.

54  Ibid., 6 Oct. 1838.

55  Ibid., 1 Apr. 1843.

56  Ibid., 9 Mar., 11 May 1839, 21 Nov. 1840, 2 Jan. 1841.

57  Ibid., 8 July 1841.

58  Ibid.

59  Ibid., 30 Apr., 4 June (poem), 16 July 1842, 12 Oct. 1844.

60  Ibid., 1 Apr. 1843.

61  James Epstein, *The Lion of Freedom: Feargus O'Connor and the Chartist Movement, 1832–1842* (London, 1982), p. 68.
62  27 June 1840.
63  Ibid., 15 May, 31 July, 23 Oct. 1841, 21 May 1842.
64  Ibid., 10 Apr. 1841.
65  Ibid., 16 Jan., 30 Jan., 20 Feb., 17 Apr., 10 July 1841. Mary Smith was the wife of Thomas Brown Smith.
66  Ibid., 5 July 1845; 4 July 1840.
67  Ibid., 20 Jan., 4 Aug. 1838.
68  Ibid., 4 Sept. 1841; 30 Jan. 1841, 8 Jan., 3 Dec. 1842.

## APPENDIX: POETS WHOSE WORK APPEARED IN THE *NORTHERN STAR*, 1838–1842

John Goodwyn Barmby (Yoxford)   24 November 1838, 4 January 1840

Philip Bevan (Newport)   2 February, 7 March 1840

George Binns (Sunderland)   9 May, 16 May, 1 August 1840

J. Bishop   17 December 1842

Arthur Boon (Plymouth)   15 May, 31 July 1841

Thomas Brown (Wakefield)   21 May 1842

Robert Buchanan (Glasgow)   2 June 1838

L.T. Clancy (London)   8 August 1840, 9 October, 4 December 1841, 23 April, 2 July, 9 July, 30 July 1842

David Cassedy (Leeds)   19 June 1841

James Clarke (Clayton West)   29 May 1841

John Cook (Ipswich)   13 June 1840

Robert Dibb   31 March, 12 May, 26 May, 2 June, 13 October, 27 October, 3 November 1838, 6 April 1839

H. Drapier   14 September 1839

Henry Dunn (South Molton)   23 May 1840

J.C. Elliot (Blyth)   24 April, 15 May 1841

John Frazer (London)   18 June 1842

James French (Newcastle-under-Lyme)   13 June 1840, 23 October 1841

Edwin Gill (Sheffield)   1 October, 29 October 1842

Thomas Gillespie (Glasgow)   23 October 1841

T. Gow (Dundee)   24 October 1840

Thomas Haig (Kinross)   7 November 1840

George Julian Harney   15 October 1842

William Hick (Leeds)    26 December 1840, 27 March, 22 May,
  5 June 1841

Alexander Huish (Uley)    20 February 1841

J. Hutchinson    22 September 1838

William Jones (Leicester)    12 December 1840, 21 August 1841

William Jones (Liverpool)    26 December 1840

Eugene La Mont (Edinburgh)    15 August, 26 September, 10 October
  1840, 11 September 1841

John A. Lawson (Sheffield)    28 November, 19 December 1840, 5 June,
  4 December 1841

Jonathan Lefevre (Bristol)    28 March, 11 April 1840

George Lindsay    3 September 1842

W. McDouall (Newton Stewart)    31 August 1839, 22 February,
  7 November 1840, 19 November 1842

Thomas MacQueen (Barras)    13 August 1842

W. Mann (Ashburton)    10 April 1841

David Mawson (Rawdon)    29 December 1838

E.P. Mead (Birmingham)    13 February, 8 May, 26 June, 16 October
  1841, 9 July, 16 July, 23 July, 17 September 1842

Joseph Middleton    14 April 1838

John Mills    15 August 1840

John Mulholland (Burton-on-Trent)    27 May 1841

G . Sheridan Nussey (Leeds)    9 April, 16 July, 27 August 1842

Feargus O' Connor    4 July 1840

W. Pargiter    6 June 1840

John Peacock (South Shields)    2 March 1839

Robert Peddie ( Beverley House of Correction)    6 March, 8 May,
  24 July 1841

Robert Peter    30 May 1840

Edwin Polin (Paisley)    28 August, 11 September 1841

Joseph Radford (Birmingham)    21 November 1840, 2 January 1841

William Rider (Leeds)    3 April 1841

William Stephen Villiers Sankey (Edinburgh)    29 February, 25 April,
  14 November, 28 November 1840, 16 January 1841

F. Saunderson    19 May 1838

T.R. Smart (Leicester)    21 August 1841

T.B. Smith (Hull)    13 January, 3 February, 3 March, 28 April, 28 July,
  6 October 1838, 12 January, 26 January, 6 July, 7 September 1839

John Smithson    6 January 1838

R. Stewart (Edinburgh)    22 January 1842

Benjamin Stott (Manchester)    17 July, 14 August 1841, 12 March,
  26 March, 16 April, 21 May, 11 June, 2 July, 27 August, 24 September,
  22 October, 12 November, 10 December 1842

James Syme    26 December 1840

John Taylor (Glasgow)    7 July 1838

P.B. Templeton (Leeds)    19 January 1839

William Thom (Inverary)    8 October 1842

Edward Thomas (Newport)    25 January 1840

W.A. Thompson    30 January 1841

C. Tunnicliffe (Baildon)    17 November 1838

Joseph Turner    11 September 1841

James Vernon (South Molton)    26 September, 24 October,
  14 November, 12 December 1840, 30 January, 13 February, 24 April,
  12 June, 2 October, 13 November, 20 November, 4 December,
  18 December 1841, 1 January, 15 January, 29 January 1842

Bradshaw Walker    5 November 1842

J.B. Walker    20 January, 3 March 1838

John Watkins (Whitby)    25 April, 1 August, 12 September,
  19 September, 26 September, 3 October, 17 October, 24 October,
  5 December 1840, 2 January 1841, 1 January, 29 January, 9 April,
  25 June, 3 September, 1 October, 22 October, 12 November 1842

Thomas Watson    2 November 1839

C. Westray (London)    20 February 1841, 5 November 1842

Thomas Martin Wheeler (London)    1 May, 15 May, 22 May, 31 July,
  7 August, 28 August 1841

Caroline Maria Williams (Bristol)    4 June 1842

Peter Williams (Sinclairston)    14 August 1841

Thomas Wilson    29 October 1842

David Wright (Aberdeen)    4 September, 2 October 1841, 9 July 1842

# 4

# *Homage to John Richards*

### ROBERT FYSON

Thirty-five years ago, Edward Thompson's essay 'Homage to Tom Maguire' focused the spotlight of history on an obscure semi-employed Leeds–Irish photographer who played a crucial role in opening the way for the Independent Labour Party (ILP) in the West Riding of Yorkshire in the 1880s and 1890s. Thompson made a passionate plea for the admission to 'full historical citizenship' of provincial radical and labour leaders.[1] Dorothy Thompson's work shares this perspective: the central section of her magnum opus explores the question 'who were the Chartists?' largely through an accumulation of illuminating details from the biographies of a great variety of individual Chartists.[2]

Due in no small part to the example set by the Thompsons, this emphasis has become familiar, as the rich Chartist historiography of the last twenty-five years amply demonstrates.[3] The biographical vein of historical enquiry into Chartism is far from exhausted, however. This essay is about a provincial Chartist leader, 'Daddy' John Richards of the Potteries, one of the oldest and most persistent Chartists, a member of the 1839 Convention, imprisoned after the riots of 1842, still active in 1848 and thereafter. Richards has been described as 'legendary', and his name, as Dorothy Thompson remarks, appears in all the standard histories, but his biography has not hitherto been explored.[4] Of considerable interest in itself, his story also sheds light on some relatively obscure aspects of Chartist history.

I

Little information is available about Richards' youth and middle age. He was born in Birmingham, perhaps on Christmas Day 1772, perhaps a year earlier.[5] In 1839 he claimed that his political principles 'had been taught him from his earliest infancy: for it was one of the instructions given to him by his father in childhood, always endeavour to secure for the people a voice in choosing their legislators'.[6] In 1843 he told the Court of Queen's Bench that 'his tutors were Charles James Fox, Major Cartwright, and other eminent men of that day'. His speech from the dock proclaimed that 'he had travelled during twenty years of his life, and had seen much of destitution. The girls of the mining districts were worse slaves than those in the West Indies. He had been in the West Indies, and spoke from personal experience'.[7] Perhaps he had been a seaman.

He married a Hanley woman, Nancy Mellor, with whom he had one son, and by 1818 at the latest was living in the Potteries and working as a shoemaker.[8] He was a lay preacher for the Methodist New Connexion, but abandoned this during the 1820s, and 'neglected the Bible for the Black Book'.[9] According to an appeal for Chartist prisoners made in 1842, he had 'on all occasions during the last twenty-four years opposed tyranny and oppression in their multiform shapes, whether national or local',[10] but there is no mention of his activities in the local press before 1830.

Richards' first recorded public appearance was at an open-air parliamentary reform meeting in Hanley in November 1830, when he spoke with studious moderation: he supported the principle of petitioning parliament for redress of grievances, but did not wish to see a 'great convulsion' in society. When reform came, he benefited from it, qualifying as a county, though not a borough, elector in the general elections of 1832 and 1837, and voting on both occasions for the Liberal candidates.[11]

Certainly some of Richards' speeches in the 1830s give an impression of a self-improving liberal artisan, prepared to accept middle-class political leadership. Thus in 1834 he was active in the cross-class agitation against high church rates, led by John Ridgway, the leading Hanley pottery manufacturer and New Connexion Methodist, and publicly commended Ridgway as 'a man whom to be able to call a friend should be esteemed one of the highest honours in social life'. In 1836 he spoke up at a meeting on the Irish Corporation Bill, saying he would like to see the House of Lords abolished, but nevertheless suggesting 'an address to ministers thanking them for their upright and honest conduct, and encouraging them to go forward'.[12]

But Richards held other views which were not at all compatible with middle-class liberal opinion. In 1831 he became a prominent speaker for John Doherty's National Association for the Protection of Labour, which made a considerable impact in the Potteries. His speeches made it plain that he saw trade unionism as the only way to protect workers' standard of living, to narrow the gap between rich and poor and avert revolution. In his view, it was not enough for the potters to have their own union, as they had in 1825–6, but they should join the NAPL and support the struggles of other workers, such as the striking spinners of Ashton-under-Lyne.[13] The NAPL was defunct by the end of 1831, but Richards had clearly established his position as a spokesman for working-class interests.

He came to the fore again in the tumultuous years 1834–6, when a new and more powerful trade union — the National Union of Operative Potters — became the main focus of working-class aspirations in North Staffordshire.[14] Largely as a result of the impetus given by the union, there was a surge of working-class involvement in local and parish affairs. Richards was the leading speaker at a meeting in Hanley, opposing the incorporation of the Potteries towns as a single borough because of the fear of centralized, unrepresentative power wielded by an élite of manufacturers and magistrates. Not least because of popular opposition, the incorporation proposal was abandoned. Richards also became an active participant in Stoke parish vestry meetings, criticizing corruption and mismanagement, and standing unsuccessfully for the post of poor-rate collector; he questioned the dismissal of the workhouse overseer for relieving the families of strikers, and was a member of a union delegation which met a visiting Poor-Law inspector in an unsuccessful attempt to secure a low financial qualification for membership of the Stoke board of guardians.[15]

In 1842 it was recalled that 'he assisted the potters to obtain an advance of price some years ago, by his writings in the defence of their claim'.[16] He spoke at union rallies to protest against the transportation of the Tolpuddle labourers, in 1834 and 1835.[17] At a public meeting in December 1836, he made a speech which demonstrated his knowledge of the pottery industry, condemning the abuses of annual hiring and 'good from oven' against which the union was contending, and recalling how his son had been driven out of the trade after a dispute with his master. He saw the bitter strike in progress unequivocally as 'a contest of money against labour', for which the only remedy, he still maintained, was a general union.[18]

The union collapsed, defeated and indebted, early in 1837. Richards, not being a potter, was not ruined by the union's failure, unlike most of its leaders. In July, he chaired a pro-Liberal non-electors' meeting, demanding the ballot and at least household, or better universal, suffrage.[19] As working-class hopes once more focused on parliamentary reform, he was well placed, with his reputation as 'a real reformer and unionist', to take the leading role locally in the new movement for universal suffrage.[20]

## II

Chartism was introduced into the Potteries at a hastily announced meeting in August 1838. John Richards, supporting petitioning once more, was the only local speaker, and probably organized the meeting. Three months of vigorous agitation throughout the Potteries followed, with Richards well to the fore as a speaker stressing the need for constitutional, peaceful action. A wave of Chartist enthusiasm swept through the district; by early November a hostile observer considered 'That a very bad spirit exists in the Potteries admits of no Question and it is one which is directed against all good Governments'.[21]

Richards took the lead: he held membership card number one of the new Pottery Political Union; he was responsible, among much else, for encouraging the formation of a separate Female Political Union.[22] When the first great open-air demonstration of Potteries Chartists was held in a field near Hanley in mid-November, with Feargus O'Connor as star speaker, Richards was the unchallenged popular choice as Potteries delegate to the National Convention. William Ellis of Burslem, in his nomination speech, described him as 'that worthy man to whom they owed the existence of the Political Union then flourishing among them. In his great exertion he had injured his health and consequently his temporal interests'. He was elected delegate by acclamation, and described by the *Northern Star*'s reporter as 'a veteran Radical with standing in all classes and strict integrity'.[23]

After a celebratory round of farewell meetings and dinners, the Potteries delegate set off for London early in February, bearing with him as his credentials an elaborately decorated and inscribed china tablet.[24] At the opening of the Convention he presented 12,000 petition signatures, and a £10 instalment of 'national rent' from the Potteries. In his mid-60s, he was one of the oldest delegates. Like other provincial radicals taking part for the first time in a national forum, he found his feet gradually and grew in confidence. At the end of the first week he proposed simultaneous public meetings throughout the country at Easter, a motion which was deferred, but finally acted upon at Whitsun. He was appointed to the Convention's fund-raising committee, and spoke at a public meeting in Holborn urging London Chartists to raise more money. He did not follow the moderate middle-class seceders from the Convention, but nor did he support the ultra-radicals, for he dissented from London Democratic Association resolutions attacking the Convention for its inaction: he was in the centre of the Convention's political spectrum.[25]

After a month in London, Richards was summoned home again by the Potteries Chartists, eager to have him back, in his own words 'to Compleat the Agitation in the Potteries and Extend it to the Neighbouring Towns', and was given leave of absence by the Convention, as 'no man could be so useful or possess so much influence in that part of the country'. Welcomed with huge enthusiasm, he promptly embarked on a high-pressure lecture tour, addressing meetings in the Potteries, and doing his best, with mixed success, to form Chartist committees in Cheadle, Leek and Stone in North Staffordshire and Congleton, Nantwich and Sandbach in South Cheshire. He visited most of these towns at least twice, usually on his own, travelling on foot, and addressed at least eighteen public meetings in a month: as he plaintively wrote to the Convention, 'you will see that I have no sinecure here but work work walk walk almost day and night'. His letters to the Convention vividly convey his impressions of poverty, hunger and threatened social breakdown, leading him to predict that 'if something be not speedily done to give a greater plenty to the working man, something of a very fearful import must follow'.[26] Already there were rumours of Chartist arming in the Potteries; and he complained that his letters were being delayed and opened in the post.[27]

Richards returned to the Convention and reported in person on his tour towards the end of April. Responding to what he had seen and to the increasingly desperate Chartist mood, he became more militant. In mid-May, after the Convention had presented the Petition and adjourned to Birmingham, he argued strongly in favour of the programme of ulterior measures, especially a run on the banks. At the end of the month he was despatched to Preston to speak at one of the simultaneous Whitsun meetings, and also, a few days later, at a demonstration on Kersal Moor, near Manchester. During June he was back in the Potteries, and when the Convention reassembled early in July he was so impressed by the great excitement in the Potteries and Cheshire that he believed the people were eagerly waiting for the Convention's instructions to begin the ulterior measures; many were already withdrawing their money from the banks, and would support the sacred month, though preferably after a few more weeks' preparation. As for the future location of the Convention, 'if they adjourned to London as speedily as possible, the Government being in such a position as they were, they should be near the House of Commons and ready to step in whenever they stepped out'. This was a remarkable opinion from a Chartist leader who was usually cautious and pragmatic.[28]

The period of maximum tension in the Potteries, as elsewhere, occurred after the Bull Ring riots and the rejection of the Petition, in the second half of July and early August, when the Convention had announced that the sacred month would begin on August 12. The police in Hanley and Burslem were convinced that arms were being made and sold, and that the Chartists were planning an outbreak.[29] Their assessments are supported by evidence from a Chartist source: many years later Thomas Dunning, a Nantwich Chartist, recalled visiting Hanley in July 1839 as delegate to a Chartist district meeting, during the week of the Bull Ring riots:

I met with many determined 'physical force' men at the meeting. While at Hanley I visited Mr. Salt's coffeehouse and arms depot. Mr. Salt had a large stock of guns, pistols, swords, bayonets, pike-heads, etc. . . . I was informed that a considerable quantity of arms had been sold in the Potteries.[30]

Charles Salt, coffeehouse proprietor, was secretary of the Han-ley Chartists.[31]

Meanwhile, as the Lord Lieutenant of Staffordshire told the Home Secretary, towards the end of July 'Richards, one of the prime Agitators is now in London—this is a daring, persuasive Man'. The daring, persuasive man was about to return from the Convention to reassess the state of his district, and finally decide whether the sacred month were practicable. After tour-ing the district for a week, he wrote from Hanley to the Conven-tion on 8 August: the run on the banks and exclusive dealing were proving effective, but although some parts had stored up provisions, others had made no preparation at all.

My opinion therefore is that the Sacred Month cannot in common providence be attempted here, there are rash spirits who would plunge head first into it, but the Majority will not move, so that I cannot think it is prudent for it to be Ordered at least at the present.

At the last minute, Richards had reverted to his usual realistic pragmatism. The majority of the Convention shared his view, and Chartism was left without a viable strategy. Even the hast-ily substituted idea of a three-day strike from 12 August was not implemented in the Potteries. Instead, an open-air demon-stration was held near Hanley, a week later on 19 August. Richards toured the coffeehouses to drum up support for this meeting, which provided some outlet for the energies of frus-trated militants, but was essentially a face-saving tactic, and as such an anti-climax.[32]

Richards, doggedly persistent, and reluctant to accept that Chartism had failed, was among the twenty or so members of the Convention who took part in its final session in London in the first two weeks of September. Initially he argued strongly against dissolution, but had, regretfully, to accept it. The Con-vention, which retained little support or interest, dissolved on

14 September, and by the end of the month, if not before, he had returned home.[33]

His participation in the Convention remained a source of pride for the rest of his life, and the contacts he had made endured: for example, in 1850 he was still in touch with George Rogers, Finsbury delegate to the Convention, and in 1851 he described himself to a census enumerator as 'retired National Convention delegate'.[34] It was, perhaps even more than 1842 and its aftermath, the high point of his long radical career.

## III

John Richards' response to the temporary eclipse of Chartism in 1839–40 is a most intriguing phase of his Chartist life. There are no press or Home Office reports of Chartist activity in the Potteries during the last three months of 1839, but the papers of David Urquhart and his associates show that at this time Richards was acting as Potteries contact for Urquhart's 'foreign policy Chartists'. In September, at about the time the Convention was dissolved, Urquhart and his friend Pringle Taylor had discussions in London with three or four Chartist leaders who warned them of plans for simultaneous risings before Christmas.[35] Subsequently an Urquhartite missionary visited the Potteries twice, in early October and late November, with Richards on both occasions setting up meetings of working men for him to address.[36] An undated letter from Pringle Taylor claimed, with characteristic hyperbole, that these efforts had 'saved Birmingham, the Potteries and London from insurrection for which all was prepared'.[37]

However, if Urquhartism was apparently making some headway in the Potteries in the autumn of 1839, the trial and sentencing of John Frost and his colleagues stimulated a resurgence of more orthodox Chartist loyalties, at least among a hard core of activists, in which Richards joined, at the end of the year. During the first six months of 1840, he was secretary of the much depleted Pottery Political Union, and local agent and correspondent for the *Northern Star*. He spoke at meetings in favour of a pardon for Frost, Williams and Jones, tried to put the Chartist case at Anti-Corn Law League meetings, and succeeded in getting the first working man elected to the Hanley

Highways Board. He represented the district at meetings in Manchester, reporting in March that the Potteries Chartists were divided between petitioning and the use of force as future strategies, but he supported petitioning. He appeared to be back in the mainstream of Chartist activity.[38]

But during July, with the encouragement of his fellow Convention delegate and shoemaker, William Cardo of Marylebone, he changed tack again and became a paid itinerant lecturer for Urquhart, apparently the last Chartist leader to decide to do so.[39] After two nights in London, he set off to the West Country, visiting, among other towns, Trowbridge where, according to his own report, he addressed a meeting of 600 men in the Chartists' room. Returning via Birmingham to the Potteries, he moved on to Manchester and Bolton.[40] By the autumn he seems to have been based in Tyneside, the strongest centre of Urquhart's movement. In October and November he spoke at Carlisle, Middlesbrough and Stockton-on-Tees.[41] At the end of November he contributed a poem celebrating the return of the remains of Napoleon from St Helena to Paris, to the former Chartist, now Urquhartite, paper, the *Northern Liberator*. At this time he was living in South Shields, very probably with his son Thomas.[42] Before the end of the year, however, Urquhart's first attempt to take over the Chartist movement was abandoned, the *Northern Liberator* folded, and Richards' employment as an itinerant lecturer came to an end.

The Urquhartite 'foreign policy Chartism' of 1839–40 is an under-researched subject, and the attraction of Urquhart's obsessions for Chartists like Richards deserves fuller consideration than is possible here. Chartists who remained loyal to O'Connor suggested that Richards and others had been bought: the *Northern Star* attacked Richards and claimed that Urquhart's lecturers were paid from £3 10s. 0d. to £4 a week. Certainly, Richards' own notes of his expenses in July reveal that he was able to travel by coach, omnibus, railway and even pleasure boat on the Wiltshire Avon, with enough money for meals, lodgings, repairs to his footwear, and payments to support his wife at home in Hanley.[43]

However, to assume that Richards was motivated solely by such considerations is unduly simplistic and inconsistent with other evidence about him. In the autumn of 1839 he must have been aware, however vaguely, of the plans for armed risings.

He was strongly opposed to the use of force, but equally strongly committed to continuing Chartist activity in some form. Urquhartism presented an alternative non-violent strategy which conveniently laid the blame for the Chartist crisis on aristocratic duplicity, Russian despotism, and foreign agitators like Major Beniowski: 'Old Corruption' on an international scale. The Bonapartist sympathies evident in Richards' poem could be related to radical anti-war pro-French views he may have held in his youth; David Urquhart may have briefly replaced John Ridgway as an acceptable leader from a higher social class; the moral and semi-religious aspect of Urquhartism may have appealed to the former lay preacher. It is entirely plausible that, as he said in Carlisle, he saw in Urquhartism not merely 'a Union based on the excitement of the moment' but 'a Union based on intelligence and cemented by mutual kindness and mutual interests'.[44]

During 1839–40 Richards vacillated between the appeal of Urquhartism and his continuing strong attachment to the Chartist movement. Even while he was lecturing for Urquhart, he never renounced Chartism. While Urquhart himself was never a democrat, Richards saw Urquhartism as a form of 'Chartism and something more' and made this plain at the meetings he addressed.[45] Thus, when organized Urquhartism collapsed he rejoined the Chartist mainstream.

## IV

It is a measure of John Richards' local standing that, even after his period of Urquhartite apostasy, he was able to resume a leading role in Potteries Chartism, though he never again enjoyed a position of unchallenged supremacy. During his absence the Potteries Chartists had affiliated to the National Charter Association (NCA), and a revival had begun in earnest, spearheaded by George Mart, a Stoke potter and a prominent local Socialist and Chartist.[46] Richards became active again soon after his return. From January 1841 he addressed open-air meetings fortnightly in Longton, walking four miles to the place of meeting, and contending at different times with harassment from the police, and stone-throwing Anti-Corn Law League supporters. By November a Chartist branch was firmly established and he had earned the support of the Longton Chartists.[47]

In Hanley, and the adjacent township of Shelton, the Chartists now largely supported George Mart and viewed their former leader with suspicion. Richards circumvented this and developed a new base of support by setting up a second Hanley Chartist grouping, the Upper Hanley and Smallthorne NCA branch, of which he was secretary from March 1841 to August 1842. Upper Hanley became the largest branch in the Potteries, with over 200 paid-up members in the spring of 1842, and possibly double that number by August.[48] Smallthorne, a mining village, became a notable Chartist redoubt; during 1841-2 the branch committee always included at least one or two colliers and ironstone miners, and generally a greater variety of trades than the Hanley and Shelton committee, which was dominated by potters.[49] Upper Hanley also boasted a separate Female Chartist Association, the only known women's Chartist group in the Potteries at this time, and its location was consistent with the encouragement Richards had given to Chartist women in 1839.[50]

Rivalry between Richards and Mart and their respective followers persisted until the spring of 1842. In April 1841 Richards' name was listed as a supporter of William Lovett's National Association; when the 'New Move' was attacked by O'Connor, Richards hastily withdrew his support, but Mart weighed in heavily a few weeks later with a denunciation of Lovett's supporters.[51] Both men's names were put forward for election as Staffordshire delegate to the 1842 National Convention, along with John Mason from South Staffordshire.[52] All the candidates addressed Chartist meetings throughout the county. Although Mart withdrew before the election, the voting figures testified to the divided allegiances in the Potteries, with Mart's supporters in Stoke and Shelton preferring to vote for Mason rather than Richards. Richards lost the election because of the overwhelming support for Mason from the huge Chartist branch at Bilston, in the Black Country, but, backed by the two largest groups in the Potteries, he once more enjoyed the support of the majority of Potteries Chartists.[53]

This was no mean achievement for a man of 70, reaching the end of his working life and living in reduced circumstances. In 1841 he was no longer a voter. He may have continued working as a shoemaker, but age and Chartist activity probably reduced his income considerably: in May 1841 he was heckled by Anti-Corn Law League supporters who shouted 'Pay your leather bill!'[54] From 1838 on, intermittent references to his declining health occur, and he was said to be lame, though this did not deter him from walking several miles to address Chartist meetings. He took a prominent role in virtually all the varied political and social activities of the Hanley Chartists, co-operating with Mart and the Shelton men when necessary. From the spring of 1842 the Potteries Chartists' internal divisions may have been put on one side. In April Richards represented the district at a conference in Birmingham, and put forward their united view that Chartists should have nothing to do with the Complete Suffrage Union: 'the Pottery men would go for nothing short of the Charter'. As the depression deepened, Chartism grew stronger still, and by the summer of 1842 there were eight Chartist branches in the Potteries district. In July, John Campbell of the NCA Executive remarked that 'Richards and the good men of the Potteries have carried Chartism into almost every hamlet in their district'.[55]

Economic depression, acute poverty and unemployment, the miners' strike and Chartist agitation built up during the summer months of 1842 and culminated in two days' destructive rioting in August, soldiers firing on the crowd in Burslem, the arrests, trials, imprisonment or transportation of hundreds of people. This was the supreme crisis of Potteries Chartism.[56]

John Richards' responses at this time of desperation and uncertainty reflected his earlier political positions. On the one hand, he still hankered after a common front with the middle classes, a view he shared with many other Chartists at this time, including O'Connor. In early July, at an open-air Chartist meeting in Hanley, he called upon the middle and working classes to 'unite to advance the rights of labour and the freedom of commerce'; and on the afternoon of 16 August, as the riots were being suppressed, he and other Chartists at last shared a platform with John Ridgway in a belated attempt to form a common front against distress and disorder, a meeting which passed Chartist resolutions before being dispersed by the military.[57]

On the other hand, as in the 1830s, Richards was also drawn to support workers on strike. Writing as the *Northern Star*'s local correspondent, he insisted that 'The Chartists, as a body, have not mixed themselves up with the colliers' turn out, nor will they. Yet we cannot shut our eyes or our ears while we see and hear the effects produced by this affair . . .'. Individual Chartists, including Richards himself, were involved. The Committee of Operative Colliers had its headquarters in a Hanley pub, the George and Dragon, which was also a Chartist meeting-place, and Richards himself sent in the colliers' public address to the *Star*. An intimidatory letter sent by the colliers' committee to a coal-owner, a few days before the riots, was said to be in Richards' handwriting. Probably, as he had done for the potters, he now drafted public statements and letters for the miners, putting his skills at their service.[58]

Writing to Thomas Cooper to arrange his itinerary as a visiting Chartist speaker in mid-August, Richards added: 'I have to say that owing to the Colliers turnout our organisation is most Sadly Deranged you will therefore be prepared to Enforce the Necessity of Union amongst us.' George Hemmings, the Hanley miners' leader, became a member of the Upper Hanley NCA Committee at about this time. At the fateful meeting held on Crown Bank, Hanley, early on the morning of Monday, 15 August, and chaired by Cooper, John Richards proposed, and Hemmings seconded, the resolution 'That all labour cease until the People's Charter becomes the law of the land'.[59] Richards played no part in the two days of rioting which followed, which was scarcely surprising in view of his age and opinions. He claimed to have spent Monday protecting the house and property of a Hanley pawnbroker; early on Tuesday morning he spoke to the crowd briefly for a few minutes, probably in an attempt to urge peace, law and order upon them; later in the day, as mentioned above, he shared a platform with Ridgway and other Chartists. He reported to the *Northern Star* that 'as a body, the Chartists have had no hand in the destruction of property that has been going on here, nor has the advice of the Chartist speakers been attended to . . . We are placed entirely under martial law, and the most absolute despotism is practised upon us'.[60]

A week after the outbreak of the riots, he wrote to Joshua Hobson, publisher of the *Northern Star*,

It now seems that I am left nearly alone, when I reflect on the cause, and see the goodly Fabrick of Chartism thrown down in these parts, my Soul sinks within me and I feel completely unmann'd . . . We are now in the midst of a Tory reign of terror. Spies and Informers are now the only persons who seem to be noticed, no matter what their Character may be . . .[61]

The next day, Richards was arrested at a coffeehouse in Hanley, with the letter still unposted in his pocket. His lodgings were searched, and various personal papers removed. He appeared before magistrates at Newcastle-under-Lyme for a committal hearing at which he was charged with seditious speaking likely to cause riot. He denied the charges against him, before a densely crowded court. One account describes him as showing 'great hardihood and bravado': as he was escorted out of Newcastle by soldiers in a carriage to the railway station at Whitmore, to be taken to Stafford gaol, he took off his hat and cheered to the crowd, and remarked 'I never was so honoured in all my life.'[62]

## V

At the age of 70, Richards' period of real political leadership in the Chartist movement was at an end. Henceforth, he would be a remarkably durable 'veteran and victim'.

He entered Stafford Gaol, overcrowded with 800 prisoners, on remand towards the end of August: for three weeks he lived on one and a half pounds of bread a day, and water. Meanwhile, his wife was turned out of their lodgings, and had to seek outdoor relief and shelter at her brother's home. When the Special Assize opened at the beginning of October, Richards found himself additionally charged with conspiracy with Cooper, William Ellis and Joseph Capper. Cooper and Richards opted to delay their trial until the Spring Assize of 1843, when they might have a better chance of a fair trial. After some delay, they were released on bail in mid-November.[63] Richards had spent twelve weeks as a remand prisoner, and now faced a solicitor's bill for £8 which has survived among Cooper's papers, suggesting that Cooper may have paid it.[64] For the next three months he resumed the life of an itinerant lecturer, visiting Wolverhampton and Birmingham, spending three weeks over Christmas with Cooper in Leicester, moving on to lecture in and around Nottingham. This provided an irregular income from collections at meetings.[65]

The trial of Cooper, Richards and Capper for a seditious conspiracy took place at Stafford Assizes, 20–30 March 1843, prolonged both by the sustained eloquence of Cooper and the number of witnesses called, over twenty for the prosecution and over forty for the defence. The defendants conducted their own defence, and the flamboyant Cooper took the limelight. Richards was quiet and thoughtful, established an alibi for Cooper's first visit to the Potteries in April 1842, when he had been at the Complete Suffrage conference in Birmingham, and did his best to discredit some of the dubious witnesses who testified against him. He was supported by a large number of Potteries Chartists; George Mart testified that he had always been 'what we call in the Potteries a milk and water speaker'. However, the judge directed that if the three men had encouraged the strike for the Charter, that in itself was sufficient ground for conviction. The jury's 'guilty' verdict, reached in five minutes, was never in doubt. Capper returned to prison with no addition to the two-year sentence he was already serving; on a legal technicality, Cooper and Richards were set free on bail for another month before appearing for sentence at the Court of Queen's Bench in London, on 4 May.[66]

Speaking before sentence was passed, Richards made an impressive speech, declaring his innocence and his opposition to violence, and reasserting his beliefs in universal suffrage, the right of public meeting, and the right to strike. He believed that he would live to see the People's Charter become the law of the land. O'Connor, who was in court, praised the speech highly; Cooper, writing thirty years later, recalled how 'the old man had fine native powers and spoke with a little stateliness that was very becoming to a white-headed, large-foreheaded man of threescore and ten'.[67]

Richards was sentenced to one year, and Cooper to two years' imprisonment. After a week in the Marshalsea prison in Southwark, where they dined with fellow-prisoner Richard Oastler, they returned to serve their sentences at Stafford prison, denounced by the *Northern Star* as a 'provincial hell hole' with an appalling diet of coarse bread, thin skilly and rotten potatoes.

ROBERT FYSON

Cooper's account of their tribulations, and his vociferous protests against the conditions, is well known. His recalcitrance benefited not only himself, but also Richards and Capper: all three were granted a better diet, and allowed the use of books and writing materials. This relaxation of the rigours of prison life must have enabled Richards to survive his ordeal in tolerable health.[68]

The available evidence on Richards' year in prison gives us two sharply contrasted impressions of his condition, both perhaps representing part of the whole truth. On the one hand, William Peplow, the leading Stafford Chartist, who concerned himself with the welfare of the Chartist prisoners, painted a bleak picture; describing Richards as nearly blind, emaciated, unable again to work at his trade, short of clothes and money, and dreading the prospect of the workhouse after his release, while his wife was now bedridden and senile. This may all have been true, but it must be borne in mind that the purpose of such letters in the *Northern Star* was to solicit contributions for the support of John and Nancy Richards.[69]

On the other hand, Thomas Cooper's memoirs portray a more buoyant Richards: after one exchange with him, 'the old man ran off, laughing'. Cooper's prison poem, *The Purgatory of Suicides*, confirms this view in a passage evidently written shortly after Richards' release:

> ... And now the blythe old man
> Is gone, who joked, and told his merry tale
> Each morning, when the prison day began
> Who spread instruction through the hours' long span
> Mingling the grave and gay with cheery tongue
> Oh how I miss the septuagenarian!
> I wonder what has kept his heart so young
> That still he dreams to live and see the end of Wrong![70]

John Richards emerged from prison on 4 May 1844 as an acclaimed hero. The day after his release, he was driven in a procession of seven carriages, from William Peplow's house in Stafford to Longton and Hanley; he was welcomed home by enthusiastic crowds lining the streets, and addressed several open-air meetings. John Moreton, a Hanley Chartist and master tailor, presented him with a new suit of clothes on his release from prison.[71]

86

Apparently given a new lease of life by this reception, he set off again in mid-May on yet another lecture tour through the Midlands, and travelled for over a month telling his audiences about his prison life with Cooper.[72] The strong links between the Stafford Chartist prisoners were a focus of mutual loyalty and support: before leaving Hanley, he initiated a petition for Cooper's early release on grounds of health, and he spoke at the homecoming celebrations of two other former fellow-prisoners, Joseph Linney at Bilston in July, and Arthur O'Neill at the Birmingham Mechanics' Institute in August.[73] Between these two events, on 5 August Nancy Richards, aged 79 or 80, died at her brother's home in Hanley. Nevertheless, a week later Richards was in Birmingham to greet O'Neill, and a week after that back in Hanley to share a platform with O'Connor.[74] In September he embarked on yet another speaking tour, this time in Lancashire and Yorkshire.[75]

He then disappears from view for several months: last heard of about to visit Keighley, it seems likely that he spent the winter of 1844–5 with his son Thomas in South Shields. On 12 March 1845 the National Victim Fund Committee voted him £1 10s. 0d. 'to convey him to his settlement'. Six months later, in one of his many appeals for funds to the various committees for Chartist victims and veterans, he said that his son was unable to support him because he had a sickly wife and a large family to maintain.[76]

His life now became a continuous struggle to find the means of subsistence, avoid the workhouse, and maintain his Chartist public life. He spent the next two years, 1845–7, mainly in the Potteries. There are scattered references in the *Northern Star* to his begging letters to the Victim Committee, and the sums of money sent to him now and then by the Committee, for whom he was only one deserving case among many, and occasionally by local Chartist branches scattered throughout England. It was a stroke of luck for him when his old friend Thomas Cooper, now out of prison, set up a separate Veteran Patriots' fund in August 1845. For some months in the spring and summer of 1846, he was receiving five shillings a week from that source and occasional subventions from the Victim Committee as well, profiting from their lack of co-ordination.[77] From February to May, perhaps because he was less acutely worried about money, he seems to have had a renewed spurt of political

energy, addressing at least five meetings: against the Militia Bill
and the Irish Coercion Bill, for the return of Chartist exiles,
especially his friend William Ellis, and for the National Association of United Trades.[78] However, in July Cooper, now at loggerheads with O'Connor, resigned as secretary of the Veteran
Patriots' fund, and was expelled from the Convention and
virtually drummed out of the NCA in early August. Richards
had lost a powerful friend in the right place, and only a letter
appealing on his behalf in the *Star* by John Shaw, a philanthropic London Chartist who had also helped Ellis's wife,
produced a new flow of donations for him.[79]

Finally in March 1847 Richards announced in a letter to the
*Star* that he had no alternative but to enter the Stoke workhouse. But as a result of his letter, the money began to flow in
again, and the Bilston Chartists, led by his prison friend Joseph
Linney, invited him to stay with them for a few weeks. Thus he
was soon able to announce that he was 'liberated from his
earthly hell'.[80] He stayed in Bilston for the next three years, and
a change of scene at the age of 75, and at a time when Chartism
was once more reviving, gave him a new lease of political life.
The Bilston men found him 'impressive and energetic', using
'sublime and powerful language'.[81] He joined in the revival of
Black Country Chartism: between May 1847 and June 1848
there are brief references to his political activities in twenty-two
issues of the *Northern Star*.

In March 1848, joining in the enthusiasm of the year of
revolutions, he revisited Hanley to propose the address to the
French people, sharing the platform yet again with Feargus
O'Connor.[82] On 10 April, he was back in Bilston, chairing
Chartist meetings and urging support for the National Convention.[83] He must have been encouraged by the activities of his
son, Thomas Richards, who became the delegate for County
Durham to the National Assembly in May and then a Chartist
lecturer in Northumberland and Durham.[84]

From the summer of 1848, however, Black Country Chartism
rapidly declined. It was Thomas Cooper who came to the
rescue again: writing to a friend at Christmas, he confided that
a few months ago he had decided to send 'the poor old Daddy'
five shillings a week, as 'the Bilston folk were about leaving him
to go to the Bastille'. Cooper raised the money from collections
at his popular Sunday night lectures, and intended to continue

doing this for the remainder of Richards' life. Thus Richards was able to struggle on, continuing to live in Bilston, even sending in a few shillings for Chartist membership cards.[85]

Once again it was the publication of a letter in the *Northern Star* which changed his fortunes. In April 1850 O'Connor came to Hanley for the last time to open the Chartist People's Hall in a former Methodist chapel. Richards wrote to his nephew in the Potteries, regretting his inability to walk to Hanley and sending greetings to O'Connor and the Potteries Chartists. O'Connor read the letter aloud to the meeting, which greeted it with 'applause till the building shook'. A month later, Richards was back in the Potteries for good. On 3 June, he chaired a well-attended lecture in the People's Hall by George Mantle of Birmingham; on 4 June he chaired an open-air meeting at Crown Bank, Hanley, called to request the government to remove from office the unpopular Potteries stipendiary magistrate, T.B. Rose. Richards was now about 78 and these two meetings were his last recorded public appearances.[86]

After 1850, we get only a very few further glimpses of John Richards. At the time of the 1851 census, the 'retired shoemaker, retired delegate to the National Convention' was living in Hope Street, Hanley, as a lodger in the house of Henry Daniel Shaw, a 37-year-old master plumber and glazier, his wife and 5-year-old daughter; Shaw was an old friend and an active Hanley Chartist. In the same year, he was listed in the new edition of *White's Directory of Staffordshire* as 'John Richards, gent, Hope Street'.[87]

Robert Gammage, who spent six weeks in the Potteries in November and December 1853 trying to form an effective miners' union, told readers of the first edition of his history of Chartism that 'Mr Richards still resides in the Potteries, full of years, but as devoted as ever to his principles'. Cooper, who was still sending him money via an intermediary, heard in March 1854 that 'Poor old Daddy Richards is growing very infirm; he seems to be decaying fast'.[88]

John Richards died in the Stoke workhouse, which he had strenuously sought to avoid for so many years, on 9 June 1856, aged 83 or 84, from 'Decay of Nature'. His death was recorded in the local paper in one brief line, and he was buried in a pauper's grave in the churchyard of St Peter's Church, Stoke.[89]

## VI

Richards is not now a well-known name in the popular perception of local history in the Potteries, where Joseph Capper, an exclusively local figure who played no part in events outside the Potteries, has, largely fortuitously, become the local Chartist best known to posterity.[90] But Richards' memory deserves to be rescued from the neglect into which it has fallen; this well-travelled radical shoemaker should be restored to his place in history.[91]

If his life before the age of 60 remains very largely a tantalizing area of ignorance, his old age is full of interest. In the 1830s, like so many other local Chartist leaders, he acquired the experience and status in his community which prepared him for leadership. His links with middle-class liberalism and his strong support for trade unionism, especially general unionism, may seem incompatible, but are a reminder that middle-class and working-class radicalism cannot be put in separate watertight compartments, which in some of the historiography of Chartism has been the Marxist version of 'compartmentalism'. As a member of the Convention of 1839, he combined devoted adherence to the Chartist cause with equally strong opposition to violence; the tensions inherent in this position in 1839–40 led him to join the Urquhart movement of those years, a little-studied phenomenon which his experience partially illuminates. He was probably the only Urquhartite to return to the Chartist fold, regain some of his former prominence, and rebuild his local support.

In 1842 he supported a general strike for the Charter, but not the violence which occurred as a result: this position was not unusual, but what distinguished Richards was the exemplary fortitude and unswerving adherence to his principles with which he suffered his trials and prison sentence in 1842–4, when he was over 70. His continuing political activity thereafter, until at least 1850, drew further on his strength of character; his strategies of survival give some insight into precisely how, and through what networks of support, Chartist veterans subsisted in their old age.

In the light of the formidably analytical social-scientific history being written now, it may seem to some to be a backward-looking, outmoded form of historical discourse to pay close attention to the life histories of individuals. This is not a view with which Dorothy Thompson has ever associated herself. The political activity of John Richards between 1830 and 1850 exemplifies the best of British radicalism in this heroic period. Homage to John Richards.

## NOTES

1 Asa Briggs and John Saville (eds), *Essays in Labour History* (London, 1960), pp. 276–316, reprinted in E.P. Thompson, *Persons and Polemics* (London, 1994) pp. 23–65.

2 Dorothy Thompson, *The Chartists* (London, 1984), pp. 89–234, *passim*.

3 The literature is too extensive to list, but see especially J.M. Bellamy and J. Saville (eds), *Dictionary of Labour Biography*, I–IX, (London, 1972–1993), and Christopher Godfrey, *Chartist Lives* (New York and London, 1987).

4 George J. Barnsby, *The Working Class Movement in the Black Country* (Wolverhampton, 1977), p. 81; Thompson, *The Chartists*, p. 181.

5 London, Public Record Office (PRO), Home Office Papers (HO) 107/2005, 1851 Census, Hope Street, Hanley. London, Bishopsgate Institute, Thomas Cooper papers, Cooper to Thomas Tatlow, 25 Dec. 1848, mentions Richards as '76 today', but two boys were baptized John Richards at St Philip's Church, Birmingham, in January 1772: Birmingham Parish Registers, information from Senior Archivist, Birmingham Public Library.

6 *North Staffs Mercury* (NSM), 26 Jan. 1839.

7 *Northern Star* (NS), 13 May 1843. T. Cooper, *The Life of Thomas Cooper* (1872, reprinted Leicester 1971), p. 234, says Richards referred to Fox and Pitt, but the *Northern Star*'s version is more likely to be correct.

8 *NS*, 10 Aug. 1844; PRO, Prison Commissioners 2/401, Stafford Gaol Register, 1841–5, Entry 972, *NS*, 24 Sept. 1842.

9 *NSM*, 22 Oct. 1842, 8 April 1843. See J. Clayson, E. and R. Frow, 'John Wade and the Black Book', *Labour History Review*, **59**, 2 (Autumn 1994), pp. 55–7 for a brief assessment and publishing history of *The Black Book*.

10 *NS*, 24 Sept. 1842.

11 *Staffordshire Mercury* (SM), 20 Nov. 1830; Poll Books, North Staffordshire Constituency, 1832 and 1837.

12   *SM*, 22 Feb. 1834; *NSM*, 25 June 1836.

13   *SM*, 5 Feb., 17 Sept., 8 Oct. 1831; *Voice of the People*, 12 Feb. 1831.

14   For a fuller discussion, see R. Fyson, 'Unionism, class and community in the 1830s: aspects of the National Union of Operative Potters', in John Rule (ed), *British Trade Unionism 1750–1850: The Formative Years* (London, 1988), pp. 200–19.

15   *SM*, 8 Feb. 1834; *NSM*, 22 March, 5, 12, 19 April 1834, 5 Dec. 1835, 26 March, 31 Dec. 1836.

16   *NS*, 24 Sept. 1842. Probably this refers to pseudonymous letters or union statements in the local press. I have not been able definitely to identify any of these as Richards' work.

17   *NSM*, 24 May 1834, 25 April 1835.

18   W.H. Warburton, *The History of Trade Union Organisation in the North Staffordshire Potteries* (London, 1931), pp. 271–2.

19   *NSM*, 8 July 1837.

20   This phrase was used by his proposer when he stood for the post of poor-rate collector: *NSM*, 5 April 1834.

21   *NSM*, 11 Aug. 1838; HO 52/38, George Keen to Lord Talbot, 3 Nov. 1838, ff. 249–50.

22   PRO, Treasury Solicitor (TS), 11/596; *NSM*, 3, 10 Nov. 1838.

23   *NSM*, *NS*, 17 Nov. 1838.

24   *NSM*, 2 Feb. 1839.

25   *NS*, 2, 9, 16 Feb. 1839; *Charter*, 10, 17 Feb. 1839; *Operative*, 10 Feb, 10 March 1839.

26   *NS*, 9 March 1839; London, British Library, Additional Manuscripts (Add. MSS), 34, 245A, Richards to William Lovett, 22 March 1839, ff. 146–7; 28 March 1839, ff. 172–3. The letter of 22 March, slightly abbreviated, is in Mark Hovell, *The Chartist Movement* (Manchester, 1918 and later editions), pp. 130–1, also in R. Fyson (ed.), *Chartism in North Staffordshire*, Staffordshire County Council Education Department (Stafford, 1981), p.10.

27   HO 40/48, H.H. Williamson to Lord Talbot, 15 March 1839, f. 5; *Staffordshire Gazette*, (*SG*), 3 April 1839; Add. MSS 34, 245A, Richards to Lovett, 28 March 1839; *NSM*, 6 April 1839.

28   *NS*, 4 May 1839; *Charter*, 19 May 1839; *NS*, 25 May, 1 June 1839; *NSM*, 22 June 1839; *NS*, 6 July 1839.

29   HO 40/48, Edward Wood to George Phillips, 20 July; George Ryles to George Phillips, 23 July; Lord Talbot to Lord John Russell, 31 July: all three letters are in Fyson, *Chartism in North Staffordshire*, pp. 12–14.

30 Reminiscences of Thomas Dunning, in David Vincent (ed.), *Testaments of Radicalism* (London, 1977), p. 136 (date misprinted as 1838).

31 Add. MSS 34, 245B, Charles Salt to anon. (William Cardo?), 19 May 1839, f. 23.

32 HO 40/48, Talbot to Russell, 31 July 1839; Add. MSS 34, 245B, Richards to T.R. Smart, 8 August 1839, ff. 125–6; HO 40/48, Staffs., August 1839, *passim*; NSM, *Staffordshire Advertiser* (*SA*), 24 August 1839.

33 HO 44/52, ff. 184, 189, 199–200; *Operative*, 1, 8, 15 Sept. 1839; NS, 7, 14, 21, Sept., 5 Oct. 1839.

34 *NS*, 4 May 1850; HO 107/2005, 1851 Census, Hope Street, Hanley.

35 Oxford, Balliol College Library, Urquhart Papers, Box 8, 1E1. MS copy of letter from Pringle Taylor to anon, 22 Sept. 1839. Southampton University Library, Wellington Papers, 4/1/10/66, letter 4, is another MS copy of the same letter which names the recipient, Hugh Cameron. The Chartist leaders concerned are not named.

36 Urquhart Papers, Box 8, 1E1, Missionary Reports 1 and 5, from Birmingham and Manchester respectively, 9 Oct., 28 Nov. 1839. There is another MS copy of the first report in Oxford, Bodleian Library: Pringle Taylor, Letters Relative to the Chartists 1839–40, Department of Printed Books, 2288. c53.

37 Wellington Papers, 4/1/10/66, Letter 1, Pringle Taylor to Mrs Stuart Hall (the unnamed missionary's aunt), n.d.

38 *NS*, 25 Jan., 8 Feb., 14 March, 25 April, 27 June 1840; *NSM*, 18 Jan., 15 Feb., 25 April, 2 May 1840; Hanley Reference Library, Hanley Highways Board Minutes, 25 March 1840; *Staffordshire Potteries Telegraph*, 30 Oct. 1852.

39 Gertrude Robinson, *David Urquhart: Some Chapters in the Life of a Victorian Knight-Errant of Justice and Liberty* (Oxford, 1920), p. 97. This book is an unsourced hagiography, but apparently drew upon original materials which are not now to be found among the Urquhart papers at Balliol.

40 TS 11/596, Richards' notebook; Robinson, *David Urquhart*, p. 97.

41 *NS*, 14, 21 Nov. 1840; *Northern Liberator* (*NL*), 31 Oct., 7, 28 Nov. 1840.

42 *NL*, 28 Nov. 1840. For Thomas Richards, *NS*, 18 March, 17 June 1848, identify him as Richards' son and give his address as 34 Brunswick Street, South Shields.

43 *NS*, 14 Nov. 1840; TS 11/596, Richards' notebook.

44 Robinson, *David Urquhart*, p. 102; *NL*, 31 Oct. 1840.

45   *NS*, 14 Nov. 1840.

46   *NS*, 19 Sept., 28 Nov., 5, 19, 26 Dec. 1840; 2, 9 Jan. 1841.

47   *NS*, 6 March, 6, 20 Nov. 1841; *NSM*, 29 May 1841.

48   *NS*, 5 March 1842; TS 11/596, pencilled note by Richards, 22 May 1842. In the quarter July–Sept. 1842, almost certainly before mid-August, Upper Hanley paid for 300 membership cards: *NS*, 12 Nov. 1842.

49   For Upper Hanley, and Hanley and Shelton, NCA committee lists, see *NS*, 10 April 1841, 29 Jan., 12 March, 6, 13 Aug. 1842.

50   *NS*, 29 Jan. 1842; *NS*, *NSM*, 28 May 1842.

51   *NS*, 17, 24 April, 8 May 1841.

52   *NS*, 6 Nov. 1841, 1 Jan. 1842.

53   Voting figures: Hanley and Shelton: Mason 96, Richards 5; Longton: Mason 1, Richards 133; Upper Hanley: Mason 2, Richards 216; Stoke: Mason 82, Richards 1. *NS*, 5 March 1842.

54   *NSM*, 29 May 1841.

55   *NSM*, 17 Nov. 1838; *SG*, 27 May 1841; *NS*, 9 April, 9 July 1842.

56   See R. Fyson, 'The crisis of 1842: Chartism, the colliers' strike and the outbreak in the Potteries', in James Epstein and Dorothy Thompson (eds), *The Chartist Experience: Studies in Working-Class Radicalism and Culture, 1830–1860* (London, 1982), pp. 194–220.

57   *NSM*, 2, 9 July 1842; *NS*, *NSM*, 20 Aug. 1842.

58   *NS*, 16 July, 6 Aug. 1842; TS 11/602, copy of letter from Committee of Operative Colliers, George and Dragon, Hanley, 13 Aug. 1842, to Mr Dean, Norton Colliery.

59   TS 11/602, Richards to Cooper, 2 Aug. 1842; *NS*, 6, 13 Aug. 1842; *NS*, *NSM*, 20 Aug. 1842; Cooper, *Life*, pp. 191–2.

60   *SA*, 27 Aug. 1842; *NSM*, 20 Aug., 3 Sept., 1842; *NS*, 20 Aug. 1842, first and fourth editions.

61   HO 45/260, Richards to Joshua Hobson, 22 Aug. 1842, ff. 374–5.

62   *NSM*, *SA*, 27 Aug. 1842; *NSM*, 3 Sept. 1842; PRO, Assizes 6:6, Depositions in case of John Richards, No. 113. The papers confiscated from Richards' home are located in TS 11/596.

63   *NS*, 13 May 1843, 6 April 1844; *NSM*, 22 Oct. 1842; *SA*, 26 Nov. 1842.

64   Lincoln, Lincolnshire Archives, Thomas Cooper Papers, bill of William Williams to John Richards for services in October and November 1842.

65   *NS*, 3, 24 Dec. 1842; 14 Jan., 4, 25 Feb. 1843.

66   The fullest account is in *NS*, 1, 8 April 1843. See also *NSM*, *SA*, 25 March, 1 April 1843. The version in J.E.P. Wallis (ed.), *Reports of*

*State Trials*, New Series, Vol. IV (1892, reprinted London, 1970), cols 1249–316, is partial and abridged, including the testimony of all prosecution witnesses, but only four for the defence. Cols 1316–330, reporting the Queen's Bench proceedings in May, entirely omits Richards' speech from the dock. Ellis was not on trial, because he had already been transported to Tasmania for another alleged offence.

67  *NS*, 13 May 1843; Cooper, *Life*, pp. 234–5.

68  Cooper, *Life*, pp. 236–53; *NS*, 20, 27 May, 17 June, 15 July 1843.

69  *NS*, 2 March, 6 April 1844.

70  Cooper, *Life*, p. 242; Thomas Cooper, *The Purgatory of Suicides* (3rd edn, London, 1853), p. 276. When this book was first published in August 1845, Cooper presented an inscribed signed copy to Richards, which was later acquired by a local bookseller: Rupert Simms, *Bibliotheca Staffordiensis* (Lichfield, 1894), p. 120.

71  *NS, NSM, SA*, 11, 18 May 1844; *Newcastle Weekly Chronicle*, 27 Sept. 1873.

72  *NS*, 18, 25 May, 1, 8, 15 June 1844.

73  *NS*, 6 July, 17 Aug. 1844.

74  *NS, NSM, SA*, 10 Aug. 1844, *NSM*, 24 Aug. 1844.

75  *NS*, 14, 21, 28 Sept. 1844.

76  *NS*, 10 May, 20 Sept. 1845.

77  *NS*, 16 Aug., 20 Sept. 1845; 13 June 1846.

78  *NS*, 7, 28 Feb., 21 March, 25 April, 9 May, 1846.

79  *NS*, 4, 18 July, 8 Aug. 1846.

80  *NS*, 13, 20, 27 March, 3 April 1847.

81  *NS*, 8 May 1847. See also the account of Bilston Chartists' hospitality to Richards in Barnsby, *Working-Class Movement in the Black Country*, p. 124.

82  *NS, SM, SA*, 11 March 1848.

83  *NS*, 22 April 1848.

84  For Thomas Richards, see *NS*, 18, 25 March, 29 April, 13 May, 3, 17 June, 12 Aug. 1848.

85  Bishopsgate, Cooper to Tatlow, 25 Dec. 1848; *NS*, 24 March, 1849.

86  *NS*, 4 May, 8 June 1850.

87  HO 107/2005, census return for Hope Street, Hanley, 1851; W. White, *History, Gazetteer and Directory of Staffordshire* (Sheffield, 1851), p. 248.

88  *People's Paper*, 22 Oct.–17 Dec. 1853; R.G. Gammage, *History of the Chartist Movement* (London, 1854 edn), p. 441; Bishopsgate, Cooper to Tatlow, 15 March 1854.

89  Death certificate; *Staffordshire Sentinel*, 14 June 1856; Staffordshire Record Office, Stafford, St Peter's Church, Stoke, Parish Registers, burial book.

90  Charles Shaw, *When I Was a Child* (London, 1903 and subsequent reprints), pp. 141–54, 172–81, and Frederick Harper, *Tilewright's Acre* (London, 1959), and *Joseph Capper* (London, 1962), two imaginative but unreliable historical novels, are the main sources of the Capper legend.

91  For radical shoemakers generally, see E.J. Hobsbawm and Joan Wallach Scott, 'Political shoemakers', *Past and Present*, **89** (November 1980), reprinted in E.J. Hobsbawm, *Worlds of Labour* (London, 1984), pp. 103–30.

# 5

## Rural Resistance: Custom, Community and Conflict in South Oxfordshire, 1800–1914

KATE TILLER

I

On Sunday morning, 21 November 1830, a large crowd gathered in the churchyard of Benson in south Oxfordshire. They were waiting for Thomas Newton, a substantial farmer who owned or occupied virtually the whole of the hamlet of Crowmarsh Battle (also known as Preston Crowmarsh) on the banks of the Thames just to the west of Benson. A notice had recently appeared in *Jackson's Oxford Journal* announcing that an application was to be made to parliament for a bill

to divide, allot and inclose, or to divide and allot only; and also for draining and improving all the open and common fields, common meadows, common pastures and commonable lands, and waste grounds, in the parish of . . . Benson, and in the hamlet or tything of Berrick Salome, in the parish of Chalgrove, and in the parish of Ewelme, all in the county of Oxford, with power to divide and allot, with consent of the respective owners, and upon just and reasonable allowances, any homesteads, gardens, orchards and old inclosed arable, meadow, and pasture land, and other ancient inclosures and lands, lying in either of the said parishes.[1]

This was widely recognized as Thomas Newton's latest attempt to transform the customary common field agriculture of the local district and, like his previous attempts, had generated concerted opposition. It was expected that Newton, his son, or a representative would that morning post the required notice of the planned enclosure on the door of the parish church at Benson. As in the case of other opposed enclosures,[2] this was seen as a critical occasion on which to manifest mass objections to the proposal. When Newton failed to appear, the protesters marched to Crowmarsh Battle Farm and, armed with sledge-hammers taken from local smithies, broke down the barn doors and demanded undertakings that neither Newton nor his son would now or in the future proceed with any enclosure. They threatened to break his threshing machines and eventually did so.[3]

These events have been briefly catalogued by Hobsbawm and Rudé[4] as part of the broader picture of the Swing Riots. The first disturbance in Oxfordshire had taken place near Henley on 20 November and on the following day the Benson protesters went on to break threshing machines at Ewelme, Berrick and Rofford. Whilst the accounts in *Captain Swing* and elsewhere[5] acknowledge the role of a local enclosure grievance, their concern is with the overall pattern of events, stressing widespread grievances about wages and the use of machinery and exploring the transmission of agitation and possibly agitators from district to district.[6] Moreover, they rely primarily on evidence from central government and national press sources, which convey a tone of anxious concern about general insurgency. When it comes to understanding the dynamics of rural resistance this external perspective is limiting. It becomes necessary and, as this chapter aims to show, possible to look not only at a flashpoint like 21 November 1830 but at both the preceding and succeeding years of frequently tense transition from a local customary and communal culture, in which common field agriculture was the key activity, to an altered landscape of private interests, independent cultivation and changed social relationships. To take this perspective was one of the challenges which E.P. Thompson perceived on the first publication of *Captain Swing*, a study of which he wrote, '[it] raises time and again questions which demand the refinement of our historical methods ... which will set local historians looking at their villages with far more subtle and complex questions in their minds; and which has placed all social historians in [the authors'] debt'.[7]

These subtle and complex questions have been posed. As the work of the generation of historians since Hobsbawm and Rudé is increasingly demonstrating,[8] rural resistance involved solidarities of greater complexity than any analysis based simply on monolithic views of class interest will allow. This study explores such alignments and identities through a local study. Its starting point is a re-examination of the events of November

1830. From detailed local evidence the communal context of
what occurred emerges, as does its genesis in a very much
longer process of actual and potential changes, some agreed,
some fiercely contested. In this respect Benson is set alongside
the adjoining south Oxfordshire parishes of Ewelme and Berrick Salome, all linked by experiences of surviving common
fields, patterns of tenure, and late and contested parliamentary
enclosure (or in the case of Ewelme, no parliamentary enclosure). The story thus stretches back into the late eighteenth
century and continues into the 1860s (and in the case of
Ewelme, into the early twentieth century). Under this sustained
pressure to enclose, which persisted for over half a century,
many realities were exposed. The evidence is clear that the
customary community was a live, working entity. Its active
survival reflected not a retrospectively rigid resistance to all
change, but rather a capacity to accommodate internal change
by local consensus. Just who were the parties to local consensus
in this evolved form of customary culture was most apparent
when that culture came under external threat. This study also
illustrates the extent and effectiveness of opposition to enclosure, much of it prior to any formal parliamentary process. In
this respect, the south Oxfordshire evidence amplifies the findings of J.M. Neeson for Northamptonshire[9] and raises similar
questions about the character of those communities which
generated opposition to enclosure. The identity of those
actively involved in opposition and their tactics in mobilizing
both those above and below them in the social scale suggests
the key role of local élites in the defence of custom (and of their
own economic interest as they perceived it).[10] Through all of
this the continued effectiveness of common field farming is
striking.

## II

Thomas Newton, who was to prove a frequent catalyst in
events in south Oxfordshire, had moved to the district in 1797,
establishing himself at Crowmarsh Battle Farm.[11] Here he refur-
bished the farmhouse and an impressive range of barns. He
rapidly became known as an enterprising and assertive farmer
whose practices were quoted by Arthur Young in his *General
View of the Agriculture of Oxfordshire* (1813). Newton set about

extending his landholding and his farming methods into the neighbouring parishes of Benson and Ewelme, which lie between the Thames and the Chiltern hills. This land was known for its fruitful soils, gravelly loams on which (as C.S. Read observed in his 1854 essay 'On the farming of Oxfordshire') 'double cropping may be carried out in a manner which reflects the highest credit on the enlightened husbandmen of these localities'. The relative prosperity and effective farming of the area within a common field system of cultivation had been noticeable in the seventeenth century. Michael Havinden[12] describes the continuing progress of south Oxfordshire farmers in the sometimes difficult period 1640–1730 and attributes it not only to the natural advantages of the terrain but also to the benefits of access to London, where wheat and barley found a ready market. Henley, Wallingford and Benson itself all had riverside wharves and malthouses. Moreover, the London to Gloucester road, turnpiked in 1736 and with links north to Oxford and Birmingham, ran less than a mile south of Ewelme and through the common fields to Benson itself. Several large coaching inns and the elegant brick and sash-windowed façades bestowed on houses along the village street bear testimony to the prosperity and extensive employment which the coaching trade brought to Benson in the eighteenth and early nineteenth centuries. This good fortune was to be increasingly challenged from 1840 when the Great Western Railway opened with a station some five and a half miles away at Wallingford, but when Thomas Newton came to Benson he found a large village with an open landholding and social structure and flourishing common fields. As a correspondent to the *Gentleman's Magazine* wrote of a visit to the village in June 1793, he was awakened at five in the morning by 'the cowherd sounding his horn to rouse the milkmaids to be prepared on his return from the common pasture with the village cows'.[13] Benson had no major resident landowners. Land tax assessments between 1785 and 1832[14] suggest the pattern of landholding. For example, in 1800, 92 units of property were assessed for the tax in Benson, although the actual number of proprietors was somewhat less, around 69. Allowing for absentee owners, the actual number of occupiers of property in the parish was around 50. This remained the case throughout the period and, until Thomas Newton began his property accumulation, no one Benson owner or occupier held property paying more than 13–14 per cent of the parish's tax. The largest single interest, some 21 per cent, was that of three members of the Shrubb family.[15]

The field system which played such an important part in the lives of the local proprietors encompassed land in three parishes (estimated in 1829 as 1,203 acres in Benson, 461 in Berrick Salome and 428 in Ewelme)[16] and was subject to extremely complex intercommoning and tithe arrangements. Benson had been the seat of a major royal manor at the time of Domesday. Its lands had extended over large parts of south Oxfordshire. When in 1628 Charles I came to sell the manor, it proved impossible to definitively unravel the linked property rights of the associated settlements in and around Benson.[17] The tenants, who held in ancient demesne a hybrid state originally falling between villeinage and full free tenure, asserted their extensive rights of common in a survey of 1606.[18] By 1800 the situation was hardly less complex. With some areas of land already in closes, as around Preston Crowmarsh, Fifield and Berrick Salome, there still remained extensive acreages of common arable and pasture run by local farmers, some of them with interests straddling the three parishes.[19] There was no active manorial jurisdiction to intervene in their determinations. This was the complex scene into which Thomas Newton came. His first attempt to promote enclosure at Benson was in 1807,[20] just one year after he first embarked on accumulating landholdings there. His name appears in the Benson land tax returns in 1806, assessed at £6 13s. 8d. of a parish total of £122 15s. 4d., a stake of 5.4 per cent in the local assessed property. Following the rebuttal of his 1807 enclosure proposal he added the outlying Potters Farm to his holdings in 1815, bringing his stake to 10.4 per cent. In 1820 this increased to four holdings (26.9 per cent), in 1827, the year of his major push for an enclosure bill, to 28.9 per cent, and in 1828 to 30.7 per cent. By 1829 Thomas and his son Robert were taxed at £40 17s. 2d., representing one-third of the land tax assessment for Benson.[21] In addition to this sizeable stake Newton had, in 1818, acquired the manor of Fifield.[22] The lands of this small hamlet, within sight of the houses at the eastern end of Benson on the one hand and those of the western end of Ewelme on the other, included parts of the three parish system. In 1827 Thomas's eldest son, Robert Aldworth Newton, then aged 29 and probably just married, moved into Fifield Manor,[23] thus bracketing Benson with a Newton family presence on each side of the village.

It is clear that the expansion of the Newtons' interests and Thomas's overt intention to enclose the local open fields met with considerable local resistance long before November 1830. The notice which Thomas placed in *Jackson's Oxford Journal* on 17 November 1827 was even blunter and less reassuring than that which appeared three years later. It informed 'proprietors of lands and estates in the parish of . . . Benson . . . and all other persons whom it may concern' that parliament would be petitioned to bring in a bill for 'dividing and allotting all the open and common fields, common meadows, common pastures and commonable lands, and waste ground in the parish of . . . Benson'. This evoked a swift and highly-organized response. A meeting was held at the White Hart Inn in the centre of Benson and was attended by the principal farmers of the parish.[24] An opposition committee was elected and resolutions passed that an Enclosure Act would not be beneficial, that it would greatly injure the local proprietors, that the waste land 'in its present state is very valuable to the proprietors', that the common fields of Benson were so intermixed with those of Ewelme and Berrick that no measure could succeed unless it dealt with all three parishes, and that it was essential that the measure should be opposed. John Franklin, Edward Shrubb and John Hutchings, all substantial farmers, Shrubb with principal interests in Benson, Franklin in Ewelme and Hutchings in Berrick, were appointed to lead the opposition committee with the energetic help of George Eyre, a member of a leading Ewelme family who was a solicitor. Eyre's letter[25] to Magdalen College, Oxford, which had landholdings in the parish, vividly conveys the feeling at the time.

Having emphasized the representativeness of the meeting (nearly every proprietor or occupier of land in the three parishes being present except for 'Ladies, persons residing out of the neighbourhood, or having only the most trifling quantity of land'), Eyre asserted that

not even a solitary individual present . . . was favourable to the intended measure . . . Mr Newton for the last quarter of a century has been endeavouring by every device that his own imagination could suggest to carry the intended measure.

These attempts dated back to September 1807 when Newton had first given notice of an intended application to parliament to introduce an Enclosure Bill. This had resulted in a similar protest meeting at the White Hart on 19 October of that year. In the light of unanimous opposition Newton had withdrawn his proposal. On the present occasion, 'Mr N. . . . has been working in the most underhand manner and concealed his intention from his neighbours as long as he was able . . . and never even asked one of them if he had any objection to the application'. Eyre alleged that Newton had exceeded the bounds of truth to obtain support but that the arguments against enclosure were compelling:

Every Proprietor's Estate in Benson is small, except Mr Newton's, and it is well known that all small Estates are invariably much depreciated in value by an Inclosure . . . to say nothing about the Expenses, but the Expenses of allotting Benson would be enormous: there are Estates and Tenures of nearly every different sort and kind mentioned in the Book of Littleton[26] . . . the boundaries of the Parish are very confused, its Lands strangely intermingled with those of Ewelme and Berrick, and its Common rights very intricate . . . the Bill . . . would greatly injure all the Proprietors excepting Mr Newton and completely extinguish those who have nothing but their Land to depend on.

Every Farmer is now able to cultivate his land as he pleases . . . and the only inconvenience is that of the Lands lying in small pieces; but it is better that the Proprietors should submit to this than to have it remedied at the Expense of their own ruin. There is no Waste Land in the Parish which is not very valuable to the Proprietors in its present state.

There is a large Heath in the parish of Benson—producing Furze, which the Poor enjoy the right of cutting, and this is very serviceable to them.

Mr Newton . . . is a large Proprietor and desirous of purchasing land; and proposes that the Bill should take power to sell the Waste Land now the Heath just mentioned adjoins his Estate, and several Proprietors should the measure be carried will be obliged to sell their Estates; as there is no Gentleman who has an estate of any consequence in the Parish . . . it is not probable there would be much competition for the Land . . . therefore Mr N. would have an opportunity of becoming the Purchaser on his own terms.

Eyre ends his letter with an eloquent appeal to the College to oppose the intended application for a bill. Both the Bishop of Oxford, on grounds of injury to the proprietors and the local poor, and Lady Stapleton, the lady of the Manor, are un-

*Table 1* The position of local proprietors on the Enclosure Bill of 1829

| | Number of proprietors | Benson | | Berrick Salome | | Ewelme | | Total | |
|---|---|---|---|---|---|---|---|---|---|
| | | Acreage A – R – P | % of Benson acreage | Acreage A – R – P | % of B.S. acreage | Acreage A – R – P | % of Ewelme acreage | Acreage A – R – P | % of total acreage |
| Assents | 2 | 298 – 1 – 13 | 25 | 105 – 0 – 31 | 23 | 64 – 0 – 0 | 15 | 467 – 2 – 4 | 22 |
| Dissents | 48 | 638 – 0 – 17 | 53 | 272 – 3 – 10 | 59 | 335 – 0 – 15 | 78 | 1246 – 0 – 2 | 60 |
| Neuters | 8 | 137 – 3 – 25 | 12 | 10 – 1 – 33 | 2 | 27 – 1 – 26 | 6 | 195 – 3 – 4 | 9 |
| Either dissents or neuters doubtful | 9 | 108 – 2 – 25 | 9 | 73 – 0 – 0 | 16 | 2 – 0 – 7 | 0.5 | 183 – 2 – 32 | 9 |
| Totals | 67 | 1203 – 0 – 0 | | 461 – 1 – 34 | | 428 – 2 – 8 | | 2093 – 0 – 2 | |

*Source:* Oxfordshire Archives, MSS D.D. Par. Ewelme c. 12.

favourable to the measure. Moreover, the College's own hold-ing is likely to depreciate in value. Finally, 'it would be very much lamented were the notorious avarice of Mr Newton to involve a whole Parish in ruin'.

This highly organized mobilization of opposition to New-ton's enclosure ended in the rebuttal of his 1827 scheme, but there were to be regular November confrontations linked to the timing of parliamentary sessions in succeeding years. In 1829 Newton got as far as formally introducing a bill and the local opposition again went to work, this time having to marshal formal statements of assent, dissent or neutrality on the bill for presentation at Committee stage.[27] The results are shown in Table 1. Only Newton and his son supported the proposal. In terms of people, the opposition was overwhelming. In terms of acreage, resistance at Ewelme, where as we shall see open field farming was most flexible and resilient, was emphatic, whilst in Benson and Berrick the lineup of acreage against Newton was impressive but potentially vulnerable in a system where neuters and doubters were weighed with assents.[28] However, in 1829 the balance of opinion was clear and parliament rejected the bill.

There followed a period of constant vigilance on the part of the opposition and in October 1830 George Eyre was again writ-ing to potential supporters[29] with proof that the vicar of neigh-bouring Chalgrove in fact opposed an enclosure because it would be 'injurious to my poorer neighbours', despite claims to the contrary and troublesome visits from Mr Newton's lawyers. Whilst acknowledging that a 'separation of the three parishes and an allotment of lands' might be desirable, Eyre reiterates that it was impossible to do so 'with equal justice to all parties and without occasioning expense or inconvenience' whilst Mr Newton was the promoter. It was at this stage that Newton claimed that some of those who had signed against his bill the previous year had changed their minds and that he published his notice of 12 November[30] with its references to drainage and improvement, to the consent of the respective owners, and to just and reasonable allowances in an enclosure. On to this cycli-cal pattern of November confrontations the mass protest of the Swing Riots was superimposed and gained local momentum.

## III

At two o'clock on the morning of Sunday 21 November 1830, Thomas Newton was wakened at Crowmarsh Battle Farm by a group of around thirty labouring men demanding that he listen to their grievances. Newton claimed[31] that they had been sent to destroy his threshing machines. Another account[32] states that they wanted his promise never to attempt an enclosure of Benson. The faces of the men were disguised, although 'some thought they knew ... their voices'. They eventually departed, allegedly having been given money to spend on beer. William Carter, a labourer from Benson, was subsequently committed to Oxford Gaol for extorting five shillings from Thomas Newton and threatening to break his threshing machine. At eleven o'clock that morning, a much larger crowd (one estimate put it at 'upwards of 1,000 persons')[33] waited at Benson parish church for a copy of Newton's notice of proposed enclosure to be affixed to the church door. When he failed to appear a throng of several hundred people made their way to Newton's farm, broke into the barn and destroyed a threshing machine. Newton promised to dismantle a machine at another of his farms the following day and not to attempt a local enclosure. He donated a barrel of beer at a neighbouring public house. The rioters subsequently called on Robert Newton, his eldest son, and 'made him pledge himself never to attempt an inclosure, and he made them a present of money'.[34] At nine-thirty p.m. Thomas Newton issued a formal notice that he would not proceed with the enclosure.[35]

Meanwhile the crowd had moved on to break a threshing machine belonging to Mr Shrubb in Benson and another at Mr Eyre's in Ewelme.[36] These men were leaders of the local opposition to enclosure. The fact that they were victims of the rioters suggests that the disturbances were more than an expression of local enclosure grievances. Threshing machines, and the threat which they posed to winter employment, figure in all the accounts. Dissatisfaction about wages is mentioned only once, in Quarter Sessions evidence against six men accused of breaking into Thomas Newton's yard and not only threatening his machinery but demanding '2s. per day, and they would have it'.[37] The Lord Lieutenant's analysis, conveyed to the Home Secretary in a letter of 5 December,[38] was that the trouble had been due to ill-disposed men coming out of Berkshire and to accounts spread by the press. His enquiries of local magistrates indicated that people were not unhappy about wages; 'most Parishes have taken measures to have the People employed'. Intriguingly Lord Macclesfield added that 'I have reason however to think that there are some Farmers who at least would not discourage' trouble. Certainly a local Benson correspondent stressed the general grievance on enclosure ('the proposed inclosure is most unpopular *with all classes* for many miles around Benson') and claimed that 'the men were orderly in their conduct, except when they broke open several smithies to obtain sledgehammers'.[39] When it came to machine-breaking, he too pointed to men from Berkshire, who 'impress into their service all the labouring people they meet with . . . The machine destroyers are headed by a man whom they implicitly obey and, after they have finished their work, he begs of the owner of the machine, and is satisfied with any trifle he may receive'. This report interestingly omits reference to the attacks on Shrubb and Eyre but ends, 'The assemblage at the church was in no way encouraged by the farmers'.

Were the Benson rioters outsiders? The fact that only two of the ten names of those arrested for taking part are readily identifiable in local records and that, unlike the long-running and contemporary enclosure disturbances elsewhere in Oxfordshire at Otmoor, there was no continued violence, suggests that those singled out by the law were from outside the three parishes. The same is unlikely to be true of the hundreds who gathered during the day.

Thomas Newton was quick to seek the punishment of his attackers. The following day he presented himself to the Oxfordshire magistrates and made a sworn deposition of his account of events.[40] He sought out and found alleged accomplices of the rioters who might be persuaded to give evidence at any subsequent trial under the terms of the reward scheme just announced[41] by a government alarmed by the rapid spread of machine-breaking and incendiarism in the southern counties. Fifty pounds was offered for evidence leading to the conviction of a machine-breaker and £500 for that of an incendiary. A free pardon was offered to any accomplice who had not committed incendiarism but was willing to give evidence. Within a week Lord Macclesfield was writing to the Home Office of the attack on Newton which 'was attended with great atrocity and extortion of Money and several Persons are in custody'.[42] The Lord Lieutenant asked that an accomplice expected to give leading evidence be granted a pardon previous to his court appearance. Newton himself undertook to engage counsel and retained as his attorney Mr Croke, also Clerk of the Petty Sessions. Of the eight men convicted at the January Oxfordshire Quarter Sessions of breaking Newton's threshing machines, four were sentenced to seven years' transportation and four to twelve months' imprisonment with hard labour. These were some of the severest punishments of the twenty-six convicted at these Sessions for machinery-breaking in the county, of whom a total of nine were to be transported for seven years and five imprisoned for twelve months.[43] An accomplice giving evidence against Joseph Wheeler, a Benson rioter, at the subsequent Oxford Assizes was met by laughter and barracking in court.[44] Undaunted, Newton pressed on to make the most of both informers and rewards. Mr Croke wrote on his behalf to the Home Office asking for an early confirmation of the convictions so that the maximum rewards could be claimed.[45] Finally, Thomas Newton himself wrote to Lord Milvill:

I humbly and sincerely thank you for your kind assistance to the Agriculturalist by order of the King's proclamation it was the wisest thing that could be done I can say it was the Salvation of the Nation . . . I have been the Prosecutor of nine men which broke my Thrashing Machine besides doing me a great deal more Dammage in pulling my barn down with the expenses of prosecutions I shall be a Loan [sic] of a great Deal more than Two Hundred Pounds as I . . . was the cause of thease men to be Convicted the Magistrates of the County of Oxford say the [sic] believe I am Entitled to the Rewards which you was so kind as to offer . . . My Lord I will not have one sixpence of these Rewards for my own private use. I hope my views will meet with your Approbation.[46]

Newton's intention was to invest the reward money in funds with the proceeds to benefit the worthy and compliant poor of Benson. He would give away coats and the residue on 'the twenty-first day of November in every Year for Ever to such Honest Good Labourers of the Parish of Bensington which shall be thought most worthy of compassion'. He did so because 'there was only one man in Bensington which came with the Mob to break my Thrashing Machine'. His intention to mark the anniversary of the riots so pointedly seems to have come to nought. There is no record of any resulting charity although his son Robert provided funds for an annually distributed dole after his death in 1879.

The promises of 1830, made under duress, were not kept. On 20 November 1833 at the Crown Inn in Benson yet another 'numerous meeting of the proprietors' was held to express continued opposition to Mr Newton[47] who had 'abandoned his aforesaid notice but intimated his intention of renewing it next year', and was seemingly undeterred by twenty-six years of resistance. A committee of opposition was formed by George Parsons, John Hutchings, Thomas Weller, John Franklin, John Eyre and William Franklin, and

the Meeting expressed their regret that Mr Newton should live in continual warfare with his neighbours and be incessantly harassing and subjecting them to heavy Expenses by his vexatious Proceedings particularly now the difficulties of the times press so heavily upon them.

The balance of opinion so carefully weighed in acreages in 1829 was re-examined. Deaths in two Benson families, notably the Shrubbs, had converted some 306 acres from dissents to neuters and created a delicate balance which might be calculated just in favour of those opposed to enclosure.[48] This proved the case and no Enclosure Act for Benson, Berrick Salome and Ewelme was successfully promoted until 1852.[49] It took another eleven years to arrive at the final award which implemented the Act. This is perhaps unsurprising given the established unpopularity of the measure. The practical and legal complexities of the property rights and rights of use which were to be replaced remained as intricate as ever. Although Thomas Newton did not live to see the Enclosure Act, his sons continued to farm actively in the area and their war of attrition, together with natural causes, inevitably changed the balance of acreage and of influence locally. The climate for agricultural 'improvement' and investment also changed, producing a surge of enclosure activity in Oxfordshire in the 1850s.[50] All of these factors in eventual change deserve further detailed examination, a task beyond the scope and size of this chapter.[51] One other factor in explaining such delayed and protracted change is clearly the vigorous viability of the existing agricultural system. This provided a workable way of life which was at the root of the effective resistance to enclosure. This was particularly apparent in Ewelme, which produced the highest proportions of resistance to enclosure, some of its most energetic leaders and, in the case of over half the parish, continued in open fields after 1863. The remaining part of this chapter will look at the balance of custom and change which sustained Ewelme in this seemingly conservative and traditional guise.

## IV

I recollect Mr Eyre had 7 yards at Woodlands...I have heard my Grandfather say it formerly used to be ploughed in three lands and a half—and that the ploughing it in three lands only would some time or other give rise to disputes...I have worked upon this Land...it appeared to me to be 7 times as wide as the yard—And I have no doubt whatever that I strided over the yard and found my Master had got his right quantity.

In the common Fields the occupiers of Lands require no Boundaries—for it is a Rule practised in these fields that all men's Lands should be the same width in proportion to the estimated quantity—that is to say—if I have an acre and my neighbour has one Land—my land must be just twice the width of his—and in order to ascertain each Man has his proper quantity an occupier has nothing to do but run the furlong...that is by taking the entire width of the furlong—so that no Man can ever defraud his neighbour without his being able at any distance of time to set the mistake right.[52]

So went the testimony of Henry Tidmarsh, an agricultural labourer from Ewelme, born locally in 1785 and called upon to give evidence of the working of the intercommoning fields following the passage of the 1852 Enclosure Act. Here custom in practice was epitomized as Tidmarsh quoted his own experience, that of his grandfather who had been 'a small farmer occupying his own estate' and a former fieldkeeper for Ewelme, and that of a succession of local shepherds. The intercommoning fields were 'broke' on the day after harvest, after which the sheep were 'always penned anywhere promiscuously...and I have seen the Sheep frequently feeding in Newton's fields between the Turnpike Road and Potters Farm'. The Eyres, who figured so largely in the opposition to Newton, seem to have exercised their common pasture rights to the full.

The heart of Ewelme's farming lay not in the intercommoned fields, actively though they were exploited, but in the Home Parish, the 1,935 acres surrounding the village of Ewelme itself.[53] Here a number of enclosures existed, close to the settlement and on land out to the east rising on to the edge of the Chilterns at Ewelme Park. This left extensive areas of arable open field arranged in strips. In 1783 this was husbanded in a considerably refined form of a three-field system.[54] The course of husbandry was three crops and a fallow. The great open field on the east had been further divided into three, Grove Field, Middle Field and Gravel Pit Field, one of which was fallow each year and the other two cultivated. Each of the other two great fields was similarly divided into three. The capacity of the system to change further was proved in May 1788 when seven signatories 'being one third in number and value of the occupiers of Lands and certain common fields within the parish of Ewelme' summoned a meeting at the Greyhound public house to alter the course of husbandry 'according to such rules and regulations as shall be then approv'd of under the Act of Parliament 13 G 3rd'.[55] This is the Act 13 Geo. III c. 81 of 1773 to which Gilbert Slater devotes a chapter of his *The English Peasantry and the Enclosure of Common Fields* (1907).[56] The legislation provided for the improvement of open fields by the agreement of three-fourths of proprietors, enabling arable to be 'ordered, fenced, cultivated or improved'. Agreements were binding for six years or two cycles of the crop rotation. Each year in May a field reeve or reeves were to be elected. Slater concludes that Hunmanby in the East Riding of Yorkshire was the only place where the Act was put into execution.[57] However, it clearly enabled the farmers of Ewelme significantly to change and improve their farming practices by agreement and without recourse to parliamentary enclosure.

Who were the signatories to this move? A comparison of their names—Thomas and John Heath, John Lane, Richard Greenwood, Robert Tidmarsh, Richard Warner and Anne Leaver—with the governing élite of the late eighteenth-century village is instructive. Taking as the principal criteria for élite membership the holding of office as churchwarden or overseer of the poor together with a rateable value of £40 or more at the parish rating of 1786,[58] four family names dominate.[59] They are Batten, Lane, Heath and Greenwood, followed by Warner,

Leaver and Eyre. The initiative in guarding and remaking custom rested with a relatively small group amongst a larger body of proprietors. Most of that group also dominated local office holding and held relatively large properties.

When anyone infringed upon this evolving custom reaction was sharp. This happened in April 1826[60] when John Eyre, John and William Franklin, M. Greenwood, James Warner, Jesse Leaver and James Ashby wrote to Joseph Heath giving notice 'immediately to throw open all the lands and grounds in your possession which have been enclosed or taken from the Waste and Commonable Land or Ground' in Ewelme. He was to cease encroachment and obstruction of rights of commons for ever for 'unless you do so you will answer the contrary at your peril'. Thus the customary community reacted against its own members and not just to outsiders like Newton. However, this does not seem to have inhibited a willingness to change, for Slater cites the proprietors of Ewelme as making voluntary divisions of land under 4 and 5 Will. IV c. 30 (1834) which facilitated the exchange of intermixed lands.[61]

At the tithe commutation of 1841[62] the accompanying map reveals a now familiar landscape with extensive open fields, strips and furlongs. Yet the data on land ownership and occupation are less predictable. Of the parish acreage of 2,348 acres 50.4 per cent was owned by one man. He was Sir John Cope, an absentee owner with estates elsewhere in Oxfordshire and Hampshire. Fifty-seven others owned property but only four (Eyre, Greenwood, Franklin and Freeman) to the tune of 100 acres or more. Forty people owned in the range four perches to ten acres. The main reality was a small number of large tenant farmers: Joseph, William and John Franklin between them ran 1,331 acres, or 56.7 per cent of the acreage of Ewelme. Joseph Heath accounted for a further 169 acres. The remaining thirty-five tenants were small operators by comparison with this. Control of land was local but polarized. The 1851 census enumerators' books[63] list eight farmers in Ewelme, farming 2,530 acres and employing 167 men. Of these, the three Franklins provided ninety-four jobs; 145 agricultural labourers lived in Ewelme, by far the largest occupational group in a total male population of 349. Whilst the landscape and farming practices of Ewelme appeared tenaciously traditional into the second half of the nineteenth century, there had been marked changes of organization and concentrations of influence within the local community.

The seemingly archaic aspect of Ewelme's landscape did not prevent its largest landholding, the former Cope estate, being bought in 1875 by Thomas Taylor.[64] He had been accumulating large areas of land between 1862 and 1876, spending over £177,000 on 4,850 acres of south Oxfordshire and Buckinghamshire, of which 2,490 acres lay in Ewelme. This included the three largest farms of the village, now tenanted by James Franklin, Thomas Franklin and Jane Orpwood. Their respective sizes, 280 acres, 452 acres and 386 acres, demonstrate the extent of polarization of landholding possible within a traditional field system. During Taylor's ownership an application was made, in April 1879, to the Inclosure Commissioners for the enclosure of 1,000 acres in Ewelme and Benson.[65] Nothing seems to have come of this and the proposal disappears from the Commissioners' reports. In 1884 an altered tithe apportionment was achieved, taking into account changes following the 1863 enclosure.[66] By this time the agricultural depression was firmly established and Thomas Taylor was in trouble. Early in 1883 his Oxfordshire and Buckinghamshire estates were valued when he sought to make them security for a £100,000 loan.[67] The survey confirmed the natural advantages of the land, especially around the village of Ewelme where the soil was of 'very fertile character growing good crops of corn and roots, is in a fair state of cultivation, and is first-rate sound sheep land'. However, the estate

as regards the arrangement of the Farms is exceedingly bad, several very large fields being divided into a great number of allotments, which are apportioned to the farms in the most promiscuous way ... each tenant has to go over the land of others to get to his own ... distances between the Homesteads and some of the outlying portions of the farms are so considerable that much time and labour are wasted in bringing home produce, carrying out manure and getting on the land to work. This evil might ... easily be remedied by more judicious apportionment of the land ... (when the existing leases expire) ... and the rents could be increased.

Perhaps such freedom of action was more apparent than real. For example, rights of pasture were still being exercised on Ewelme Cow Common between 12 May and 11 October each year,[68] and here the Taylor estate did not dominate. Thirteen properties had between them the right to graze fifty-eight cows. Of these, seven were Taylor's tenants (with twenty-four cow commons) but five were not and had rights to thirty-four cow commons. So Ewelme passed into the twentieth century with 'rather more than half this parish . . . legally in the condition of open common fields, and . . . besides a very extensive "cow-common" '.[69] Gilbert Slater, in 1907, confirmed that local farmers still enjoyed 'certain rights of common and of shooting over one another's land' but added that no labourers enjoyed rights of common. Slater was clear that after the 1863 enclosure the commonable waste of the local field system had been lost to the poor and that, although allotments in consideration of these cottagers' rights had been made, in practice (just as George Eyre had surmised in 1827) these allotments had been subsumed into ordinary farms and 'the poor simply lost their supply of fuel without any compensation'. Slater clearly felt that the central Enclosure Commissioners appointed to regulate the implementation of the General Enclosure Act of 1845, under the terms of which the local enclosure had been made, had failed in their duty not only to facilitate enclosure but 'to prevent any injury to the class least able to guard its own interests'. The fact that the Commissioners' original Provisional Order for Benson, Berrick Salome and Ewelme in November 1852 had allotted just twelve acres for the labouring poor[70] but that in the final settlement this was reduced to three of the 2,450 acres affected by the act[71] suggests that Slater's strictures were justified.

## V

Slater wrote a hundred years after Thomas Newton's first attempt to enclose Benson, Berrick and Ewelme. Virtually all the farming names Newton knew had disappeared, although *Kelly's Directory* for 1915 lists eleven farmers in Benson, compared with nine in 1852.[72] At Ewelme the number of farmers had dwindled, from seven to three. The Cow Common at Ewelme survived but as a golf course. In Benson the former coaching inns offered hotel accommodation close to the leisure delights of the River Thames. At Gould's Grove Farm, part of the Newton holdings, Jerome K. Jerome, author of *Three Men in a Boat*, was in residence, although in 1910 the interest in the surrounding land remained with T.D. Newton whose address was Union Stock-yards, Chicago, USA.[73] Succeeding generations of Newtons apparently continued to seize commercial opportunities, even if they lay in a direction threatening to home agriculture. Locally, too, Newton's successors were acting 'on the basis of a cool, economic calculation' as John Orr, surveying Oxfordshire agriculture in 1916, found.[74] Crowmarsh Battle had been famous for its flock of Hampshire Down sheep. In 1897 all stock-keeping had been abandoned on economic grounds. Orr found Crowmarsh Battle out of step with other local farmers who had determinedly stayed with mixed farming, corn, sheep and bullocks. Nevertheless, Orr found that

to cross the district . . . is to be impressed by the achievements as well as by the possibilities of English agriculture. The appearance of the fields, with scarcely a fence, and with trees relegated so often to the neighbourhood of villages, to the banks of rivers, or to the roadside, suggests decks cleared for action. It is possible that these decks are not so fully manned as they once were . . . but progress is being made.[75]

If some prospered in farming, what of the agricultural labourers? The census returns for Ewelme are telling. In 1851 the population had been 673, of whom 145 were agricultural labourers; in 1891 it was 540, of whom 86 were agricultural labourers. Not only had farming employment dwindled drastically but the age structure of the workforce had changed markedly from 38 farmworkers under 20, 56 aged 21–40, and 51 over 40 in 1851, to 16 under 20, 25 aged 21–40, and 45 over 41 (including 7 almsmen) in 1891.[76] Overall population figures[77] show Benson growing rapidly, by 45 per cent, in the first three decades of the nineteenth century, barely sustaining that growth in the middle years, and suffering absolute decline in numbers from 1871 onwards. In Ewelme there was more gradual growth, reaching a 41 per cent increase by 1871, and thereafter even more rapid decline than at Benson. It was in the 1870s too that many traditional farming names disappeared from local records. The communities suffered not just in numbers but in a decline in the vigour of village life, as at Benson, a distinctly open village, which

had once the reputation of being a very rough place. Fights were a frequent occurrence during the days of the old Benson Benefit Club . . . the great day was Whit Tuesday and it was a pleasant sight to see the old and young men in their blue ribbons marching behind the brass band down the village street to church. The day finished up by a large banquet of roast beef and beer at the Crown. A small Fair was erected in the open space near the latter and here unfortunately some of the lively ones got out of hand as the day closed, and fighting (minus gloves) was the order of the day. I believe the old village police preferred to give this corner of Benson a wide berth at these exciting times.[78]

The Benefit Club was dissolved around 1890.

This study has pursued the levels of historical understanding to be gained from a close scrutiny of local evidence. Insights into the processes of rural change emerge at both specific and general levels of question and debate. The south Oxfordshire experience suggests that enclosure could be redundant, much delayed or partial as a mechanism of change. Factors in its late or incomplete implementation were absentee lordship, diversity of landholding, the complexity of existing rights, natural advantages of soil quality, access to markets and the capacity of the open-field system to survive by itself changing. Custom continued to provide a framework for this internal modernization, which was achieved by local consent. However, the parties to that customary consent were increasingly limited. Rural custom did adapt to changing contexts. Local élites of small and middling farmers played the key role. This was most apparent under the galvanizing effect of an outside pressure to change. The continuing gulf of attitudes and farming practice between the leaders of the customary community and the Newton family throughout the nineteenth century demonstrates the depth of difference. Opposition to parliamentary enclosure was effective. Its full extent emerges only outside formal parliamentary procedures. The farmers of the common fields, with their influence and resources, were at the centre of opposition. They appealed both up and down the social scale for partners in consensus but neither their clerical, collegiate and landholding allies nor the numerous wage labourers already part of the local economy were full partners to the customary society. Men like Henry Tidmarsh, whose family slipped from small independent farmers to labourers in the early nineteenth century, were imbued with the custom of the common fields as a working system, yet played a diminishing role within it. The Swing Riots of 1830 provided an occasion to further local opposition to enclosure but also a rare chance for some insiders, boosted by outsiders, to air different grievances. It was in the 1870s that the viable customary society really began to disintegrate in south Oxfordshire. That these changes occurred in areas of early enclosure, recent enclosure and no enclosure suggests that wider economic shifts and agricultural depression lay at the root of this change.

# NOTES

Owen Ashton, David Eastwood, Bob Fyson, Michael Holroyd and Rex Leaver have all read and commented on this paper. I am grateful to them for their valuable help and advice.

1  *Jackson's Oxford Journal (JOJ)*, 20 Nov. 1830.
2  E.g. Michael Turner. 'Economic protest in rural society: opposition to parliamentary enclosure in Buckinghamshire', in *Southern History*, **10** (1988), 103 recounts incidents at Stewkley (1803), Oakley (1819–21), Princes Risborough (1823), and Towersey (1822–5) of opposed enclosures during which the posting of notices to church doors was physically prevented.
3  *JOJ*, 27 Nov. 1830; Bodleian Library GA Oxon 4° 49, p. 233; Public Record Office (PRO), HO 52/9/414, letter from W.H. Ashurst, chairman of the Oxfordshire Sessions, to Lord Melbourne, 22 Nov. 1830.
4  E.J. Hobsbawm and G. Rudé, *Captain Swing* (London, 1973 edn), pp. 110–12.
5  E.g. Bernard Reaney, *The Class Struggle in 19th-Century Oxfordshire* (History Workshop Pamphlets 3, 1970), pp. 42–3.
6  Andrew Charlesworth, *Social Protest in a Rural Society* (Historical Geography Research Series, no. I, 1979) emphasizes the role of the London highways in the spread of the Swing Riots (pp. 21 and 52), 'For it is in these settlements on the London highway and in studies at the community level that the history of the revolt may really begin to be unravelled'.
7  Quoted on the cover of Hobsbawm and Rudé (1973 edn).
8  As David Eastwood writes in 'Communities, protest and police in early 19th-century Oxfordshire: the Otmoor riots reconsidered', *Agricultural History Review* (forthcoming 1996), 'we encounter a rural England comprised not of static, or normative, class conflicts but rather of mutable social alignments'. Other recent work with a similar approach includes J.M. Neeson, *Commoners: Common Right, Enclosure and Social Change in England, 1700–1820* (Cambridge, 1993); J. Archer, *'By Flash and Scare': Arson, Animal Maiming, and*

*Poaching in East Anglia 1815–70* (Oxford, 1990); K.D.M. Snell, *Annals of the Labouring Poor: Social Change and Agrarian England, 1660–1900* (Cambridge, 1985); Alun Howkins, *Reshaping Rural England: A Social History 1850–1925* (London, 1991); Bob Bushaway, *By Rite: Ceremony and Community in England 1700–1880* (London, 1982).

9   J.M. Neeson, 'The opponents of enclosure in 18th-century Northamptonshire', in *Past and Present*, **105** (1985), 114–39; Neeson, *Commoners*.

10   As Neeson 'The opponents to enclosure', p. 138, puts it, 'The organisation of work in the open field system encouraged co-operation; and defence of common rights required the protection of lesser rights as well as greater'.

11   Oxfordshire Archives (OA), QSD L 33, land tax assessment for Crowmarsh Battle, 1797.

12   M.A. Havinden, 'The rural economy of Oxfordshire, 1580–1730' (unpublished B.Litt. thesis, Oxford, 1961).

13   Quoted in Grace E. Chamberlain, *Benson Past and Present: A Scrapbook* (unpublished Notes and Collection, Benson, 1937)

14   OA, QSD L 32, land tax assessments for Benson (or Bensington), 1785–1832.

15   OA, QSD L 32, assessment for 1832.

16   OA, MSS DD Par. Ewelme c. 12 (b).

17   Rev. M.T. Pearman, *A History of the Manor of Bensington (Benson, Oxon), a Manor of Ancient Demesne* (London, 1896), pp. 125–6.

18   PRO, LR 2 224, ff. 29–33, 153–9.

19   OA, MSS DD Par. Ewelme a. 4. 'Survey of the Open Fields and some Old Enclosures in the Tithing of Benson together which [*sic*] such open Field land in the Tithings of Berwick and Ewelme as lay intermixed with the above' (1788).

20   Magdalen College Archives, Estate Papers 249/6 (1). Letter from George Eyre of Ewelme to the Steward of Magdalen College, Oxford, 23 Nov. 1827.

21   OA, QSD L 32.

22   OA, H II a, Deeds of the manor of Fifield, 1623–1836.

23   OA, QSD L 34. Land tax assessments for Fifield. The remodelling of the manor house and the construction of the massive barns at Fifield date to these years. I owe this information to Dr Malcolm Airs.

24   Magdalen College Archives, Estate Papers 249/6 (2).

25   Magdalen College Archives, Estate Papers 249/6 (1).

26   Sir Thomas Littleton, *Tenures* (c.1480), a standard treatise on the law of real property. Coke's *Commentary on Littleton* appeared in 1628.

27   OA, MSS DD Par. Ewelme c. 12 (b).

28   Mr Rex Leaver first drew my attention to the growing practice of counting neuters with assents in disputed enclosures. His study of

Princes Risborough, Bucks, yields the following comment by the parliamentary agent to the promoters of the local enclosure in a letter of 3 Dec. 1819:

there is no fixed proportion of Assents required for passing a Bill through a Committee. Some years back when Inclosure Bills were more numerous than at present 4/5ths in number of Acres or Value where the state of the property was taken from the Land Tax or Poor Rate were considered such a Majority as would insure the bill, but within the last four or five years Parliament has so much favoured Inclosure Bills that it is now very difficult to find a Member to oppose an Inclosure where the usual terms of the County where lands be are complied with. Where the Lord of the Manor and the Tythe Owners are concurring with as many others as make up 2/3rds in Number or Value as aforesaid I consider there is no chance of the opposition stopping the Bill unless some powerful Parliamentary Interest can be exerted for them. Of late years Bills have been passed where a less proportion than 2/3rds have been consenting...Neuters are stated as such by the Committee to the House but they are looked upon in the light of Consents and the judgment of the House I have always considered to be formed upon the actual strengths of the opponents only (Bucks CRO IR/M1/7/446).

29   OA, MSS DD Par. Ewelme c. 12 (b).
30   *JOJ*, 20 Nov. 1830.
31   PRO, HO 52/9/414.
32   Bodleian Library, GA Oxon 4° 49, p. 233.
33   Ibid.
34   *JOJ*, 27 Nov. 1830.
35   GA Oxon 4° 49, p. 233.
36   *JOJ*, 27 Nov. 1830.
37   *JOJ*, 8 Jan. 1831.
38   PRO, HO 52/9/384. Lord Macclesfield to Lord Melbourne, 5 Dec. 1830.
39   GA Oxon, 4° 49, p. 233 (author's emphasis).
40   PRO, HO 52/9/414.
41   Reported in *JOJ*, 27 Nov. 1830.
42   PRO, HO 52/9/410, letter of 29 Dec. 1830. Evidence was subsequently given by a Richard Reade.
43   *JOJ*, 5 Feb. 1831.
44   *JOJ*, 5 Mar. 1831. 'The witness is a greater rogue than the prisoner' was the cry.
45   PRO, HO 52/15/507.
46   PRO, HO 52/15/509. Letter from Thomas Newton to Lord Milvill, 21 Mar. 1831.
47   OA, MSS DD Par. Ewelme c. 12 (b).
48   Ibid.
49   Act 16 Vic. c 3.

50  See J.R. Walton, 'Aspects of agrarian change in Oxfordshire 1750–1880 (unpublished D.Phil. thesis, Oxford, 1976). On the absence or late occurrence of parliamentary enclosure in south Oxfordshire, see M. Turner, *English Parliamentary Enclosure* (Folkestone, 1980), Ch. 3.

51  It is hoped to make the villages of south Oxfordshire in the nineteenth century the subject of a full-length study.

52  OA, MSS DD Par. Ewelme c. 12 (b).

53  OA, MSS DD Par. Ewelme c. 11. In January 1834 the Home Parish lay in nine fields, whilst a further 800 acres (of a total of 1,935) were enclosed.

54  OA, MSS DD Par. Ewelme e. 3. Rector's memorandum of glebe and tithes, 1783–1813.

55  OA, MSS DD Par. Ewelme, c. 12.

56  G. Slater, *The English Peasantry and the Enclosure of the Common Fields* (London, 1907), Ch. IX, pp. 86–90.

57  Slater, *The English Peasantry* p. 90. W.E. Tate, *The English Village Community and the Enclosure Movements* (London, 1967), p. 80, fn. 1, comments 'the powers given by the Act were used much more widely than most writers on agrarian history have supposed'.

58  OA, MSS DD Par. Ewelme, b. 10.

59  Barry Fletcher, 'The politics of the parish: Ewelme in the 18th century' (unpublished Oxford University Summer School for Adults project, 1994).

60  OA, CH/E/I/iii/5.

61  Slater, *The English Peasantry*, p. 51.

62  OA, tithe award no. 159.

63  PRO, HO 107/1690.

64  OA, Ta VIII/iii/10.

65  Inclosure Commission. Thirty-fifth annual report of the Commissioners. Parl. Papers (PP) 1880, XVIII, 489, p. 7. I owe this reference to Mr Michael Holroyd.

66  OA, tithe award no. 159 a.

67  OA, Ta XI/i/5. The Ewelme estate included land in Swyncombe, Nuffield, Watlington, Berrick Prior and Dorchester.

68  OA, Ta VIII/iii/13.

69  Slater, *The English Peasantry*, p. 50.

70  Inclosure Commission. Special Report of the Commissioners, 1852. PP 1852–3, XL, 661, p. 7.

71  Return of all Inclosures since the Inclosure Act of 1845. PP 1870, LV, 151, p. 15.

72  R. Gardner, *History, Gazeteer and Directory of the County of Oxford* (1852), pp. 811–13; *Kelly's Directory of Berkshire, Buckinghamshire and Oxfordshire* (1915).

73  OA, DV IV/27.

74  J. Orr, *Agriculture in Oxfordshire* (Oxford, 1916), p. 23.

75  Orr, *Agriculture in Oxfordshire*, pp. 25–6.

76  PRO, HO 107/1690; RG 12/0986. Benson's peak population was 1,248, Ewelme's 691.

77  Decennial figures for 1801–1901 in *Victoria County History of Oxfordshire*, Vol. 2 (1907), p. 220.

78  Letter of 1935 from A.R. Littleboy to Mrs G.E. Chamberlain quoted in her scrapbook of Benson past and present (1937).

# 6

## Narratives of Control: Informalism and the Workplace in Britain, 1800–1900

### CLIVE BEHAGG

The structure and organization of industrial work in the nineteenth century has attracted the attention of increasing numbers of historians in recent years. In particular attention has been drawn to the uneven nature of development, with the continuation of supposedly 'archaic' forms of organization, alongside the reconstruction of skill and its role in a highly fragmented labour force.[1] Some historians have argued that the history of nineteenth-century workplace relations may be seen as a continuous process of contestation around the control of work.[2] It has been argued by others that such an approach relies too heavily on Braverman's theoretical framework, particularly that provided by the notion of 'autonomous regulation' at the expense of other perspectives. At particular points, it is argued, labour and capital were constrained to co-operate with each other rather than relentlessly contesting the territory of work: instead of a 'contested terrain', a 'terrain of compromise' has been identified.[3] Whatever the points of disagreement this growing body of work has identified the social relations of production, and the contingencies surrounding their reproduction, as an important area of concern in the continuing debate on the pace of British industrialization. As Whipp puts it, in examining the pottery industry, 'Students of work are therefore now obliged to explore in their own right the mixture of values and motivations which both employer and employed bring to the workplace'.[4] The broad economic and social context within which work was situated clearly changed as the century unfolded, reflecting the development of the market, or shifts in other factors of production. Nevertheless, the sense that the workplace was the location of a range of versions of what constituted work, what work was for, and how it should be structured has been widely recognised.[5]

Despite this recognition, however, the culture of the workplace remains frustratingly difficult to gain access to at any point that is beyond the chronology of oral history.[6] This is largely because the relationships between workers, the object of analysis, were constructed only on the basis of informal agreements and tacit understandings, reinforced by daily practice. Employers certainly found these networks to be highly intrusive. We know, for example, that workers in the early industrial workplace frequently intervened to slow the pace of production, punctuating the working day with a series of activities which were clearly not work. The exaction of 'footings', the holding of workplace 'courts', the extensive observance of 'Saint Monday', and the existence of a popular culture which assumed a year that could be marked by unofficial holidays all suggest that the early industrial workforce carried with it the expectation that it would control its own time at work.[7] The organization of work within the day, the week and the year were all subject to decisions made by workers amongst themselves. Often this was driven by the perceived need to share work within the workforce. By 1850, for example, a third of the pits in the Northumberland and Durham coalfield were restricting output through controls at the coal-face. This was said to be 'a rule among the men themselves' rather than a trade union intervention.[8]

The work that has been carried out on the subject of worktime suggests that workers were loath to see the employment contract as a simple exchange of time for money wages. There were other contingent factors involved. In many cases workers appear to have clung to their identity as independent contractors selling finished goods, even beyond the point where such independence possessed little substance in reality. This construction of independence was encouraged by the resilience of piecework operating in conjunction with the subcontracting system in many trades. Most workers operated in small workgroups, within which they produced goods and then 'sold' them to the employer within the workplace. The workgroup co-owned the product up to the point of sale and this gave them the right to control labour time and significant elements of the labour process. Co-ownership of the product was reflected in the workgroup's temporary possession of it during its production within the territory of the workplace. Hence the common view that the workplace was not necessarily an appropriate place for the employer or his manager to appear.[9] However irksome this defence of space may have been to employers, there were some advantages for them. Cross's work in this area has provided an important corrective to the one-dimensional view of irregularity as entirely worker-led. In fact, in a changeable market a workforce that worked irregularly might be advantageous. For example, it might allow a large order to be met without recourse to overtime.[10] Similarly, worker self-management, as Lazonick points out, reduced the need for management organization.[11] The great disadvantage, of course, lay in the manufacturer's inability to predict product volume.

Glimpses of this network of informal agreements may appear through worker testimony in autobiographies, parliamentary enquiries or court records. More commonly, such informalism was seen to constitute the object of reform and innovation in the testimony of employers or middle-class observers of the workplace, of which evidence there is, conversely, a good deal. There is clearly a place for the history of informal workplace organization, but most of the evidence for it has arrived through the medium of the disapproving observer. In addition, full study of this aspect of productive relations has been obscured by existing and well-established narratives which carry their own chronologies and which have become orthodoxies in their own right. We may identify two such approaches which have been developed through the existing interpretations of the workplace and its development through the nineteenth century. First, there is the narrative of management, which might be called 'factory discipline and the world's first industrial workforce'. This relates the way a modern workforce was created from the unlikely material of the labouring poor of the eighteenth century. An alternative narrative covering the history of the workplace in the same period may be called the 'rise of labour'. Within this a modern trade union movement emerges from a newly created industrial working class. There are some similarities between these two narratives, the most significant of which is that both search for a moment when modern industry began.

Within the narrative of management and its evolution in the nineteenth century, employers are seen to have learned the hard way that the 'carrot' is often a better management tool than the 'stick'. For their part, workers gradually threw off their plebeian origins and adapted to their new circumstances, accepting 'factory discipline' as something from which they might benefit.[12] A systematized structure to work would bring a clearer distinction between work and leisure.[13] Some agreement is seen to have been possible between the classes on what constituted respectable values[14] and from this consensus the legal position of trade unions and friendly societies could be confirmed as part of the more ordered structure of social relations in the second half of the century. For the narrative of management, the second half of the century represents something of a watershed, demarking a point after which we may expect our historical characters to have learned, and to be increasingly acting upon, the lessons of the first half of the century. 'Saint Monday', it is argued, was 'eroded' in this period, the working week and the working year became more ordered, and the state intervened to limit hours and improve conditions, protecting more and more workers as the century unfolded.[15] At this point this analysis of work, and its successful management, makes contact with a wider, liberal interpretation of social reform and welfare which hinges on the growth of humanitarianism in an increasingly ordered society.[16] The close affinity of this narrative of work and that of social reform may be seen in the identification of industrial paternalism as a significant factor in the new relationship between employers and employees in this period.[17] Sometimes the narrative is characterized by the assumption that the organization of work to maximize profit and compete efficiently is invariably positive, whilst management techniques which bring this about have an in-built legitimacy.[18] In some accounts workers even adopt the values of their employers in this period. Thus, in its most extreme expression, this narrative projects factory paternalism not as a form of control but rather as the expression of an agreed set of values, or a consensual view of the natural order.[19]

An alternative narrative covering the history of labour in the workplace in the same period charts the development of formal industrial relations. In this account few of the above assumptions are accepted. Nevertheless, there are points of similarity. Here the significant moments are those which signal the emergence of a formal workplace relationship through the development of trade unions and the legislation that enabled them to be effective. Workplace strife does not disappear, but the ground to be fought over is increasingly laid out in a formal way. Although, in fact, for most of the period most workers were not represented directly by trade unions, nevertheless the history of the workplace has often been the history of trade unions. Again, 1850, or thereabouts, is a crucial moment. The mid-century was originally set by the Webbs as the significant moment in the shift from primitive or ephemeral forms of bargaining to the effective formalism of the 'new model'. This approach can be seen to display the Fabian presuppositions of much early labour history, and these have been reinforced by the pragmatic need for historians to operate with the kind of written evidence which formal organizations provide. There is an expectation built into much labour history that after the 'new model' informal organization became very marginal except in its manifestation as 'rank and filism'. A militant workplace culture, with its home on the shopfloor and its aggressive class consciousness growing directly from the experience of work, is seen in many instances to have reacted against the inertia of a trade union movement whose collective hands were increasingly tied by the legal and bureaucratic framework that was the price of its formalism.[20]

To some extent these two narratives can be seen to be drawn together in the recent call by Zeitlin for a 'neo-institutionalist' interpretative framework for understanding employer–employee relationships.[21] The argument, from some points of view, is compelling, since the formal structure of the relationship between capital and labour within the workplace has been analysed through two frameworks of interpretations which overlap but remain divergent. Nevertheless, further emphasis on the institutional would simply compound the difficulties inherent in both narratives. Both work with a similar chronology, and with an important break around the mid-century, since both are primarily concerned to chart the advent of a 'modern' society. For most historians these narratives are so well established that it is difficult to work outside of them.[22] Judging by output, most historians of industrial relations are more comfortable charting the apparent certainties of formal trade unions and their actions than with the less accessible activities of workers inside the workplace but outside the formal organizations of 'the trades'. In this way the Webbs' original chronology has been confirmed by practice. In a similar way historians of 'management' are clearly happiest in accentuating the positive; and so histories of 'enlightened' employers tend to predominate. Yet as feminist historians have explained, one of the demonstrable weaknesses of both narratives is that women are, more or less, shut out from both. In the first, they are constructed as the, largely passive, raw material of the workforce that is 'managed' increasingly effectively as the century unfolds. In the second, they are simply excluded.[23] The absence of women in these accounts draws attention to the way these well-established narrative traditions only partially reconstruct the lived experience of the workforce. What is most frequently missing from these accounts is the informal structuring of authority within the workplace itself, and the way this was mediated by both the employer and the workgroup involving all workers. In particular, the experience of the wider workgroup has been ignored because work has so often been read in terms of the skilled worker. In recent years, the emphasis of feminist historians on the value structures which operated within the workplace has effectively challenged many of the underlying assumptions of the existing narratives of work.[24] The strength of this revision lies in a willingness to place emphasis on the less formalized aspects of workplace culture. Lown, for example, opens up a whole range of cultural contingencies by analysing the employer's approach to the style of dress adopted by female workers and the taking of meal-breaks at Courtauld's Essex factory in the second half of the century.[25]

This chapter is an early contribution to the opening of the broad issue of informalism within the nineteenth-century workplace, arguing that this may provide a focus for an approach which begins to integrate an analysis of the experience of skilled labour into that of the less skilled. The central concern here is less with the idea of discontinuity: a decisive moment, or series of moments when the early industrial workplace became 'modernized', when, for example, an early industrial concept of time was replaced with a time-frame more appropriate for an industrial society. Rather, certain continuities of experience may be identified throughout the century. The dialogue within a wider workplace culture, with its roots in the informalism of the working community, was a constant factor of production, though its nature changed from moment to moment. Above all, it should be acknowledged that both of the narrative traditions identified above are essentially nineteenth century in their nature, drawing as they do their significant characteristics from aspects of the contemporary debate. It is easy for historians, in using contemporary sources, to miss this contextual relevance. This is to say, many aspects of these historical narratives rely for their conceptual framework on a very partial contemporary view evolved in the nineteenth century to make a particular case about the workplace whilst the debate was taking place. To appreciate fully the debate in the period we need to reconstruct the arguments against which these narratives evolved.

## CONSTRUCTING THE FAIRYLAND OF WORK: CONTROL AND THE LANGUAGE OF WONDER

In its own way the management narrative of workplace relations between manufacturers and the workforce is a heroic story. In no small part this is because it is technocentric in its nature, equating a controlled workforce with the development of mechanization. This was an important connection for middle-class observers in the nineteenth century, for whom the well-organized workplace became a metaphor for an ordered society. This idealization of the workplace often took on a mythic quality, and this was often reflected in the language of unashamed wonder which it utilized.

When Queen Victoria looked down from the gallery on the machinery and its products in the Great Exhibition of 1851 she described the scene as possessing 'quite the effect of fairyland'.[26] To some extent her reference to 'fairyland' echoed those of Andrew Ure in the 1830s, who described the child labourers whom he saw in the textile mills of the 1830s as 'little elves at play'. In a similar way, Harriet Martineau was commissioned by Dickens to write a series of articles for *Household Words* on the nature of the workplace which would exploit the public enthusiasm for machinery, and its application, which the Great Exhibition had encouraged. Through her family links with Birmingham she found it easy to gain access to some of the town's larger factories, around which she was carefully guided by the manufacturers. Her articles reflect a breathless enthusiasm for mechanization. In 'What There is in a Button' she describes a production process focused on 'This exquisite machinery' described as a 'truly wonderful and beautiful apparatus' which could cut buttons at a remarkable rate: 'The number cut out and pushed aside in a minute is beyond belief to those who have not seen it done.'[27]

On introducing the operation of a brassworks she invites the reader, 'Now let the imagination follow this...and we shall be full of wonder'.[28] This contemporary reinvention of the workplace as wonderland was only an extreme version of the workplace as the representation of an ideal society. In an article, significantly entitled 'The Wonder of Nails and Screws', Martineau reported on a visit which she made to a highly mechanized screw manufactory. Here, she draws the links explicitly between systematized work and its implications for society outside the workplace:

These six score women are neatly dressed; hair smooth, or cap clean—handkerchief or little shawl nicely crossed over and fastened behind; faces healthy and countenances cheerful... As we turned away from the hundreds of women thus respectably earning their bread, we could not but hope that there was no screw loose in their household ways, that the machinery of their daily life might work as truly and as effectually as that dead mechanism which is daily revolving under their care for so many hours of every day.[29]

Martineau stresses the importance of correct dress, particularly for female workers, in the display of an appropriately ordered workplace. Gray has shown that such comments, made by observers in textile factories, were part of a wider debate about cultural identity.[30] At the heart of this was the connection made between dress and morality. Middle-class observers preferred factory women to wear what was simple, clean and comely.[31]

Creating the image of the workplace as a scientifically constructed wonderland was, of course, fraught with difficulties. Martineau visited Osler's glassworks, of particular significance since this was responsible for the distinctive fairy fountain which had formed the centrepiece of the Crystal Palace in 1851 and which had been identified by the *Art Journal* as 'the most striking object in the Exhibition'. But Osler wrote to her afterwards asking her 'not to notice' that a particular process was being carried out by women, fearing this might lead to a questioning of the quality of the product.[32] Osler's concern is a reminder of the context within which the contemporary debate about work was taking place. In an increasingly competitive marketplace the public image of the firm was a crucial element in commanding market share. One important element in the image of the firm was always the way that it controlled its workforce, since the ability to meet orders and predict productive capacity depended upon such control. Publicly, employers stressed the unity of their workers with the productive processes upon which they were engaged, rather than the difficulties they experienced in organizing work. For this reason the iconic representation of the workplace, by which 'new model' employers were happy to be known and which appears so often in contemporary prints, was the image of the rows of machines operated by well-ordered and respectably dressed workpeople. Joseph Gillott's large steel-pen manufactory in Birmingham was considered by the *Morning Chronicle*'s observer to be 'a model of its kind', and he clearly felt that on entering it he had crossed a threshold into a place where systematic production and social order were synonymous:

Ranged in double rows along a large and roomy workshop, with windows at both sides, and scrupulously white and clean, in floor, roof, and walls, are seated from fifty to a hundred girls and women, from the age of fourteen to that of forty or upwards. Unlike too many of the women employed in the manufactories of Birmingham, they are extremely neat in person and attire. They present an air both of cleanliness and comfort seldom to be met with. There is no talking in the room.[33]

The significant elements in this, fairly typical, example of the language of extreme approval are the integration of the worker with the systematized labour process, and the fact that the relationship had been established by the intervention of a humane and benevolent employer. Here was a female workforce that was healthy, clean, productive and, apparently, passive. Eleanor Gordon's work on the Dundee jute mills has done much to question this image of a passive female worker.[34] But to contemporary observers this was an essential ingredient of a successfully ordered workplace. At all times the control of work involved a close monitoring of personal behaviour both inside and outside the workplace. Gillott would sack a female worker, 'if the charge of immoral life is proved against her', and in the

eyes of most observers order in the workplace and high standards of personal morality on the part of the workforce were
necessary concomitants. This was to be taken to its extremes by
the Cadbury family in their Bournville works established in the
1880s. Much was made of the healthy location; the Cadburys
liked their works to be referred to as 'the factory in a garden'. In
this, much admired, model factory the Cadburys would not employ married women and the factory was designed to separate
male and female workers completely. On appointment a female
worker was issued with sufficient fabric to make two white
working uniforms. So, at Bournville, rows of unmarried women,
dressed in spotless white uniforms, made and packed a product
which was sold on the basis of its purity. The firm's advertising
slogan was 'Absolutely Pure, therefore Best'.[35]

From a management point of view, the Cadburys' great
achievement was to interlock the product and productive process by which it was made so inextricably that it was difficult to
see where one ended and the other began. This was the apothe-
osis of the view that the systematization of work was essentially
benign in its impact. In this way the link between machinery,
science and systematized work was used to reinforce the notion
of the factory as a place of wonder. Thus Angus Reach, the
*Morning Chronicle*'s investigator in Lancashire wrote in 1851 of
'the exquisite perfection' of the machinery and its impact upon
the operatives: 'So far from being degraded to the level of the
machines amongst which he works, he rather seems to elevate
them to his own perceptive and reasoning powers.'[36] Some of
these assumptions were built into the design of some of the
'new model' factories. Eccles Shorrock's India Mill in Darwen,
opened in 1869, was built to an elaborate Italianate design with
a chimney which was designed to look like the Campanile in
Venice. The links between the 'civilizing' values of the Renais-
sance and the benefits of industrial society were thus clearly
drawn by the architecture of the factory.[37] The corollary to this,
however, was a recognition of the employer's right to manage.
Shorrock explained to the workforce in 1879: 'What is to be
done to diminish the costs of production? There are only two
ways—lower wages and longer hours...I think the factory
laws will have to be altered again.' The strike and riots that
occurred in Darwen in the same year suggest that his view was
not necessarily shared by his workforce.[38]

It is important to note that this promotion of the workplace as a place of scientific wonder was taking place at a time when Marx was developing his theory of alienation. The belief in the benign influence of machinery was widely contested. Working people devised informal means of subverting the systematization of their labour partly to help deal with the mind-numbing monotony of work in a factory. Frederick Forrest noted, with some disapproval, that the machinery provided a cover for the development of an alternative culture in the Dundee mill in which he worked in the 1820s:

The noise caused by machinery is so great, that the most unhallowed dialogues may be conducted by two persons near to each other, without anyone knowing what is going on. This circumstance I found to be the most favourable one for the mutual circulation of anecdotes and ideas which spread and maintain moral contamination amongst young factory workers.[39]

The alternative culture included the singing of what Forrest refers to as 'obscene songs', passed between female workers at moments when the supervisor was not in evidence. In a similar way Joseph Brooks remembers that the spinning mill, in Radcliffe, where he worked in the 1880s contained four members of a popular local minstrel troupe. The drawing-in room provided a useful location for them to rehearse to an audience during the working day: 'And so all the songs and jokes for the forthcoming performances were rehearsed in our hearing.' These activities were likely to be disrupted and Brooks recalls that 'They scattered as quickly as the rest when it was whispered that "Owd Garstang" was coming'.[40] There are some echoes here of the textile workers from the Amoskeag Mill in New England, interviewed by Hareven and Langenbach, like Yvonne Dionne who began work in 1920 and recalled 'I learned to dance in number 4 mill'.[41] Certainly, in Britain there is a good deal of evidence to suggest that factory workers used song as a way of commanding, or signifying the command of, space within the workplace during the working day and that this had particular significance for women workers.[42]

Eventually management would emerge as a science in its own right, with the publication of the work of, among others, Frederick Taylor. In many ways this represented an extension of the technicist justification for employer control, focused on the machine and signalled in much nineteenth-century literature. As Taylor put it, 'The best management is a true science, resting upon clearly defined laws, rules, and principles, as a foundation '. There is some significance in the fact that Taylor's development of 'scientific management' was based on his own experience of workplace informalism on the shopfloor of the Midvale Steel Company of Philadelphia. Working as part of a small workteam he found that 'the shop was really run by the workmen, and not by the bosses'. He identified the informal networks of understanding between workers that made such worker control possible as 'soldiering'. Under his proposed 'scientific management' the planning of work would take place in a separate department, away from the shopfloor. Since the heart of the problem was, as he saw it, the collectivity of the small workgroup this would be replaced by a system through which the workforce could be reconstructed as individuals, each part of a management-centred collectivity of shared objectives. By this means, informalism, which revolved around common experience, would be destroyed by emphasizing the difference between members of the workforce, in terms of tasks, workrate and wages.[43] Although Taylor's management techniques were never implemented in Britain in the pure form that he might have wished, nevertheless, his analysis of the nature of the problem is significant. The need to control production in the face of what he called the 'systematic soldiering' remained a common and persistent problem for employers throughout the nineteenth century.

## DEALING WITH INFORMALISM

The informal structures of tacit understanding by which workers attempted to influence their work situation for their benefit were, thus, far from being a transitory hangover of an early industrial workforce. Rather, they remained an essential element in the economic framework of the firm throughout the nineteenth century. In fact, the need to deal with informalism became more important in the changing market situation of the later decades of the century. Some of this can be seen in the case of the well-established and successful Birmingham brassfounding firm of Best and Hobson. Faced, in 1901, with increasing competition and the expiry of a patent on their most lucrative line (the 'Surprise' chandelier), the firm appointed as a new works manager an American, with a brief to increase productive efficiency by introducing what were referred to as 'more up to date methods of production and marketing'.

What the incomer found was a nightmare scenario for anybody who hoped to work within the general context which was fast being defined as 'scientific' management. The factory in question was large, but it had grown almost organically, as the firm expanded in the second half of the century. It was also clear that spatially the factory was predicated upon the assumption that only a minimum of work supervision would ever take place. The new manager recalled: 'As one moved around the works and suddenly opened a door into many of the shops there was sure to be a scuffle and an effort to look busy.' As he approached the shops early in the morning he was hit by the smell of sizzling bacon on the soldering hearths, 'and again as one o'clock approached, but then the aroma changed to one of chops and steaks'. In the course of his inspection he discovered a hole in the back wall of the factory where 'the morning beer was pushed through'. The working day was also punctuated by a series of sporting activities including the baiting with dogs of rats caught in traps laid in the factory the previous night. Over the course of the next five years he introduced what he referred to as 'a hundred reforms' including timing machines, a piecework bonus scheme and a works canteen.[44] Yet, even allowing for exaggeration on the part of a missionary for scientific management, this analysis of factory life, and the perceived need to induce a recalcitrant workforce to adopt a more regular pattern of work reprises, in a number of ways, the debates that took place in the 1850s and 1860s surrounding the ending of 'Saint Monday'.[45]

The need to deal with informalism as a factor of production remained a real issue for employers in the second half of the nineteenth century. Workers continued to assume a relationship to the product and to the territory of the workplace which often ran counter to the sytematization of work necessary for efficient labour utilization in an increasingly competitive market. Labour may have been learning the new 'rules of the game' but in doing so it did not forget the old regulations of trade. The collection of perquisites, despite moves to criminalize it as theft from the workplace, continued to be a problem.[46] George

Bassett the Sheffield confectionery manufacturer, cut rather a sad figure at the Children's Employment Commission of 1867 when he reported that he had found no way of preventing his workforce, which consisted mostly of children, from eating the product. 'There is a rule forbidding this,' he lamented, 'but of course it cannot be really enforced.' By his own reckoning he was losing around 80 pounds of sweets per week in this way.[47] In fact, it was widely felt amongst employers that the best way to deal with informalism was by a process of formalization. Thus Huntley and Palmer introduced a rule by which every worker could take home a pound of broken biscuits a week.[48] Such agreements put a limit on the removal of perquisites and might, in some cases, be allied to fairly stringent use of gate searches as workers left the premises.

Yet, informalism was, by its very nature, amorphous and would expand to occupy any spare, unsupervised, space within the working day. This can be seen in the case of meals taken within the workplace. The cooking of both breakfast and lunch eroded the formally agreed working day. Certainly, for employers one of the great attractions of the shorter working day was that it involved workers eating breakfast at home.[49] William Watson writes of this as a contested area in the early twentieth-century engineering industry. A worker would arrive at a new job with a makeshift Bunsen burner which would be tapped into the gas supply. With a nail banged into the wall and a pot hung over it refreshment would be available on demand. He remembers the characteristic strategy of formalization: 'To regularize tea-making, some employers installed an urn and the shop boy was detailed to make the men's tea.'[50] The second half of the nineteenth century was the age of canteen provision, celebrated by Elizabeth Gaskell as the action of an enlightened employer.[51] In fact, the creation of a works canteen was more likely to be about an employer reclaiming the space of the workplace during meal times. Richard Tangye, a Birmingham manfacturer, made it clear that this was an issue of control when he introduced a canteen into his factory in the 1860s:

Great loss was sustained by large numbers of men preparing and cooking their meals during working time, before the arrival of the meal hour. The foremen usually went to their homes to their meals, so that the shops were left without sufficient superintendence, advantage often being taken of this want of oversight to indulge in 'larks' and games, and in wandering around the various departments, the result frequently being the loss of valuable tools and materials.[52]

These unsupervised moments were the times when workers engaged themselves on 'jobs for the king': the making of tools or household implements for home use or sale.[53]

The strategy of formalizing the informal was often accepted by the workforce as providing positive benefits. Workers certainly seemed to see canteens as an improvement on the ad hoc arrangements that previously existed. Similarly, Reid has demonstrated, the formal structuring of the working week to eliminate 'Saint Monday' involved a good deal of worker support. This was, at least partly, motivated by the knowledge that, however formal the new system, space would still exist to recreate informal structures via tacit agreements between work groups. Samuel Courtauld's provision of a canteen in his Bocking Mill in 1873 came with firm regulations that the use of the silk mills, furnaces or stoves for 'any but business purposes' was explicitly prohibited. Lown argues, however, that despite this clear injunction 'instances continued of quiet subterfuges'.[54]

Similarly, when W.G. Riddell reported to his first job, in a Glasgow engineering works in the years preceding the First World War, he found the factory deserted. 'I did not know,' he explained, 'that the men never started work after the holiday on the appointed day.' And he later discovered: 'At some places they used to assemble at the gate and throw a brick in the air: if the brick stayed up they started work, but if it came down again they went for a drink.'[55] This is a reminder that the existence of formally agreed structures of work did not necessarily reflect either a fully structured routine to work or the existence of an unyielding complicity on the part of the workforce: that agreement on the structured working day, week and year might be tempered by circumstances and simply represent a moment in the continuing process of negotiating work control.

Formal agreement on any aspect of the work routine was not the end of informalism, it simply created a new baseline upon which the workforce would impose a layer of informality. This does not mean that the workforce attempted to control the totality of the labour process; rather it sought to have a say in its operation. Through the networks of informalism the wider culture of the working community entered the workplace. Through this medium, work was gendered, skill was constructed, and relations within the workforce and with capital were reproduced through concepts of territory and time. Existing narrative traditions have drawn upon this dialogue as it occurred, inevitably prioritizing certain aspects of it above others. The presentation of the firm as a corporate body whose shared values were expressed by the existence of an ordered workforce was employer wish-projection in the late nineteenth, as it still so often is in the late twentieth, century. The connection that was so often made between 'disruptive' behaviour in the workplace and working class immorality was, similarly, part of a wider debate about particular notions of order, in which the workplace stood as a metaphor for an ideally ordered society, and should be read within this wider context. Above all, the notion that informalism can be seen as either deviant or marginal is worthy of reconsideration within a fuller history of the workplace than has hitherto been attempted.

## NOTES

1   R. Samuel, 'The workshop of the world: steam power and hand technology in mid-Victorian Britain', *History Workshop*, 31 (1977), 6–72; R. Penn, *Skilled Workers in the Class Structure* (Cambridge, 1984); P. Joyce, 'Work', in F.M.L. Thompson, *Cambridge Social History of Britain 1750–1950* (Cambridge, 1990) Vol. 2, pp. 131–94.

2   R. Price, *Masters, Unions and Men: Work Control in Building and the Rise of Labour* (Cambridge, 1980); 'The labour process and labour history', *Social History*, 8, 1 (Jan. 1983); 'Theories of labour process formation', *Journal of Social History* (Fall 1984), 91–111; C. Behagg, *Politics and Production in the Early Nineteenth Century* (London, 1990) pp. 104–57; R. Edwards, *Conflict at Work* (Oxford, 1986).

3   H. Braverman, *Labor and Monopoly Capital: The Degradation of Work in the Twentieth Century* (New York, 1974); C.R. Littler and G. Salaman, 'Bravermania and beyond: recent theories of the labour process', *Sociology*, 16, 2 (May 1982), 251–69; B. Elbaum, W. Lazonick, F. Wilkinson, and J. Zeitlin, 'Symposium: the labour process, market structure, and Marxist theory', *Cambridge Journal of Economics*, III (1979); P. Joyce, 'Labour, capital and compromise: a response to Richard Price', *Social History*, 9, 1 (Jan. 1984), 67–76; 'Languages of reciprocity and conflict: a further response to Richard Price', *Social History*, 9 (1984); M. Savage and A. Miles, *The*

*Re-making of the British Working Class 1840–1940* (London, 1994), pp. 8–10, 41–56.

4  R. Whipp, *Patterns of Labour: Work and Social Change in the Pottery Industry* (London,1990), pp. 4, 195–212; M. Buroway, *The Politics of Production* (London, 1985)

5  P. Joyce (ed.), *The Historical Meanings of Work* (Cambridge, 1987), pp. 1–30, and the many innovative essays in this volume.

6  The contrast in focus between the histories of the workplace based on oral evidence and those based on written evidence is marked. For studies which reconstruct relations at the point of production see, for example, Andrew Phillips, 'Women on the shop floor: the Colchester rag trade 1918–1950', *Oral History*, **22** 1 (Spring 1994), 56–65; J.D.. Stephenson and C.G. Brown 'The view from the workplace: women's memories of work in Stirling *c*.1910–1950', in E. Gordon and E. Breitenbach, *The World is Ill Divided: Women's Work in Scotland in the Nineteenth and Twentieth Centuries* (Edinburgh, 1990), pp. 7–28; M. Glucksman, *Women Assemble* (London 1990).

7  J. Rule, *The Experience of Labour in the Eighteenth Century Workplace* (London, 1981); D.A. Reid, 'The decline of Saint Monday', *Past and Present*, **71** (May 1976); H. Cunningham, *Leisure and the Industrial Revolution 1780–1880* (London, 1980); R.W. Malcolmson, *Popular Recreations in English Society 1700–1850* (Cambridge, 1973).

8  J. Ginswick (ed.), *Labour and the Poor in England and Wales 1849–1851: Letters to the Morning Chronicle* (London, 1983) Vol. 1, p. 68.

9  C. Behagg, 'Controlling the product: work, time and the early industrial workforce in Britain, 1800–1850', in G. Cross (ed.), *Worktime and Industrialisation: An International History* (Philadelphia, 1988).

10  Cross (ed.), *Worktime and Industrialisation*, pp. 3–19.

11  W. Lazonick, 'Industrial relations and technical change: the case of the self-acting mule', *Cambridge Journal of Economics*, **III** (1979), 231–62; M. Freifeld, Technological change and the "self-acting" mule', *Social History*, **11** (1986).

12  S. Pollard, *The Genesis of Modern Management* (London, 1965); E.J. Hobsbawm, 'Custom, wages and work-load in nineteenth century industry', in *Labouring Men* (London, 1964), pp. 344–370; Reid, 'Decline of Saint Monday'.

13  G. Gross, *A Quest for Time* (Berkeley, 1989), see generally.

14  T.R. Tholfsen, *Working Class Radicalism in Mid-Victorian England* (London, 1976); T. Laqueur, *Religion and Respectability: Sunday Schools and Working Class Culture 1780–1850* (London, 1976), pp. 187–239; F.M.L. Thompson, *The Rise of Respectable Society* (Glasgow, 1988)

15  Reid, 'Decline of Saint Monday'.

16  O. MacDonagh, *Early Victorian Government 1830–1870* (London, 1977), pp. 22–77; U. Henriques, *Before the Welfare State: Social Administration in Early Industrial Britain* (London, 1979), pp. 66–116.

17  P. Joyce, *Work, Society and Politics* (Brighton, 1980); D. Roberts, *Paternalism in Early Victorian England* (London, 1974).

18  J. Zeitlin, '"Rank and Filism" in British labour history: a critique', *International Review of Social History*, **XXXIV** (1989), 42–6. In responding to this article Price comments that 'the history of institutions is the history of the winners in history': R. Price, '"What's in a name" Workplace history and "Rank and Filism"', *International Review of Social History*, **XXXIV** (1989), pp. 62–77, 76.

19  D.A. Reid, 'Labour, leisure and politics in Birmingham, *c.*1800–1875' (unpublished Ph.D. thesis, University of Birmingham, 1985); E. Hopkins, 'Birmingham during the industrial revolution: class conflict or class co-operation?', *Research in Social Movements, Conflict and Change*, **16** (1993), 117–37.

20  See the debate between Zeitlin and Price cited above, and J.E. Cronin, 'The "Rank and File" and the social history of the working class', *International Review of Social History*, **XXXIV** (1989), 78–88.

21  J. Zeitlin, '"Rank and Filism" and labour history: rejoinder to Price and Cronin', *International Review of Social History*, **XXXIV** (1989), 89–102, 101.

22  In earlier work on the secret traditions of the workplace in the 1830s I argued that this was simply a stage which workplace organizations went through on the way to formalization. It would be more useful to see this as a temporally specific kind of informalism, fashioned to meet the needs of the moment, replaced by other forms as the moment changed: C. Behagg, 'Secrecy, ritual and folk violence: the opacity of the workplace in the first half of the nineteenth century', in R.D. Storch (ed.), *Popular Culture and Custom in Nineteenth Century Britain* (London, 1982).

23  See J. Purvis, *Hard Lessons: The Lives and Education of Working Class Women in Nineteenth Century England* (Cambridge, 1989), pp. 9–21.

24  For example, A. John, *By the Sweat of Their Brow* (London, 1984); S.O. Rose, 'Gender at work: sex, class and industrial capitalism', *History Workshop Journal*, **21** (Spring 1986).

25  J. Lown, *Women and Industrialization: Gender at Work in Nineteenth Century England* (Oxford, 1990).

26  A. Briggs, *Victorian Things* (London, 1988), p. 61.

27  H. Martineau, 'What There is in a Button', *Household Words* (1852), 106–12.

28  H. Martineau, 'The Wonder of Nails and Screws', *Household Words* (1851–2), 138–42.

29  Ibid.

30  R. Gray, 'Factory legislation and the gendering of jobs in the North of England 1830–1860', *Gender and History*, **5** 1 (Spring 1993), 59–80, 73.

31  See the discussion of dress in relation to prostitution in J. Walkowitz, *Prostitution and Victorian Society: Women, Class and the State* (Cambridge, 1980), p. 26.

32  Osler to Martineau, 10 Feb. 1852, Martineau Papers 713, University of Birmingham.

33  *Morning Chronicle*, 16 Dec. 1850.

34  E. Gordon, 'Women, work and collective action: Dundee jute workers 1870-1906', *Journal of Social History*, **21** (1987).

35  E. Cadbury, *Experiments in Industrial Organisation* (London, 1912); C. Dellheim, 'The creation of a company culture: Cadbury's, 1861–1931', *American Historical Review*, **92** (1987).

36  Ginswick (ed.), *Labour and the Poor*, p. 9.

37  J. Marshall, 'Eccles Shorrock, his biography: an experiment in literary form' (unpublished M.Phil thesis, West Sussex Institute of Higher Education, 1994).

38  E. Shorrock, *Letter to the Working Men of Darwen* (Manchester, 1979), in Marshall, 'Eccles Shorrock'.

39  F. Forrest, *Chapters in the Life of a Dundee Factory Boy*, edited by David Phillips (Dundee, 1980), p. 14.

40  J. Barlow Brooks, *Lancashire Bred: An Autobiography* (Oxford, 1951), p. 122.

41  T.K. Hareven and R. Langenbach, *Amoskeag: Life and Work in an American Factory City in New England* (London, 1979), p. 200.

42  See C. Behagg, 'The song of the factory: singing, dancing and contested space in the nineteenth century workplace' (forthcoming).

43  F.W. Taylor, *The Principles of Scientific Management* (New York, 1913), pp. 1–10; 48–94; F.W. Taylor, *Shop Management* (New York, 1911) pp. 30–3.

44  R.D. Best, *Brass Chandelier: A Biography of R.H. Best of Birmingham* (London, 1940), pp. 152–5; this predates the publication of Taylor's work, but he was publishing in an established context of debate; William Watson, an engineering worker remembers, 'The system came to Britain about 1900, and for years the employers were scientific system mad': W.F. Watson, *Machines and Men: An Autobiography of an Itinerant Mechanic* (London, 1935), p. 90.

45  Reid, 'Decline of Saint Monday'; W.R Lambert, 'Drink and work: discipline in industrial South Wales c.1800–1870', *Welsh History Review*, **7** (1975).

46  D.C Woods, 'Customary rights and popular legitimation: industrial stealing in the Victorian Black Country', *West Midlands*

Studies, **17** (1984), 7–11; D. Philips, *Crime and Authority in Victorian England* (London, 1977), pp. 176–94.

47 *British Parliamentary Papers: Children's Employment Commission, Appendix to the Fourth Report of the Commissioners on the Employment of Young Persons in Trades and Manufactures* (1865), p. 53.

48 S. Yeo, *Religion and Voluntary Organisations in Crisis* (London, 1976), p. 100.

49 Cross, *A Quest for Time*, see generally.

50 Watson, *Machines and Men*, pp. 27–9.

51 E. Gaskell, *North and South* (Harmondsworth, 1970 edn), p. 445. This novel was originally published in 1855.

52 R. Tangye, *'One and All': The Autobiography of Richard Tangye of the Cornwall Works, Birmingham* (Birmingham, 1889), p. 112.

53 Watson, *Machines and Men*, p. 33.

54 Lown, *Women and Industrialisation*, pp. 125–6.

55 W.G. Riddell, *Adventures of an Obscure Victorian* (London, 1982).

# 7

## 'Levelled to the Same Common Standard'? Social Class in the Lunatic Asylum, 1780–1860

### L. D. SMITH

## INTRODUCTION

Attitudes to mentally disordered people have always been characterized by a complex pattern of perceptions. The insane may be feared as dangerous, or be pitied as unfortunate and hopeless. They may be stigmatized, and even ostracized. They may be looked upon as the inevitable casualties of rapidly changing social and economic conditions, or as the embodiment of individual vulnerability. They could be lost souls to be rescued, or damaged people to be restored to some conception of 'normality'. At different periods in history particular constellations of attitude have predominated, leading on to either a more restrictive or a more open approach to the care and treatment of people with mental disorders. A range of other influences have also helped to determine how individuals have been cared for and treated. One of the more significant has been the person's position, or perceived position, within the social hierarchy.

In late Georgian and early Victorian England, significant shifts were taking place in the social structure and in its interrelationships. A society which had numerous subtle gradations and delineations of 'rank' or 'order' became gradually transformed into one where the existence of distinct classes became clearly acknowledged. Many interacting elements contributed to the structural changes. The processes of commercial development and industrialization fostered a growing middle class, as well as a larger and more diverse industrial working class. The upheavals of continental revolution and war, complemented by political struggle in Britain, consolidated the formation and development of both the middle classes and the working classes as powerful forces within society, each with influence to wield, though by different means.[1] Throughout each stage of the transition, position in the rank or class hierarchy could determine opportunities for employment, marriage prospects, and social relationships. It could also determine the means of access to personal services, such as health care, and the ways in which these were to be delivered.

By the latter part of the eighteenth century, institutional provision for people deemed insane had attained a certain level of sophistication. A network of private madhouses, some dating back to the early part of the century, had been established around the country, particularly in the hinterland of the growing urban centres. These houses were catering primarily for the mad offspring of the upper and middling classes. There had also been some development of public asylum provision. In London, Bethlem hospital, with its origins in the sixteenth century, had been joined in 1753 by St Luke's. Cities such as Manchester, Liverpool, York, Newcastle and Exeter had established asylums based on public charitable subscriptions. These catered mainly for the relatively impecunious, some of whom were supported by their parishes. Most deranged paupers, however, were still contained within their community or, if unmanageable, in workhouses or more custodial institutions like bridewells or prisons.[2]

The incipient system was, however, being placed under increasing strain by the growing numbers of 'pauper lunatics' who could not be maintained in the community, and who were too disturbed and disruptive to remain in the workhouse. Market forces led some madhouse owners to widen their clientele and to admit paupers. From the 1780s onwards this became a growing trend. New houses were opened to cater for this new source of demand, some negotiating bulk contracts with parish authorities, as did the Droitwich lunatic asylum which opened in 1790, with space for 100 inmates, a majority of whom were to be paupers. Commercial considerations were increasingly coming to dominate patterns of care.[3]

Standards of care and treatment varied significantly between asylums and madhouses, public and private. Some proprietors and managers set out with the explicit intention of providing a regime and conditions geared towards promoting the recovery and consequent discharge of their patients. Apart from the celebrated Quaker-run Retreat at York, founded in 1796, there were other establishments which attempted to provide a humane and therapeutic environment. Some, however, demonstrated no such intent. The best that could be hoped for in these was long-term confinement in spartan conditions, with neglect and ill-treatment often the norm.[4]

The prevalent abuses were highlighted by select committees in 1807 and again in 1815–16, which reflected and further stimulated the exertions of an influential lobby of reformers. The most significant legislation of the period, the County Asylums Act of 1808, attempted to redress some of the evils of the private madhouse sector and of neglect in the workhouse. It enabled county magistrates to establish a county asylum, funded by a county rate, and laid down basic standards for the design and arrangements of the building. The influence of the Act was limited, as local opposition both to the large expenditure entailed and to the spectre of state intervention resulted in widespread inaction. Nevertheless, a number of counties did adopt the provisions of the Act, and by 1820 there were seven county asylums, with a few more following before the mandatory legislation of 1845. These early county asylums became highly influential in the evolution of methods of management of insane people.[5]

This pattern of asylum care, with its combination of public, charitable and private provision, continued until after 1845. During this time the system was subjected to a continued pressure of growing demand, mainly for the accommodation of pauper lunatics. The result in the county asylums was that they were allowed to become ever more crowded, until finally the buildings had to be expanded by the addition of extra wings or storeys, a precedent for the huge structures of the later nineteenth century. The private sector continued to grow to take advantage of the market opportunities, with a steady stream of new asylums opening in the provinces, geared to accommodate mainly pauper patients, many under contract from local boards of guardians. The shortcomings of a ramshackle system were finally confronted in the 1845 Asylums Act, which required each county to provide an asylum, either on its own or in combination with other counties, and also enabled boroughs to set up their own asylums. Over the next few years a national network of pauper lunatic asylums was developed. Projected and built on a tide of optimism as to what the 'new model asylum' could achieve, the county asylum system formed the basis of psychiatric care for almost a century and a half. The betrayal of that optimism, and the gradual atrophy of the great monolithic asylum during the succeeding decades of the nineteenth century, has been amply highlighted by Andrew Scull and others.[6]

## SOCIAL CLASS AND MENTAL DISORDER

The images of insanity in the late eighteenth and nineteenth centuries were overwhelmingly negative. It was viewed as a severe affliction, perhaps the most serious that a person, and his or her family, could suffer. In its more extreme presentations it was seen to reduce the sufferer to something approaching bestiality and to destroy all normal relationships. Even in its less stark forms, it could lead to a profound upheaval in the person's life, and pose a serious threat to future ability to earn a livelihood. If the onset of insanity was viewed as a calamity, the degree of calamity might be compounded by the person's social position. The more elevated the status the greater was the loss suffered by the individual, and the more profound was the disgrace experienced by the family.

The relative susceptibility of the different social classes to insanity, or particular types of insanity, was a focus of ongoing speculation. As Michael Donnelly has argued, the question became bound up with wider debates about the nature of civilization and the advance of society. People who were more cultivated were seen as more liable to succumb, and as society advanced so insanity increased. Certainly, as Roy Porter has shown, there was a widespread belief in the eighteenth century that people from the higher ranks were more prone to mental disorder, particularly melancholy, than the poorer classes. The social excesses of the affluent, combined with preoccupations with success in trade and financial affairs, served to make them liable to the 'English malady'. The apparent greater propensity of the wealthier classes to fall prey to insanity was later observed by the influential nineteenth-century Scottish alienist and asylum superintendent, W.A.F. Browne. While acknowledging that all classes were exposed equally to the possible physical causes of mental disorder, he argued that the wealthy were more liable to fall victim to the moral (or social) causes. He cited as evidence the large number of 'Retreats' which had been opened as speculative ventures to cater for the disordered rich. The burdens of public affairs and of political strife, Browne suggested, served as particular moral causes which might precipitate their disorders. The problems could be further exacerbated within the 'affluent and exclusive classes' by intermarriage, accounting for the tendency towards madness of numbers of the English peerage. Later in the nineteenth century, the ground shifted more to focus on the liability of the labouring classes to insanity, rendered vulnerable by degradation and excess. In the absence of sound data, the arguments remained inconclusive.[7]

By the late eighteenth-century, class was a key determinant of whether institutional care might be available to an insane individual. The wealthy mad could have their specialist care provided in a madhouse. Increasingly, by the end of the century, pauper lunatics also had some prospect of being financed to enter a madhouse or asylum. The sector of society who were most disadvantaged were some of those in between—the lower and middling classes, the small farmers, tradesmen, shopkeepers, artisans and others who were not paupers but whose means were not sufficient to enable them or their families to pay for care within a private madhouse. These people attracted the special attention of lunacy reformers, and particularly of those influential local people who were instrumental in trying to establish asylums. Provision for them had been among the main purposes of the public subscription asylums that had been opened in a few cities, such as the one at Manchester, which sought to give assistance to 'many persons of middling fortunes'.[8]

In most county towns there were attempts by some of the leading citizens to establish a subscription lunatic asylum, usually following the successful founding of a hospital. However, in many instances the level of public indifference to the consequences of mental disorder precluded the raising of sufficient funds. Progress came after the 1808 Act, which provided the stimulus in some counties, by promoting the option of combined action by county magistrates and voluntary subscribers. Where they were formed, the new joint bodies were intent on providing for the relatively poor working non-paupers. As the joint committee responsible for the opening of the Staffordshire asylum told the public in 1818:

Persons of this description are objects of peculiar pity, as they are too poor to avail themselves, out of their own means, of the benefit of this establishment, and not poor enough to claim the support of their parishes. They must, therefore, unless assisted, remain a helpless burden upon families ill able to manage them.

Similar sentiments motivated the infirmary governors in Nottingham, in considering their response to the 1808 Act. Although the projected asylum was to cater mainly for paupers, they were conscious of the particular virtues in providing for the working poor, who were 'fit objects of beneficence'. The preoccupation with the needs of this group remained a constant theme in the ideas of lunacy reformers.[9]

The growing political influence and predominance of the middle classes further concentrated attention on the desirability of addressing the needs of their casualties. The wealthier private patients and paupers had been the main beneficiaries of the expansion of asylum places in the 1830s and 1840s. Concern about provision for the intermediate groups led ultimately to the development of second asylums in several counties, such as Staffordshire in 1854 and Nottinghamshire in 1855. These were specifically intended for the middle classes, and led to the abandonment of the principle of 'General' asylums. The private and charity patients were all removed to the new asylums, with the original deteriorating buildings being relinquished to the paupers. The expressed objective, as laid down for the new Coton Hill asylum at Stafford, was still 'to afford relief to insane persons of limited means and reduced circumstances'.

The development of a facility for people who 'in education and in character were yet above the rank of the pauper' was an objective of the leading lunacy reformer, Lord Shaftesbury, and of the most influential psychiatric practitioner of the era, John Conolly. Conolly had become convinced from his work at the Middlesex asylum that, after the 1845 Act, it was the middle classes who had the greatest unmet needs:

That class comprehended persons of education and respectability, whose means of living depended on their own exertions, and the moment they were struck with insanity, that moment their means of livelihood were cut off, and they became in reality more helpless than the poor. Such a condition as this, in which the middle class were placed, was as distressing as any they could well conceive, as no provision was made for such cases.

Conolly's plea was designed to tap into the fear that mental illness could, more than anything else, threaten the hard-earned goal of middle-class respectability. The separation of the sufferer from the degraded pauper lunatic might at least go some way towards redressing what had been lost.[10]

Many mentally disordered people who came from the ranks of the lower middle classes, however, did not have the opportunity to enter one of the few special new asylums like Coton Hill. They were left to fend for themselves, untreated, until impoverishment drove them into a pauper asylum. Some of the new post-1845 asylums did initially make limited provision for impecunious private patients. However, the spiralling demand for admission of paupers soon ended the practice. The superintendent of the Warwickshire County asylum, William Parsey, regretted in 1859 that his asylum had been obliged to cease taking private patients. This penalized a class who 'above all others' were denied facilities for proper care and treatment at a cost they could afford. They were excluded from private asylums because their payments were not sufficiently remunerative, and because their presence among higher-class patients was considered 'objectionable'. By being forced to come to a pauper asylum they would suffer 'consequent social degradation'. This was particularly painful to contemplate for the middle-class officers of the new asylums.[11]

The apparent continuing preoccupation with the importance of protecting the integrity of those above the level of pauper may perhaps mask a more complex debate about the nature of insanity. There was, on the one hand, a widely held belief that the sufferings of the better off and their families were somehow greater when insanity struck, with the loss of earning power, of social position, and very probably of respectability. The provision for them of types of institutional care which matched social aspiration was an attempt at compensation. However, there was an opposing perspective that all this was of little point, for mental derangement had effectively cancelled any class pretensions. This position was articulated by Edward Latham, the president of the Royal College of Physicians and a leading witness to the select committee in 1815. He argued that social rank was of little importance, for the disease 'levelled to the same common standard the peer and the beggar'. Insanity was completely unlike any other diseases which could afflict a man, for it destroyed 'those consolations which are to be derived from his superior means and rank in society'. It rendered the person's former distinctions of status irrelevant, because

the mind being equally lost in all, the man can feel no more actual gratification who possesses such distinctions, in reality, than the poor wretch who is constantly fancying himself in possession of them; for everything is either false in perception, or perceived to no salutary or proper purpose, by both of them.

The lunatic had, in effect, sacrificed his class by virtue of his madness. Consequently, Latham dismissed any possible benefits of private establishments making special provision for the wealthier classes. These could be positively harmful, by reinforcing an imaginary social distinction that had ceased to exist by virtue of the mental disorder. Here was an argument that lent intellectual respectability to inherent public prejudice on the manifestations and effects of mental illness.[12]

## THE SEGREGATIVE ASYLUM

If there were elements of double or conflicting standards in conceptions of how insanity determined or altered the sufferer's social status, these would be translated into the operation of social structures within the madhouse and the asylum. In terms of practical policy, from the later eighteenth century onwards, proprietors and managers were becoming steadily more conscious of the perceived desirability of replicating and reinforcing within the asylum the norms of class relationship of the wider society outside the walls. In the private sector, this was largely a commercial decision, based on presumptions as to what the customers would expect. In the charitable and public sector, the impetus came more from a sense of responsibility to meet the expectations of the patrons and projectors.

It was, above all, the increasing influx of paupers into the madhouse system from the latter part of the eighteenth century that made social rank an issue of major significance in asylum management. Even before their advent, there was an increasing amount of differentiation between houses as to the rank of

customers, reflecting society's fine social gradations. Some proprietors targeted particular segments of the market. Clientele
was partly determined by the nature of local and regional
demand, and by the reputation established by the proprietor,
which would be represented in the levels of fees charged. The
house of George Chadwick in Lichfield, for example, established by the 1770s, was catering for people of moderate means.
His eight patients in December 1779 comprised four farmers,
two grocers, a gentleman, and a (female) mantua maker. In June
1808, his twenty-three patients included three yeomen, four
farmers, and one each of apothecary, buttonmaker, machine
maker, grocer, ironmonger, potter, shoemaker, and builder.

Other houses were rather more select, such as that of Mrs
Gibbs at Wootton Wawen in Warwickshire, established in the
1790s. At Wootton Villa asylum she received eight ladies 'exclusively (of) the first class'. As Charlotte Mackenzie has described
in detail, the important private asylum at Ticehurst in Kent,
opened in 1792, geared its services toward an increasingly select
clientele.[13]

The growing admission of paupers into both public and private asylums forced more careful consideration of management
arrangements. Asylum managers and madhouse proprietors had
to find ways to bring about some semblance of order among the
different types of wayward and unpredictable individuals who
peopled their establishments. The idea of 'classification' became,
from the later eighteenth century onwards, a key component in
the creation of a system of asylum management. Essentially it
meant a separation of patients by different categories. These
might relate to the person's type of illness, or their behavioural
presentation. Patients who were 'dirty' or 'refractory', for example, were likely to be kept segregated. The classification might
be based on the stage reached on the road to recovery; for
example, 'convalescent' patients were often separated from
others. There would normally be segregation, of varying strict-
ness, by gender. Above all, social factors like the separation of
private from pauper patients, or other more subtle distinctions
according to background, became key elements. Over time the
idea of classification developed into a doctrine that was seen to
have therapeutic, as well as organizational, value.[14]

Classification of patients by social class was part of the normal
arrangements in both private and public asylums by the latter

part of the eighteenth century. Many private madhouses were continuing to admit only private patients. Those that had widened their customer base to attract parish paupers would take care to separate them, as far as possible, from the more lucrative private patients. The nature and degree of the separation was dependent on the size of the establishment. In some larger houses, such as Laverstock near Salisbury which catered for forty pauper and sixty private patients, the two groups were housed in completely different buildings. At others they would be accommodated in distinct parts of the same building, as at the Droitwich asylum. It provided a separate 'Department' for the paupers, who formed the majority of its patients. Similar arrangements operated in the large teeming private madhouses in the east end of London, in Hoxton and Bethnal Green. In Warburton's 'White House' in Bethnal Green in 1815 there were 360 patients, of whom 230 were paupers. In his adjoining 'Red House' there were 215 paupers in a total of 275 patients. In the latter, the private patients occupied the large central part of the house, the male and female quarters being divided by a staircase; the paupers were housed in the wings.[15]

In the larger establishments, class differentials could be further stratified. Private patients were far from being a monolithic group. They could range from people whose means were barely above those eligible to become charity patients in a public asylum to dependents of wealthy, aristocratic families. The Droitwich asylum's scale of charges and facilities reflected these variations. As its proprietor, William Ricketts, explained to the Select Committee in 1814:

I have accommodations according to the different classes; according to their pay; patients of a superior class pay, some four guineas a week, some three, some two and a half, some a guinea, and fourteen shillings a week pauper lunatics, except the town of Birmingham, they pay only ten shillings, and the major part of the pauper lunatics are from the town of Birmingham.

Not only were there gradations of private patients at Droitwich, it seems, but also of paupers. Ricketts had made a contract with the Birmingham parish authorities whereby they could bulk-purchase places in the asylum at a favourable rate. Other large private asylums, such as Brislington House near Bristol, Laverstock House, and the increasingly exclusive Ticehurst, operated similar arrangements to Droitwich, with scales of charges for their patients, according to their means and expectations.[16]

The critical shortage of asylum places in the 1830s and 1840s stimulated the opening in the provinces of several large new private asylums, geared to accommodate substantial numbers of paupers, alongside a nucleus of lucrative private patients. Duddeston Hall, near Birmingham, for example, was opened in 1835, with space for thirty private patients and sixty paupers, mainly taken from the Birmingham and Aston workhouses. The huge Haydock Lodge asylum in Lancashire, which opened in 1844, had capacity for fifty private patients and 400 paupers. These and other similar establishments were strictly speculative commercial ventures aimed to tap a buoyant market. Their proprietors took advantage of the accepted norms of class separation. The private patients would be accommodated in reasonable standards of comfort in the central part of the building, where the proprietor and his family might also live. The paupers were likely to be consigned to spartan conditions in dormitories, in out-buildings, or in converted stables. These discrepancies in standards of care were overlooked by many hard pressed boards of guardians, until scandals and exposures contributed to the pressure to bring about reform in provision for the insane.[17]

Differential provision according to rank had become the norm in the later eighteenth-century public asylums. Distinct class accommodation became a key element in the management arrangements of those of the new post-1808 county asylums which were set up as 'General' asylums. A due regard to social order was seen as essential, as was the cultivation of an image of respectability for the asylum. This meant ensuring that the less desirable attributes of the paupers did not obtrude excessively into the view of outside observers. Such considerations clearly influenced the projectors of the first county asylum, at Nottingham. A meeting of the infirmary governors in October 1808 was advised by Dr John Storer, the chairman of the committee set up to build the asylum, that the pauper patient should be offered 'every accommodation and comfort that his situation admits'. Treatment should endeavour to restore him as a 'useful member, perhaps even an ornament to Society'. The governors were reminded that there was always the possibility that, behind the façade of the deranged pauper, there might be rather more promising material, for it has been remarked that among the victims to this deplorable disease, there is very considerable proportion of Persons endowed with the rarest gifts of genius and sensibility.

If there were to be paupers in the asylum, there had at least to be some standards. The Nottingham committee consequently tried to ensure that their intake of paupers was controlled to a degree by the exclusion of criminal lunatics.[18]

In the development of their plans for the Nottingham asylum, the committee sought advice from various sources. Interestingly, they entered into detailed correspondence with a leading private practitioner, Edward Long Fox, the respected Quaker proprietor of Brislington House near Bristol. One of the chief concerns they raised with Fox was the possibility that the mix of patients might have damaging effects on the willingness of people to send their insane relatives into the asylum, particularly if it were to contain criminal lunatics. Fox in his response acknowledged the possible dissonance between reason and prejudice in public perceptions:

Insanity to a certain extent, reduces all men to a par, it raises Peasants to Emperors and Kings & vice versa. On that account it would seem, at first view, unnecessary to attend to any arrangement, according to the rank of the individual in Society when sane, but, as frequently, nay generally it happens that persons have perceptions and are aware of the relations they bear in Society; as, many are only wrong upon one or two Topics and sometimes not always upon those—it seems proper to consult prejudice so far, as well to wound the feelings of such by an indiscriminate admixture.

The committee were clearly impressed by Fox's arguments, and attempted to make their plans in accordance with his recommendations. The private subscribers to the asylum were able to ensure that they retained a strong influence in its government.[19]

Other authorities on the management of mental disorder were also urging clear class distinction in the new public asylums. A prominent asylum architect, William Stark, lamented in 1807 at the mixing of classes in 'common receptacles', where it happened that:

persons of liberal education, and of respectable rank in society, are unavoidably mixed with those of the lowest rank, of the most brutal manners, and of the most profligate habits . . .

He proposed plans which isolated the classes from one another. This approach proved influential. In practice the distinctions of class and rank exemplified in many private madhouses and some charitable asylums were replicated, even magnified, in the early county asylums. The norm was to divide the patients into three classes—first, second and third class. The first class were those private patients of adequate or even ample means, whose relatives were able to bear the full costs of their residence and care in the asylum. The second class were those private patients of lesser means who were unable to meet the full charges, and who were eligible to receive subsidy from the charitable fund associated with the asylum subscribers in a 'General' lunatic asylum. The third class were the pauper patients, whose care was paid for by their parish or, after 1834, board of guardians. Within the first and second classes there might be further distinction and gradation. At the Nottingham asylum payments for patients were to have 'some relation to the rank and circumstances of each', taking account of the 'nature of the apartments and table expected'. At the Stafford asylum, opened in 1818, the first-class patients, referred to in the initial publicity as being lunatics 'of a superior rank', were subsequently subdivided into three groups. Those of the 'highest rank' were to pay not less than two guineas per week; those of the 'middling ranks' not less than one pound; and those of 'inferior rank' not less than twelve shillings per week, a rate that was very competitive with the charges in many private madhouses.[20]

With the mix of classes in these county asylums, the managers strove to ensure that they were kept apart as far as possible within the building, both physically and in their patterns of activity. The classes were separately accommodated, in due deference to the expectations of the higher-class patients and their families. The standards of accommodation were intended to bear some relation to what the person had experienced outside the asylum. The usual arrangement was to house the first-class patients in the central block, with the second-class and paupers in the wings, females on one side and males on the other, a precedent which was set at Nottingham. At Gloucester, the first-class patients were housed in a rather grand crescent that formed the centrepiece of an imposing building.[21]

The segregation of the classes in public asylums was lent intellectual backing by the prominent Scottish alienist, W.A.F. Browne, who went on to put many of his ideas into practice at the well-endowed Crichton Royal asylum, near Dumfries. In his influential book *What Asylums Were, Are, and Ought To Be*, published in 1837, Browne placed great emphasis on the essential place of classification in developing management arrangements that were conducive to a therapeutic regime. The classification should take into account the nature and state of the illness. It should also relate to the rates of board paid by the inmate. As Browne argued, the accommodation, food and attendance provided for the rich could not and should not be extended to the poor:

The pauper could not appreciate, nor prize, nor derive benefit from the refinement and delicacies essential to the comfort, and instrumental in the recovery of the affluent. Most fortunately this arrangement, which is called for by the usages of society, is found to correspond with those higher and less artificial distinctions which are dictated by philosophy.

Browne was prepared to concede that ability to pay might exclude some worthy patients from the benefits of association with the more refined, and that individual cases might be entitled to receive special treatment:

Wherever the poor lunatic has been well educated, accustomed to the courtesies and amenities of good society, and retains amid his hallucinations, the feelings and tastes which characterize that condition, he should be raised from the grade of paupers, and placed among those who still cherish similar feelings and tastes.

People in this situation had suffered the degradation of a 'loss of caste'. To elevate them in the social hierarchy of the asylum was, Browne argued, likely to have a curative effect. He could hardly have more clearly articulated the vulnerabilities of the middle classes and the case for special consideration of those who had lost their place as they lost their senses.[22]

In practice, the principle of class separation had its limitations, and could be expendable. There were certain behaviours which were considered unacceptable, the manifestation of which would lead to the sacrifice of class privileges and pretensions. The better behaved could not be expected to share their quarters with those who were 'dirty' or 'refractory'. Refractory wards tended to house people of all classes, while dirty private patients might be confined in the basement with the worst of the pauper patients. Expediency might also lead to the abandonment of hierarchy. The incessant demand for accommodation for paupers by the late 1830s led to compromises, with some being placed in accommodation for second-class, and even first-class patients. Equivocation over the true social position of second-class, or charity, patients was increasingly likely to lead them to be placed with the paupers. These lapses from the norms of differentiation of the classes were accepted with little protest by the asylums' committees of management. When necessity intervened the social niceties were dispensed with, and the lunatic was declared classless.[23]

## CLASS, CARE AND TREATMENT

Social class, as a key determinant of the nature of the asylum experience, exercised an influence on the nature of the facilities and the treatment that were provided. In the best private asylums catering solely for the wealthier classes, the services on offer made them something akin to a recuperative country house. The contrasts between what the different classes might expect were most clearly exemplified in the mixed madhouse or asylum, private or public. Here the distinctions of rank or class were not only reflected in physical separation. The whole management regime, and all the arrangements for care and treatment, were delineated according to the social position of the inmates.

It was not only that the pauper patients were generally housed in a lower standard of sleeping accommodation, particularly in private asylums. Distinct day areas for the different classes were the norm, with the paupers invariably placed in inferior day rooms that were cold, bare, ill furnished, poorly ventilated, and crowded. The room might have more than one purpose, as at the private Hereford lunatic asylum in the 1830s, where a pauper day room doubled up as a laundry. The private patients there had benefit of a parlour, where they took their meals, while the paupers were required to spend most of their days and eat their meals outside in the yard, even in the middle of winter. At Fonthill in Wiltshire, in 1814, the day room for those of the 'better class' was 'a small hall with a good fire, and decent', while that for the paupers was a small kitchen, in which the meals for the proprietor's family were cooked. The early county asylums provided reasonable pauper day rooms, albeit more basic and less comfortable than those for the private patients, but the paupers' rooms could be expendable when the demand for the reception of growing numbers of patients meant that they had to be taken over as dormitories, as had occurred at Stafford by 1840.[24]

Access to outdoor recreation areas marked a clear distinguishing feature between classes, especially in private asylums, many of which were converted country mansions with several acres of land attached. The 'pleasure grounds' were publicized to the families of prospective customers as an important aspect of the therapeutic benefits the establishment had to offer. However, these benefits were rarely available equally to all inmates. The discrimination was epitomized at the well-regarded Laverstock House near Salisbury. The 'superior patients' had the benefit of all nine acres, whilst the paupers were restricted to rather less than an acre. The contrast was yet more stark at Duddeston Hall near Birmingham, where the pauper patients (the great majority) were offered 'one dull yard' for each sex for exercise. The private patients had access to the extensive gardens and grounds, lauded by one poetically inclined private patient for 'the variety and richness of its plantations, and ... the occasional scenes of perfect and luxuriant solitude' which were a match for any setting in Britain or Switzerland. In those asylums where the poorer patients were permitted access to the surrounding land, it was usually for purposes more productive than the purely recreational.[25]

The therapeutic value of activity and occupation in the asylum was well recognized by the end of the eighteenth century, and was highlighted by the Tukes at the York Retreat. The inculcation of the work ethic and of work rhythms into those who had lost the habit became a primary element of the treatment programme of many asylums, public and private. It was presented as a means of taking the mind of the lunatic away from irrational thoughts or delusional ideas and of re-establishing patterns of normality. During the early decades of the nineteenth century, the employment of active patients became an increasingly integral part of asylum life. However, class norms acted as a brake on offering this means of therapy to all patients.[26]

Whilst it was acceptable to employ paupers, and other poorer patents, on the land attached to the asylum, at various trades within the asylum, or (for women) in the laundry or cleaning the wards, none of these was seen as appropriate for the wealthier or first-class patients. Edward Long Fox remarked how it was 'much more difficult to give employment to gentlemen'. Some commentators lamented the great disadvantage which the wealthier patients thereby suffered, by being deprived of one of the main means of achieving a cure. Edward Latham in 1814 deplored as a 'fact not to be controverted' that people in asylums for those of 'superior rank and opulence' were less likely to experience recovery from their illness than poorer patients who had the benefit of asylums where labour was an integral part of the treatment regime. Thomas Bakewell, the proprietor of a well-known private asylum in Staffordshire, also concluded that pauper patients were easier to cure because they could be engaged in work. He would discourage refusal by the alternative of confinement in a dingy yard or day room, in an atmosphere of disgrace. He did not feel it proper to offer similar options to his private patients, considering that a requirement to work for those not used to it would be a degradation. However, if they would voluntarily undertake some lighter work such as horticulture, or supervising the paupers in their work, this was seen to have considerable therapeutic value.[27]

For the more privileged there were recreational options to employment. Inside the house there would be musical instruments, games such as chess or backgammon, playing cards, and books and periodicals to read. For outdoor exercise there might be long country walks, and games like croquet or bowls. Several private asylums, and even some public asylums, made available a carriage for the use of the better-off private patients, so that they might be taken for drives. Use of a carriage, with servants, was one of the most obvious symbols of an attempt to preserve the semblance of the trappings of gentility. Edward Latham derided these misguided attempts:

Painful indeed it is to see a man, devoid of all mental energy waited upon by a number of servants, supplied with all the luxuries of life, and carried about in a coach with all the accustomed pomp and grandeur of elevated rank; who, had he but the least glimmering or reason, would tell you, that he derives not any enjoyment from such indulgencies.

These indulgencies, he contended, were futile in the context of the loss of reason. Another common manifestation of privilege was in the arrangements for taking meals. In a number of mad-houses or asylums, private patients who were in a period of 'convalescence' were likely to be awarded the honour of eating their meals at the same table as the proprietor and his family. Indeed, the creation of a supportive family-like environment could be an essential element in the therapeutic programme, and to be treated like a house guest was part of the reward for behaving with the sort of manners and decorum that only the more cultivated patient could demonstrate.[28]

One recurrent obstacle, however, to maintaining the social standards of private patients in both private and public asylums was the staff providing the direct care The keepers, attendants or nurses were universally poorly paid, untrained, and tended to come from the lower social strata. Whilst it is clear that many did their best to adopt a caring approach to their charges, they had their limitations. Edwin Rickman, a former private patient at Duddeston Hall, was generally favourable about the treatment he had received. However, he was scathing about the standard of staff in asylums:

Nothing is more calculated to disgust and increase the excitement of a convalescent and sensitive mind, than to be subject, to the low, and necessarily ignorant talk of even the most civil, and for their station in life, the best informed of the class almost invariably chosen . . .

John Perceval, the periodically deranged son of the assassinated prime minister Spencer Perceval, was even more dismissive of the staff. He felt degraded by being cared for and controlled by 'menials', who showed a 'gross want of respect' to rank or situation. In some asylums private patients would be allowed to bring their own servants in with them, so minimizing contact with the asylum's own keepers. A recognition of the issue in the Gloucester asylum in 1841 led the superintendent to arrange for some medical students to be employed, in order to do away with some of 'the objectionable, but previously unavoidable' services of keepers 'belonging in fact to the class of menial attendants'. Their attentions were concentrated on the first-class patients, with whom, together with the superintendent and his family they formed 'one domestic party', who would 'daily assemble for meals and for amusement'. The pauper patients, not invited to these exclusive gatherings, at least had the consolation of regular singing lessons with their more refined fellow inmates.[29]

If what were deemed the moral aspects of treatment were mediated by the social origins of the patients, the same could not be said for the more physical treatments. The armoury of the mad-doctor included blisterings and bleedings, shaving of the head, contraptions like the rotating or swing chair, and the use of water administered by various means—hot and cold showers, douches or plunge baths. Practitioners also made use of medicines, sometimes of a drastic nature, particularly narcotics, emetics and purgatives. The employment of these treatments and preparations did not differentiate between class. Neither did the use of the celebrated techniques of the mad-doctor, such as 'the eye'—the use of a piercing gaze, designed to intimidate and cow the patient into submission to his will. The treatment meted out to King George III by the mad-doctor Francis Willis exemplifies how the means of therapy paid scant regard to rank or status.[30]

The aspect of patient management that most aroused the ire of the lunacy reformers was the employment of physical or mechanical restraint. The use of chains, leg locks, wrist locks, straps, restraint chairs, strait-jackets, and a number of other contrivances, was widespread in private and public asylums, despite the well-publicized success of the more liberal regime of the York Retreat, and the later application of the 'non-restraint' system in public asylums from the late 1830s onwards. Restraint was always more prevalent, as a means of maintaining control, in asylums where numbers of staff were limited by the need to keep costs down. For some mad-doctors, like Thomas Arnold of Leicester, the issue involved principle as well as money:

Chains should never be used but in the case of poor patients, whose pecuniary circumstances will not admit of such attendance as is necessary to procure safety without them.

A similar position had been expressed by Thomas Monro of Bethlem Hospital in 1815. Patients there were routinely manacled as a means of reducing staff costs. However, in his private asylum Monro adopted a different approach; chains were not used as they were 'fit only for pauper lunatics; if a gentleman was put in irons he would not like it'. In reality it was mainly in those asylums or wards with pauper patients that low levels of staffing led to high levels of mechanical restraint. However, these means of control were available and used for all classes of patient. The records of public and private asylums demonstrate that there was frequently little hesitation in employing the techniques of restraint even for the wealthiest or most socially exalted. The need to exercise due control over the wayward superseded most observances of class status.[31]

## CONCLUSIONS

Any historical consideration of the nature of class structures and class relations is always liable to become rather complicated. In the late eighteenth and nineteenth centuries, these structures and relations were in a state of almost perceptible transition, as the idea of class superseded the legacy of rank and order. To try to analyse the interaction between class and mental disorder, with its stigma and the range of other attitudes which surrounded it, becomes a complex exercise, replete with obstacles. The resulting picture is inevitably mixed and inconsistent.

Clearly, within both the public and private asylum sectors, there were attempts to retain at least the pretence of distinction between social classes. In the public asylum, with its altruistic base, there was the objective of providing a public service unblemished by commercial considerations. To do so had to include a reflection of the social norms of the wider society. For the private asylum proprietor, this approach made sound business sense in the drive to attract custom. The families of those confined, burdened by the loss they had experienced and by the fear of social disgrace, expected some semblance of standards to be maintained within the asylum. They also expected efforts to enable the patient to retain his or her dignity, in case they should recover sufficiently to resume a place in society. However, the impression remains that demarcations of facilities and of aspects of service provision often formed a superficial veneer over a system that was rather less discerning. The façade was exposed by Select Committees, by Lunacy Commissioners, by articulate ex-patients, and by polemical novelists like Charles Reade.[32]

The reality is probably that attitudes towards the lunatic, in the nineteenth century as in the twentieth century, were characterized by double standards. The loss of reason was likely also to mean the loss of status, which 'cure' could never quite bring back. It was not only the illness itself which brought about this loss. The nature of the treatment which mentally disordered people received served to reinforce this further. Heroic treatments, like bleeding, blistering and purging, and the administration of cold baths, were great equalizers. Mechanical restraint, with all its connotations of punishment and degradation, served to place a question mark over the recipient's humanity. A person whose loss of reason led to behaviour which required severe measures to keep it under control had at least temporarily sacrificed the entitlement to be treated as a civilized being. In this circumstance, the nobleman was scarcely better off than the pauper.

With the triumph of the lunacy reform movement, epitomized in the legislation of 1845, there was a serious attempt to impose a more enlightened, albeit paternalistic, ethos on the care of the mentally disordered. The new model asylum offered the opportunity to provide an alternative to the 'less eligibility' philosophy of the workhouse for at least one section of the disadvantaged poor. These asylums were constructed, furnished and equipped with the intention of providing standards well above what most of the inmates had been used to in their own homes. In many cases this meant a deliberate attempt to inculcate some attributes of middle-class respectability.[33] At the same time, the segregation of classes became almost complete, as private patients were moved out of county asylums and paupers were removed from private asylums. The class delineations characteristic of a mature, industrializing society would remain at the core of the lunatic asylum system for generations to come.

# NOTES

I should like to thank Roy Porter for his comments on the original draft of this chapter. Thanks also to the Wellcome Trust; and the County Record Offices of Gloucestershire, Hereford and Worcester, Nottinghamshire and Staffordshire and the Lichfield Joint Record Office for permission to cite from their archive collections.

1 R. Porter, *English Society in the Eighteenth Century* (Harmondsworth, 1982) pp. 63–112; H. Perkin, *The Origins of Modern English Society* (London, 1985 edn), pp. 18–38, 176–216; J.C.D. Clark, *English Society 1688–1832* (Cambridge, 1985), pp. 68–106; R.S. Neale, *Class in English Society l680–1850* (Oxford, 1971); E.P. Thompson, *The Making of the English Working Class* (Harmondsworth, 1968 edn), 'Eighteenth-century English society: class struggle without class?', *Social History*, **III**, 2 (May 1978), 133–65.

2 R. Porter, *Mind Forg'd Manacles: A History of Madness in England from the Restoration to the Regency* (Cambridge, 1987) Ch. III.

3 Ibid.; W.L. Parry-Jones, *The Trade in Lunacy* (London, 1972), pp. 9–15, 39–42, 121–3; C. Mackenzie, *Psychiatry for the Rich: A History of Ticehurst Asylum, 1792–1917* (London, 1992), pp. 6–16; *Berrows Worcester Journal*, 24 Nov. 1791.

4 Porter, *Mind Forg'd Manacles*, Chs III–IV; Parry-Jones, *Trade in Lunacy*, Chs VII–VIII; A. Digby, *Madness, Morality and Medicine: A Study of the York Retreat, 1796–1914* (Cambridge, 1985).

5 *Report of Select Committee to Enquire into the State of Lunatics*, (Parliamentary Papers (PP) (1807), II; *Select Committee on the State of Madhouses*, PP (1814–15), IV; *Select Committee on Madhouses*, PP (1816), VI; 48 Geo. III, cap. 96; A. Bailey, 'The founding of the Gloucestershire county asylum, now Horton Road hospital, Gloucester, 1792–1823', *Trans. Bristol and Gloucs. Archaeological Society*, **XC** (1971), 178–91; A. Foss and K. Trick, *St Andrews Hospital, Northampton: The First Hundred and Fifty Years, 1838–1988* (Cambridge, 1989), pp. 7–39; B. Cashman, *A Proper House: Bedford Lunatic Asylum, 1812–1860* (Bedford, 1992), pp. 1–41; K. Jones, *A History of the Mental Health Services* (London, 1972), pp. 89–96.

6 A. Scull, *The Most Solitary of Afflictions: Madness and Society in Britain, 1700–1900* (London, 1993), Chs III, VI; *Report of the Metropolitan Commissioners in Lunacy to the Lord Chancellor* (1844); P. McCandless, 'Build! Build! The controversy over the care of the chronically insane in England, 1855–1870', *Bulletin of the History of Medicine*, **LIII** (1979), 553–74.

7 R. Porter, 'The rage of party: A glorious revolution in English psychiatry?', *Medical History*, **XXVII** (Jan. 1983), 35–50, at 42–7; W.A.F. Browne, *What Asylums Were, Are, and Ought To Be* (Edinburgh,

1837; repr. London, 1991), pp. 59–61; M. Donnelly, *Managing the Mind: A Study of Medical Psychology in Early Nineteenth Century Britain* (London, 1983), pp. 124–39.

8   N. Roberts, *Cheadle Royal Hospital: A Bicentenary History* (Altrincham, 1967), pp. 6–7; A. Digby, 'Changes in the asylum: the case of York, 1777–1815', *Economic History Review*, Second Series, **XXXVI**, 2 (May 1983), p 218–39, at 219.

9   Porter, *Mind Forg'd Manacles*, pp. 129–32; Bailey, 'Founding of Gloucs county asylum'; Hereford and Worcester County Record Office (CRO), Hereford branch, 560/8, Lady-Day, 1799, Nottinghamshire CRO, SO/HO/1/1/1, 1 Nov. 1803, 5, 12 Oct. 1808, SO/HO/1/3/1; Staffordshire CRO, Q/AIc, *Considerations on the Lunatic Asylum Intended to be Erected in the County of Stafford*; *Staffordshire Advertiser*, 21 Mar. 1812, 26 Sept. 1818.

10  *Ninth Report of the Commissioners in Lunacy* (1855), app. B, p. 67; *Charitable Institution for the Insane of the Middle Classes: Proceedings at a Public Meeting* (Stafford, 1851, copy in William Salt Library, Stafford), pp. 4, 5, 8 (main quote).

11  Birmingham Reference Library, *Birmingham Borough Lunatic Asylum, Second Annual Report* (Feb. 1853), p. 14, *Sixth Annual Report* (Jan. 1857), pp. 28–9, Warwickshire CRO, CR1664/30, *Warwickshire County Lunatic Asylum, Annual Report 1859* (Jan. 1860), p. 6.

12  *S.C. on the State of Madhouses* (1814–15), p. 128.

13  Lichfield Joint Record Office, D25/3/3, 29 Dec. 1779, 2 June 1808; Warwickshire CRO, QS24/I/i/xi; Mackenzie, *History of Ticehurst*, pp. 35–75.

14  Donnelly, *Managing the Mind*, pp. 38–9; W.A.F. Browne, *What Asylums Were*, pp. 199–202.

15  *S.C. on the State of Madhouses* (1814–15), pp. 50–2, 81; *S.C. on Madhouses* (1816), p. 37; *Journal of the House of Lords*, **XL**, (1828), 721.

16  *S.C. on Madhouses* (1814–15), p. 51; Mackenzie, *Ticehurst*, pp. 70–5, 90–1.

17  Parry-Jones, *Trade in Lunacy*, p. 58; A. Scull, *Most Solitary of Afflictions*, pp. 81–2; L.D. Smith, 'Duddeston Hall and the "trade in lunacy", 1835–65', p. 17, *The Birmingham Historian*, **IX** (1992), 16–22; *Report of the Commissioners in Lunacy Relative to the Haydock Lodge Lunatic Asylum*, PP (1847), XLIX, pp. 3–14; *Metropolitan Commissioners in Lunacy* (1844), pp. 41–2.

18  Nottinghamshire CRO, SO/HO/1/1/1, 12 Oct. 1808, hand-bill, 'An address on the subject of an intended asylum for lunatics' (quote), 7 Dec. 1808; Roberts, *Cheadle Royal Hospital*, p. 29.

19  Nottinghamshire CRO, SO/HO/1/1/1, 29 Apr. (quote), 15, 29 Nov. 1809, 4 Oct. 1810.

20   W. Stark, *Remarks on Public Hospitals for the Cure of Mental Derange-ment* (Edinburgh, 1807), pp. 14 (quote), 16, 19; Nottinghamshire CRO, DD177/1/2, *Sixth Annual Report of the General Lunatic Asylum* (Oct. 1816); *S.C. on the State of Madhouses* (1814–15), evidence of Rev. J.T. Becher, p. 177; Staffordshire CRO, D550/2, 27 Mar. 1819; *Staffordshire Advertiser*, 26 Sept. 1818.

21   *S.C. on the State of Madhouses* (1814–15), p. 177. The former Glouces-ter asylum on Horton Road was standing derelict at the time of writing, awaiting development for commercial purposes. The grandeur of the original central part of the building is still clearly visible.

22   Browne, *What Asylums Were*, pp. 153–5; A. Scull, *The Asylum as Utopia: W.A.F. Browne and the Mid-Nineteenth Century Consolidation of Psychiatry* (London, 1991); M. Williams, *History of Crichton Royal Hospital 1839–1989* (Dumfries and Galloway Health Board, 1989), pp. 19–27. The term 'alienist' had tended to replace the earlier mad-doctor', as 'asylum' had replaced 'madhouse'.

23   Staffordshire CRO, D550/63, 17 Oct. 1829, D644/10/3, J. Wilkes to H. Philips; Gloucestershire CRO, HO22/1/1, 23 Dec. 1839; *S.C. on the State of Madhouses* (1814–15), p. 177.

24   *Report from Select Committee on the Hereford Lunatic Asylum*, minutes of evidence (PP 1839, IX), pp. 5, 47, 48, 53, 62, 66, 73, Appendix, pp. 182, 187; *S.C. on the State of Madhouses* (1814–15), p. 43; *S.C. on Madhouses* (1816), p. 52; Gloucestershire CRO, HO22/1/1, 22 May 1823; Staffordshire CRO, D550/1, *Report of the Visiting Justices as to the Necessity for Erection of Additional Buildings at the Staffordshire General Lunatic Asylum* (February 1848).

25   *Oulton Retreat, near Stone, Staffordshire* (hand-bill in possession of the author); *S.C. on the State of Madhouses* (1814–15), evidence of E. Wakefield, pp. 51–2; Smith, 'Duddeston Hall', p. 17; E. Rickman, *Madness, or the Maniac's Hall* (1841), pp. iii, 247.

26   Digby, *York Retreat*, pp. 60–6; Browne, *What Asylums Were*, p. 196.

27   M. Fears, 'The moral treatment of insanity: a study in the social construction of human nature' (unpublished Ph.D thesis, Univer-sity of Edinburgh, 1978), pp. 129, 230–62; *S.C. on the State of Mad-houses* (1814–15), p. 21, evidence of E. Wakefield, p. 126, evidence of T. Bakewell, p. 128, evidence of E. Latham; *Imperial Magazine*, Mar. 1828, cols 230–1; L.D. Smith, 'To cure those afflicted with the disease of insanity: Thomas Bakewell and Spring Vale asylum', *History of Psychiatry*, **IV** (1993), 107–27, at 123.

28   Digby, *York Retreat*, pp. 34–53; Mackenzie, *Ticehurst*, pp. 53–6, 70, 90, 140–1; Smith, 'Thomas Bakewell', pp. 121–3; L. D. Smith, 'Eighteenth-century madhouse practice: the Prouds of Bilston', pp. 46, 51–2, *History of Psychiatry*, **III** (1992), 45–52; *S.C. on the State*

*of Madhouses* (1814–15), p. 128 (quote); *S.C. on Madhouses* (1816), p. 52, evidence of W. Ricketts; Staffordshire CRO, D550/6, 3 May 1852, Q/AIp/6, 29 Oct. 1845.

29  L.D. Smith, 'Behind closed doors: lunatic asylum keepers, 1800–1860', pp. 305–9, *Social History of Medicine*, **I**, 3 (1988), 301–27; Rickman, *Madness*, pp. 219–20; J. Perceval, *A Narrative of the Treatment Experienced by a Gentleman During a State of Mental Derangement* (London, 1838), pp. 180–1, 191–2, 200, 231 (London, 1840), II, pp. 227–8; Mackenzie, *Ticehurst*, Chs 3, 5; Gloucestershire CRO, HO22/8/1, *Annual Reports of Gloucestershire County Lunatic Asylum*, 1841, 1842.

30  I. Macalpine and R.A. Hunter, *George III and the Mad Business* (London, 1969), pp. 269–72; Porter, *Mind Forg'd Manacles*, pp. 209–11, 220–2.

31  J. Conolly, *Treatment of the Insane Without Mechanical Restraints* (London, 1856, 1973 edn), pp. 136, 143, 299–326; Porter, *Mind Forg'd Manacles*, pp. 125, 142; Parry-Jones, *Trade in Lunacy*, pp. 174–9; T. Arnold, cited in R.A. Hunter and I. Macalpine, *Three Hundred Years of Psychiatry, 1535–1860* (London, 1964), p. 469; *Select Committee on Pauper Lunatics in the County of Middlesex and on Lunatic Asylums* PP (1826–27), VI, pp. 78–92; Staffordshire CRO, D550/62; Hereford and Worcester CRO (Worcester branch), b125, BA710/l(i).

32  N. Hervey, 'Advocacy or folly: the Alleged Lunatics' Friend Society, 1845–63', *Medical History*, **XXX** (1986), pp. 245–75; J. Perceval, *A Narrative of the Treatment Experienced by a Gentleman*; R. Paternoster, *The Madhouse System* (London, 1841); T. Mulock, *British Lunatic Asylums, Public and Private* (Stafford, 1858); C. Reade, *Hard Cash: A Matter of Fact Romance* (London, 1863).

33  J. Cranmer, *Asylum History: Buckinghamshire County Pauper Lunatic Asylum: St John's* (London, 1990), pp. 35, 39, 47; *Birmingham Borough Lunatic Asylum, Sixth Annual Report*, p. 27; Warwickshire CRO, CR1664/30, *Annual Report* (1858), p. 7.

# 8

# Henrietta Stannard and the Social Emancipation of Women, 1890–1910

## OWEN ASHTON

It was the prominent late Victorian novelist, Henrietta Eliza Vaughan Stannard (1856–1911), who, in the last years of the nineteenth century, first accorded the radical-journalist William Edwin Adams (1832–1906) a measure of public recognition and respectability for his contribution to movements of progress, culture and humanity. Writing in March 1893 in her own *Winter's Magazine*, a nationally circulating penny weekly for women, she paid warm tribute to Adams's diverse talents, breadth of interests and causes which he championed in and through the world of provincial journalism. Stannard's biographical résumé, accompanied by a portrait of her subject taken in old age, made great play in juxtaposing Adams's present 'days of matured serenity' with the decidedly turbulent character of his Chartist past, in order to emphasize his remarkable upward social mobility and public influence on Tyneside. Next, she fulsomely acknowledged his skills in investing the *Weekly* with 'all the charm of a first-class family magazine' which had made it, in words borrowed from fellow journalist and novelist, Joseph Hatton, 'the most wonderful, the most interesting and the most remarkable paper that ever was produced in England or anywhere else'.[1] Pride of place, however, for Stannard in assessing Adams's work focused on two related activities: firstly, the formation in 1876 of his 'Dicky Bird Society' in the 'Children's Corner' which, in stressing kindness to animals as its main aim, had by 1893 secured a world-wide membership of nearly a quarter of a million; and, secondly, within the broad spectrum of campaigns against the cruelty of fashion that exploited animals for decorative purposes, his unequivocal support for her own successful nation-wide dress reform crusade known as the 'No-Crinoline' League agitation.

An obvious but intriguing question must surely be this: who exactly was this famous woman who had so much in common with a radical like W.E. Adams? No one, to date, has accorded Henrietta Stannard, better known by her pseudonym, 'John Strange Winter', the rightful recognition she deserves as an eminent Victorian, although Helen Black did devote a chapter to the author in her influential *Notable Women Authors of the Day* (1893), and the *Strand Magazine* in February 1895 featured her in one of their long-running series on Victorian celebrities.[2] Save for a brief eulogy by Adams in his *Memoirs of a Social Atom* (1903), a hagiographical biography by her author-friend Oliver Bainbridge in 1916, and a *Dictionary of National Biography* entry in 1920 outlining her contribution to public life, Stannard's reputation virtually died with her.[3]

It is not difficult to explain why historians and literary scholars have long found Mrs Stannard insufficiently important to merit attention. On the one hand, she was an accomplished professional married woman to whom other writers and journalists of her sex turned both for comment and inspiration on 'the woman question'. On the other hand, however, whilst a signatory to the women's suffrage campaigns of the decade, she did not figure prominently enough because she was too much of a singularity and too little inclined to join in other recognizably feminist causes, such as those embracing working-class women's employment or middle-class women's education. Nor was she in literary terms one of the 'new women' novelists of the 1890s, whose self-image and work featured a strong measure of independence in the public sphere of the time. The subject matter of her novels, of which over 100 were published, focused principally on garrison life and women and the regiment, and the wives and children of military heroes; but such fiction, with its association with the late Victorian and Edwardian imperial age, did not translate well after the carnage of the First World War.[4]

In recent years a hint of recognition has at least surfaced in a number of ways. Firstly, in a crop of scholarly writings on the modern novel and its readers, we catch a glimpse of Stannard's creative and literary talents.[5] Peter Keating, for example, exploring author–publisher relations, cites how aspiring writers of the day were advised by Leopold Wagner in *How to Publish* (1898) to establish a reputation for specialist fiction and added in support of this advice: 'Mr. Kipling is identified with Indian life, Mrs. Stannard ('John Strange Winter') with cavalry life, Mr. G.R. Sims with London life (of a sort), while Mr. Anthony Hope, Mr. Machen, and others are all specialists in fiction.'[6] More substantial is the information on the range of Stannard's interests as outlined in entries in women's biographical dictionaries compiled by Janet Todd (1976) and Joanne Shattock (1993).[7] From both we begin to learn about those often interconnected issues which she embraced. These included the agitation as a women's dress reformer against the reintroduction of the crinoline; her concern for animal rights, child welfare and charitable work in general; her business flair and interest in journalism and the sale of toiletries; and, arguably, the general extent of her radicalism on women's rights as set out in *Winter's Weekly* or expressed amongst the sisterhood of London-based literary clubs.

Born in York on 13 January 1856 into a solidly middle-class family and within a stone's throw of the York Cavalry Barracks, Henrietta was the only daughter of Henry Vaughan Palmer, rector of St Margaret's, York, and his wife Emily Catherine Cowling. Before taking holy orders her father had been an officer in the Royal Artillery and was one of those selected to attend the coronation of Queen Victoria. Among the ancestresses of the Palmers was the celebrated actress, Hannah Pritchard, to whose memory a monument was erected in Westminster Abbey.[8] As a child, she appears to have displayed something of a rebellious streak and later recalled to Bainbridge: 'I never missed an opportunity of playing truant and attending a review. Races also were my keen delight, and I would ostensibly go to school, in reality watch a big race from some safe and unseen coign of vantage [sic].'[9]

Her high spirits at Bootham House School, York, resulted in being 'sent down'[10] and finishing her education under the supervision of 'masters at home'.[11] Here life was not entirely conventional. Whilst she was expected to conform by attending church regularly, her insatiable appetite for novels and poetry met with no parental restriction[12] — a practice that was highly unusual amongst Victorian children, particularly of her background.[13] Her vivid imagination and intimate knowledge of military mannerisms — two key features which millions of readers of her novels were later to enjoy— were first kindled by her father's stories about the prowess of the family's own ancestors and then by meeting uniformed neighbours and visitors, who told tales of army life at home or in the empire.[14] At fourteen she began a ten-year span of periodical writing, at first for the *London Society* and the *Yorkshire Chronicle*, and then for a longer period for the *Family Herald* under the pseudonym of 'Violet Whyte'; for the latter periodical she contributed over eight years a total of forty-two novelettes or short stories issued as supplements, besides many long romantic serials.[15] After her father's death in 1877 when she was twenty-one, she started writing in earnest. Her first successful publications in volume form were a collection of military sketches, composed in York, entitled *Cavalry Life: or Sketches and Stories In Barracks and Out* (1881), followed by *Regimental Legends* (1883).[16] Given the masculine culture both of the age and her subject matter, Henrietta's publishers induced her to adopt the *nom de plume*, 'John Strange Winter', the name of one of her own fictional characters in the novels; it was felt that both would 'stand a better chance of mercy at the hands of the critics'[17] if perceived to be the work of a man rather than a woman—the public immediately thereafter assumed the author to be a cavalry officer![18]

Following a whirlwind romance in the autumn of 1883—she became engaged within five days—Henrietta married Arthur Stannard, a civil engineer and ex-soldier who had served under General Gordon, on 26 February 1884 at Fulford, York.[19] Both emotionally and materially the marriage appears to have become more a partnership of equals or, as Helen Black puts it, 'the two—so perfect as one—working as it were hand in hand'.[20] The reason for this modification, so that husband and wife came to share common ground in the business domain, is attributable largely to Henrietta's remarkable talents and fame as an up-and-coming novelist. Shortly after their marriage and move to Putney, London, Arthur Stannard secured a contract to work in Brazil as an engineer in charge of sugar factory construction at a salary of £1,000 a year, but political troubles in Brazil precipitated the bankruptcy of his future employers, and an embarrassed Stannard suddenly found himself without employment. Whilst seeking new work he filled some of his spare time successfully negotiating the sale of his wife's last York-inspired manuscript, *Bootles' Baby: A Story of the Scarlet Lancers,* in August 1884 to the *Graphic*, in which periodical it appeared in serialized form during the spring of 1885.[21] Another tale of military life, *Bootles' Baby* was to become her best-known and most successful work, one which began to provide the young couple with an income equal to their needs.[22] Released subsequently in a one-shilling volume series in 1885, it sold over two million copies within ten years, was also dramatized at the Globe Theatre, London in 1889[23] and remained on tour until at least the end of 1893.[24] This commercial success coincided not only with Arthur Stannard's own in finding an engineering position with the Great Western Railway Company,[25] but also with more for Mrs Stannard as she again triumphed with yet another serialization of her fiction in the *Graphic*: in 1885 the story entitled *Houp-la*, which this time indicated her familiarity with and interest in the lives of children, appeared and attracted considerable attention; it, too, was then published in a cheap volume in London in 1886.[26]

Her reputation as a writer both on army life and now on children established, the couple took two important and joint decisions: firstly, they decided to remain and rear their young family in London rather than move to the post offered to Arthur in Cornwall; secondly, they began a highly unusual and complete partnership which in itself blurred the conventional boundaries for their social class and suggested a different conception of womanhood, that of the married professional mother. Thus Henrietta became the principal bread-winner who wrote novels, mixed in literary and cultural networks, whilst Arthur, 'who was an excellent man of business', managed from his study 'all his wife's affairs'.[27]

Between 1885 and 1904 Henrietta Stannard wrote prolifically and always under the pseudonym of 'John Strange Winter', even though the disclosure of her real identity to a curious reading public and her literary critics had become a well-known fact in the wake of her first flush of success.[28] From her pen came a steady stream of novels, including *Army Society* (1886), *Pluck* (1886), *Mignon's Secret: A Story of a Barrack Bairn* (1886), *Mignon's Husband* (1887), *A Siege Baby* (1887), *Beautiful Jim of the Blankshire Regiment* (1888), *Good-Bye* (1891), *The Major's Favourite* (1895), and *Cherry's Child* (1904).[29] Others, such as *Buttons* (1889) and *The Other Man's Wife* (1889), first appeared in serialized form, accompanied by flattering details of her literary accomplishments, in W.E. Adams's *Newcastle Weekly Chronicle*,[30] by this time a newspaper known locally as 'the pit-men's bible'; its readers also voted Stannard their fourth most popular author behind Mary Braddon, Walter Besant and Rider Haggard in a piece of Adams-inspired market research.[31] Still more, such as *A Fairy on Horseback* (1887) and *A Pair of Young Things* (1900) were published respectively as novelettes in the journals *Belgravia* and *Cassell's*.[32] Occasionally, too, as with *Confessions of a Publisher* (1885) — a light tale about a vanity publisher whose son loved a lady author writer — Stannard enjoyed commercial success in the United States, with a reprint of the novel in New York during 1892.[33]

Stannard's inspiration as a novelist came in part from the style of a number of authors including Wilkie Collins, Charles and Henry Kingsley, Whyte Melville and Charles Reade;[34] but ultimately the greatest influence was John Ruskin.[35] Not surprisingly, the two become firm friends and regular correspondents; she also visited him at his home in Sandgate, whilst he, in a letter to the *Daily Telegraph* on 17 January 1888, pronounced her to be 'the author to whom we owe the most finished and faithful rendering ever yet given of the character of the British soldier'. Part of her popularity, too, according to Janet Todd, stemmed from 'the light-hearted simplicity and tender pathos of her writings, for she expressed a preference for Anglo-Saxon over Latinate diction'.[36] But for Helen Black, who knew her intimately by the 1890s, it was a special mix of a number of talents that gave her a unique and mass appeal as a novelist: 'Fertile in imagination, acute in observation, sprightly and wholesome in style, there is a freshness and life in her books which charm alike old and young, rich and poor, at home and abroad.'[37] The practical and material results of Stannard's literary success found expression in all the trappings and realities of a solidly middle-class family way of life. Her rapid output, nurtured by the business acumen of her husband-manager, brought a level of income sufficient to maintain servants and 'a charming residence' at first in Putney,[38] and then in 1890 an even more spacious house with gardens in the villadom of Nevern Square, Earl's Court;[39] there also followed a long lease on a summer home at Wix on the Essex coast and, later in life, a residence in Dieppe in France.[40]

An active member of the Society of Authors by 1888,[41] first president by 1892 of the Writers' Club,[42] a Fellow of the Royal Society of Literature by 1893,[43] and a regular patron in the 1890s of the London stage,[44] Henrietta Stannard was at the same time an extremely devoted and caring mother. Indeed, she attributed her success in part to her happy marriage and the inspiring company of her offspring.[45] The first child, a daughter christened Audrey Noel, was born on Christmas Day, 1884; then came twins, a boy and a girl, who were named Eliot and Violet Mignon after two of their mother's creations in fiction; the fourth child, another girl, was christened Olive Nancy.[46] All four appear to have enjoyed a privileged yet progressive and creative childhood. Like their mother, the children were encouraged from an early age to express themselves on paper and to adopt a catholic taste in reading.[47] In adult life her son at least is known to have been an actor.[48]

However much the accomplished authoress, society woman, devoted mother and upholder of what both Black and Bainbridge then and others since have perceived to be a zealous domesticity,[49] Stannard displayed nevertheless a restless streak and, like Adams, was driven by a sense of duty to others outside of home and family. A woman of great industry, versatility and courage, she had a strong social conscience, enjoyed a challenge and had outspoken views on a number of contemporary social issues. Her biographer records, for example, how she intervened on two occasions whilst walking in the London streets to prevent a number of women and children from being further beaten either by irate spouses or drunken parents.[50] By outlining her activities as a journalist, rational dress campaigner, animal rights lover, philanthropist and purveyor of women's toiletries for hair and skin, we can begin to assess her modest contributions to the cause of middle-class married women for whom the possibility of embracing both a professional career and yet still acting as the centre of family life was beginning to be realized in the last decade of the nineteenth century.[51]

Early in 1891, at a time of unparalleled expansion in the market for women's journals,[52] a shrewd and business-like Mrs Stannard, sensitive to the new trends, launched her own illustrated penny weekly magazine for women under the title *Golden Gates*; it was altered after forty issues to *Winter's Weekly* 'in deference to the opinion of those who objected to the somewhat religious sound of the former name'.[53] This little magazine was, according to Janet Todd, the first weekly periodical to be exclusively owned, edited and published by a popular novelist.[54] Apparently, its 'fresh, frank individuality'[55] appealed not only to a growing army of single and lower-middle-class women readers,[56] for whom the spread of industrialism created new opportunities chiefly in a range of clerical posts and the retail distributive trade, but also to professional married women in paid employment for whom the domestic sphere was important but no longer perceived to be the scene of their only acceptable domain in life.[57]

Amongst the paper's regular features was an attractive mix of articles covering the world of dress, fashion, etiquette and beauty culture; fictional material in the form of serialized stories, romantic novelettes and inspirational poems by invited authors, as well as pieces by Stannard herself; entertaining snippets on society gossip, word puzzles, competitions, anecdotes, palmistry, and correspondents' letters; and, to complete the appeal to the family circle, instructive articles on child care and a children's corner in language directed to the young readers themselves. Whilst a great deal of attention was clearly paid to the concept of hearth and home, Stannard also offered readers a varied and stimulating diet which was both outgoing, improving and different. In the 'Editor's Thoughts' column, supplemented elsewhere in the paper by a feature entitled 'Subjects for Debate', she offered, for example, her own perspective on a wide range of topical issues. These included paid employment, as well as leisure activities, suitable for middle-class women, the question of their political equality with men, charity work in general, and two other rather idiosyncratic concerns which can only be alluded to here, namely her continuing defence of the ordinary British soldier against charges of drunkenness in barrack towns[58] and, secondly, her support for John Henniker Heaton, the Conservative MP for Canterbury (1885–1910) and leading postal reformer, and his campaign for an imperial penny postage charge to be common currency throughout the British empire.[59] One extra dimension to all these crusades was the provision of a portrait gallery giving lively biographical features of interesting people who were carefully selected by Stannard, in order to underline her admiration not only for their professional success, but also for the fact that they shared her goals. Included were the veteran novelist and active member of the Writers' Club, Mrs G. Linnaeus Banks, the leading English actress Ellen Terry, the famed English beauty Mrs Lillie Langtry, and the scientific dress reformer Dr Gustave Jaeger — all of whom were campaigners against the tyranny of fashion — the outstandingly successful newspaper and magazine proprietors, Cyril Arthur Pearson and Joseph Cowen, Jr.; the Irish dramatist and writer of fairy tales, Oscar Wilde; and, not least, the journalist friend and animal rights activist, W.E. Adams.[60]

Despite the fact that in September 1894 Stannard was forced by ill health to give up the 'double strain' of following her writing profession and editing the magazine,[61] the latter enjoyed a degree of success under her assistant, Florence White, until its final demise in 1895. Circulation figures do not exist by which to measure its success, but Stannard frequently referred in gratitude to the 'many thousands of readers' both in England and overseas, where it was listed as being on sale in New York, Toronto and Cape Town.[62] One correspondent summed up its appeal with these revealing comments: 'It is so suited to women like myself in what I may call the "lower middle class"—women with large families and small incomes. We cannot afford the expensive society papers but yet like to know how the world wags.'[63] Another indicator is the perceptive comments of fellow members of the English press: *The Lady's Pictorial* described it as 'now the best journal for the home';[64] *The Yorkshire Post* as 'having a decided individuality of its own'; the *South Wales Liberal* as exhibiting 'No namby pambyisms, but careful editing, vigorous writing, and interesting matter', and Adams's *Newcastle Weekly Chronicle* declared that 'it is already an assured success'.[65]

The key issues on which Stannard as editor offered her thoughts — the paid employment of women, their level of involvement in politics and how they might occupy their leisure time — all suggest that she was at least a cautious advocate of their increased emancipation and participation in the public domain. In her view the middle-class ideal of the leisured female was to be eschewed: 'The woman who exists only for the society treadmill and for the purposes of seeking pleasure and of social ambition, must in time grow utterly narrow and cramped in her mind.'[66] Moreover, she was not averse to offering a class perspective by reminding fellow privileged readers of the un-enviable plight of more unfortunate labouring sisters:

Nobody splutters about the women who make nails or the women who go hoeing potatoes and turnips. But let a widow woman in a higher sphere of life take to journalism or novel-writing or the study of medicine, or any other profession by which she can make a decent living, and at once there is an outcry from the unapproachable men that she is taking the bread out of their mouths.[67]

Stannard believed that 'the irresistible force of circumstances' was encouraging the spread of opportunities for all women, but particularly those in salaried and clerical-based employment, albeit at low rates of remuneration.[68] A champion, too, of equal pay, she urged women to utilize their own power in order to do what the men had achieved:

Women, the world over, are numerically stronger than men, and could rule the universe if their strength and energy were properly organized and directed . . . It would be an easy matter for lady workers to band together their now scattered forces, and insist on a fair and equal remuneration being granted them.[69]

This sense of belonging to a sisterhood of working and professional women found expression in Stannard's unswerving commitment to, and membership of, a special community of literary and press-based women's clubs.[70] Associated with the Writers' Club at 190 Fleet Street from its inception in 1892, Mrs Stannard strove as its first president both to give it a broad foundation and to offer help to the cause of struggling women writers.[71] She instituted a weekly Friday afternoon *rendez-vous* for house-teas in their third floor rooms, provided a reference library, built up club finances and used the platform of *Winter's Weekly* to report on proceedings, as well as comment on the increase and nature of the membership.[72]

A similar spirit informed her work of improving the status and condition of women journalists. Aware of the extremely busy and often mentally demanding workaday world of fellow professionals — one that demanded much 'staying power'[73] — she wholeheartedly welcomed and publicized the founding in June 1894 of the Society of Women Journalists, a women's press club with rooms in New Bond Street,[74] which was intended to provide both a business centre and social retreat for all members. Elected to its executive committee, she also became president between 1901 and 1903 in which post she helped promote 'a policy of professionalism as distinct from cliquism and made membership a sort of freemasonry which impressed the outer world with the solidarity of women journalists'.[75] Historians in recent years have indicated how the 1890s were important for the proliferation of women's clubs in expanding members' career horizons.[76] What is pinpointed here in the specific networking activities of founding members like Henrietta Stannard is the growing independence not only of the middle-class woman whose education and professional experience had given her a taste of her own capabilities, but also the phenomenon of the married woman who was determined to pursue a worthwhile career outside the home and family.[77]

Stannard's strong sense of the social solidarity of professional women was not matched by a similar level of political awareness on behalf of her class and gender. Up until 1892 at least, it is abundantly clear from reports in *Winter's Weekly* that she took virtually no interest in the women's franchise movement and little for that matter in politics generally.[78] Yet her position began to change in May 1892 following an article by the well-known journalist, G. A. Sala, advocating the franchise for all qualified women in the wake of the political furore provoked by Sir Albert Rollit's women's suffrage bill which excluded married women.[79] Stannard's reaction to Sala's article reveals a mixture of innate caution and political pragmatism:

It is so clear and forcible, and so full of commonsense. It has almost converted me; for up to now I have been a most lukewarm thinker on the subject. I don't want the franchise for myself, but at the same time if any other women do want it, I don't see why they should not have it, when they possess the necessary property qualification.[80]

Thereafter, *Winter's Weekly* carried occasional political features such as postcard competitions on the 'question of women's political equality with men'[81] and commentary on the slow progress of women's suffrage petitions;[82] but the whole subject of politics tended to be treated as low-key and certainly compartmentalized from other concerns, not least her most prominent cause—the agitation against the revival of the crinoline.[83]

In Chapter LX of *Memoirs of a Social Atom* entitled 'People of Some Importance In Their Day', Adams recorded that 'Mrs.

Stannard deserves credit for a great public service when she scotched and crushed a threatened revival of the crinoline'.[84] In the world of dress reform Stannard had long campaigned against the cruelty of women's fashion, both in terms of the controversial issues of tightly laced corsets[85] and millinery decorations derived from the plumage of native or exotic birds.[86] In her magazine she also offered her own views on the need for more practical and healthy dress for work and recreation, particularly in relation to the new and liberating cycling craze,[87] and was very much in favour of the work of Lady Harberton, fellow member of the Writers' Club and president of the Rational Dress Society, the leading pressure group for the modernization of women's underwear and outer garments between 1881 and the late 1890s.[88]

In the whimsical world of fashion, the threatened re-appearance in 1893 of the crinoline or steel-hooped petticoat, symbolic of women's dependency and for many what was debilitating, deforming and dangerous about the nature of their dress in the 1860s, posed a new and considerable challenge to all concerned. Aware of the fact that money had actually been invested in anticipation of the fashion reappearing, Mrs Stannard and Lady Harberton rapidly found themselves at loggerheads over the best strategy to adopt to circumvent the threat.[89] Such a division may also help explain why in the history of the Rational Dress Society the work of Mrs Stannard has been ignored. According to Bainbridge, their contemporary, Harberton held to the belief that

if women really wish to avoid crinolines, the way to do so is not by the formation of leagues. That was tried with regard to the 'dress improver' fashion of four or five years ago, and was absolutely useless. The only way in which the 'anti-crinoline' apostles could hope to succeed would be their beginning at once — each one alone — to refuse to have any skirt made more than three yards in circumference. For without a crinoline the wider skirts are only uncomfortable, but do not look very different when on.[90]

To Stannard, this position was both complacent and contradictory to the very spirit and activities of the Rational Dress Society itself. She firmly believed that only by their social solidarity could women conduct their own agitation, make their protest known and effectively resist the unacceptable face of fashion.[91]

Anything less would, in Stannard's own words, mean that: 'it will be held up against her as a proof that, after all her declarations and efforts to prove the contrary, she is *not* a creature to be taken seriously.'[92] Unresolved, the outcome was Stannard's unilateral action in forming the 'No-Crinoline' League and leading what Bainbridge refers to as the 'Anti-Crinoline Crusade'.[93]

She launched the agitation via the platform of *Winter's Weekly* towards the middle of January 1893 with a call for women to send in written pledges and to do all in their power to oppose the crinoline's revival.[94] Astonishingly, within three weeks over 21,000 women had rallied round the cause of persistent and public declarations against the male-run fashion houses' plans.[95] Support was drawn not only from all parts of the villadom and suburbdom of Britain, but also from titled ladies in Italy and Switzerland, from dress reform activists in the United States and sympathizers in the outposts of the empire.[96] Leading signatories in England whose names were emblazoned across the pages of her magazine included, amongst others, the Countess of Strafford, Lady Hornby and Lady Foster, the wives of millowners in Blackburn and Bradford respectively, Henrietta, Lady Brooke of Warwick, the Dowager Lady Lighton, the Hon. Mrs Livingstone, Mrs Lillie Langtry, and Mrs Samuel Plimsoll, wife of the Liberal MP.[97] She also claimed the backing of two women's pressure groups, the Ladies' Health Society and the Women's Progressive Society.[98] As part of her campaign of consciousness-raising, Stannard diligently published lists of members' names and addresses, wrote inspiring prose and poetry on the perils of readopting 'The Crin', organized the production and distribution of members' 'No-Crinoline' League paper and dress insignia, and carried reports of drawing-room meetings on discussions about 'the history, absurdity, and evils of the crinoline'.[99]

Although Stannard saw the campaign to be 'solely a women's strike against the tyranny of a certain set of men',[100] she shrewdly looked to extend her range of support by campaigning in an influential quarter: the world of male-dominated journalism. In London, she attempted to influence, for example, the content of the new cycling magazine *Wheeling* with the argument to its editor that if the reintroduction of the crinoline went ahead women would find it virtually impossible to mount their bicycles; in turn the cycling boom would falter and sales of magazines dependent on that new leisure interest would suffer.[101] In the provinces, Stannard found some of her warmest support in the columns of W.E. Adams's widely read *Newcastle Weekly Chronicle*, by now a paper with a reputation for combining innovation with a range of personal interest stories.[102] One pioneering aspect, according to John Saville, and certainly a novel feature in British journalism generally at the time, was the publication in the *Weekly* of a 'Ladies Column'. Here, Adams, joined in 1889 by his talented daughter Ada, who wrote under the pseudonym of 'Geraldine', became a keen supporter of the 'No-Crinoline' League.[103] Such a position, of course, fitted in well with Adams's long-term campaigning against the cruelty of fashion, particularly that which stemmed from killing animals for their skins for beauty garments and birds for their plumage.[104]

Metropolitan–provincial links of this type help explain why Stannard's protest movement met with such widespread and spontaneous support. Their first sign of success came with the news in March 1893 that Alexandra, HRH the Princess of Wales, an influential figure in court fashion circles and beyond, had unequivocally declared against wearing the crinoline in any form.[105] By the end of the year, such was the head of steam built up and level of resentment manifested by Stannard's publicity work amongst the middling classes that the obnoxious project was quietly dropped by the leading London dress houses, though she remained ever vigilant lest the threat might return.[106]

Stannard was the first to admit that with regard to the crinoline agitation women had 'united over a comparatively small question'.[107] Yet the significance of the success should not be missed. Firstly, as the suppression of the crinoline was the only object of the League, it should now be ranked alongside the phenomenon of the new bicycle boom in explaining the revitalization in 1894 of the fortunes of the Rational Dress Society.[108] Secondly, the League gave apolitical women like Stannard a greater degree of self-confidence and awareness, a feeling which she shared with her readers:

I have, like a great many other married women, very little sympathy with the Women's Rights movements, and detest anything which suggests comparison and competition between the sexes; but I do rejoice to think that the women of to-day have learned to judge for themselves on the subjects primarily interesting them.[109]

Lastly, the composition of the 'No-Crinoline' League is of interest to historians of social movements. Geoffrey Crossick has observed that the emergence of the British lower middle class — shopkeepers and small businessmen, managers, clerks, teachers and civil servants — has been neglected because of 'their sheer lack of heroism . . . They fail to do anything striking'.[110] The activities of Stannard's 'No Crinoline' League, drawn as it was from the many pledges of the wives, mothers and sisters of this broad social group, must surely suggest, at the very least, an important caveat to the received view of their inactivity on the historical stage.

For Mrs Stannard, dress reform activity was also inseparable from support for animal rights. She was, like Adams, both a staunch supporter and publicist for the campaign led by the Society for the Protection of Birds against the use of any bird's feathers for decoration or fashion-based purposes.[111] Elsewhere in her writings, as in the novel *He Went for a Soldier* (1890), she made 'indignant comments' on the issue of overloaded hackney carriages with broken-down horses, which led to the passing of by-laws by Fulham Borough Council to bring such vehicles under effective police supervision.[112] So intense was Stannard's love of animals that Bainbridge described her as 'a red-hot anti-vivisectionist', following her membership then presidency of the Clapham Branch of the National Anti-Vivisection Society in the 1890s.[113] At about the same time another honour befell her: she was made an honorary member by Adams of his 'Dicky Bird Society' which ran in the 'Children's Corner' of the *Newcastle Weekly Chronicle*; it stressed kindness to animals and all living things as its basic objective; it also numbered John Ruskin, Lord Tennyson, H.M. Stanley, Baroness Coutts and Sir Henry Irving amongst its eminent honorary officers.[114]

Other social concerns claimed her crusading zeal, too, not least one involving kindness towards children. When, for example, Adams first introduced Stannard to his younger readers in 1890, he described her as 'a well-known lady, who is excessively fond of children, and who is therefore just the person to be connected with our army of boys and girls'.[115] It was precisely through the public work of influential middle-class women like Henrietta Stannard that attitudes towards children were beginning to change in the last years of the nineteenth century. Norman McCord writes on the subject: 'Instead of treating them essentially as immature adults, society came to see them rather as a special category of individuals which required separate consideration. There was increased awareness, fed by an accumulation of evidence, that many children were in need of protection.'[116] Stannard was a life-long campaigner against corporal punishment for children and read a paper on the subject before members of the Pioneer Club, a haven for women of advanced views,[117] on 7 June 1894.[118] She also supported the work of the National Society for the Prevention of Cruelty to Children (founded 1889),[119] the financial upkeep of the Plaistow Day Nursery for working mothers in the East End,[120] and gave all the revenue derived from her novel, *A Soldier's Children* (1892), for the benefit of the Victoria Hospital for Children, Chelsea.[121]

Stannard's other charities included fund-raising for the Brompton Hospital for Consumption,[122] the League of the Silver Cord, an organization concerned with secret and excessive drinking, and all its attendant miseries for families in the middle-class home,[123] and the Girls' Guild of Good Life at Hoxton Hall, a philanthropic establishment for the educational and cultural improvement of factory girls in that district.[124]

In 1896 the ill health of both her husband and youngest daughter prompted Mrs Stannard to move to the seaside, and for the next five years the Villa des Rosiers at Dieppe in northern France became their family home; thereafter, until 1909, they alternated between residing in Putney and Dieppe during the summer months.[125] Life in Dieppe, as in London, was full and interesting. Stannard continued to write, but also branched out in new directions. Firstly, she became involved in the cultural affairs of Dieppe itself, particularly by publicizing the town's tourist attractions to prospective English visitors; it was also due to the joint efforts of her and a recovered Arthur Stannard, who became secretary, that the local golf club, a favourite venue for those from across the Channel, was founded.[126] In appreciation, the townspeople presented her in 1897 with a diamond ring 'for having written and induced others to write so favourably about the town, and for her zealous and practical interest in the efforts of those who desired to make Dieppe as attractive as possible to visitors'.[127]

Secondly, she turned her favourite hobby of making toilet preparations into a business, a move that became central to earning a livelihood after her publishers went bankrupt at the turn of the century and Stannard was left 'heavily in debt, and an unsecured creditor for a very large amount'.[128] Beauty culture, like dress reform, it should be remembered, had long been disapproved of, although a discreet use of cosmetics for skin enhancing was becoming generally acceptable by the end of the nineteenth century.[129] Here again Stannard was something of a pioneer and trend-setter. Overcoming criticism and indeed some public hostility for embarking on her new business venture,[130] Stannard's toilet preparations for both hair and skin came to be 'almost as much liked as her stories'.[131] She went on to win public recognition with the award of gold medals for her beauty lotions at, for example, the Colonial and Indian Exhibition held in London in 1905, the Food and Health Exhibition in London in 1906, the International Hygiene Exhibition in Vienna in 1906, and the Festival of Empire in London in 1911.[132]

Whilst getting out of a lift at Earl's Court station in the spring of 1911, Mrs Stannard slipped and fell on her elbow, damaging her arm very seriously. The wound never healed and complications followed. Confined to her bed for over twenty weeks at York House, Hurlingham Gardens, Putney, she died, aged 55, on 13 December 1911. According to the *Daily Chronicle*, it was her expressed wish to be cremated; this was subsequently carried out and the ashes interred at Woking Crematorium.[133]

Henrietta Stannard was a remarkably talented woman. Her detractors might suggest that she was no more than a self-publicist and shrewd middle-class woman intent on making a lot of money. What has been argued here, however, is that she deserves recognition for the fact that she took a prominent and active position in improving the status of professional and often married women writers of her time, worked at the centre of an embryonic sense of female collectivity which foiled an attempt by male-run fashion houses to revive and foist on them the crinoline, and was a tireless campaigner both for animal rights and children's welfare. What is also fascinating is the fact that she reconciled these demanding public activities with an equally strong commitment to domestic life and a virtual eschewal of politics as a form of action.

However much she might be viewed as an activist on the margins of women's causes, Stannard's career is nevertheless of some importance. An examination of her activities in this chapter helps throw more light on the nature of both the connections and shifting boundaries between the public and private spheres of a married, educated woman of the middle class;[134] it also suggests that educated and independent-minded women, like Stannard, went in for types of emancipation which they perceived to be more far-reaching than the immediate impact of the parliamentary vote could achieve.[135]

## NOTES

I wish to thank the following for their help or advice: Linda Coleing, Barbara Garlick, Kay Howard, Angela V. John, Clare Midgley, Ann Parry, David Rubinstein, Anne Scott, and Joanne Shattock.

1   *Winter's Magazine*, 25 March 1893, **V**, 104, 'Mr. W.E. Adams'. The paper was later called *Winter's Weekly*.
2   Helen C. Black, *Notable Women Authors of the Day* (Glasgow, 1893, repr. Temecula, CA, 1974), for Stannard see Ch 5, pp. 45–57; and 'Portraits of Celebrities', the *Strand Magazine*, 9 February 1895. p. 187. See also V.G. Plarr, 'Mrs. Arthur Stannard', *Men and Women of the Time: A Dictionary of Contemporaries* (London, 1899, fifteenth edn), p. 1028.
3   W.E. Adams, *Memoirs of a Social Atom* (London, 1903, 2 vols, repr. in 1 vol. with an introduction by John Saville, New York, 1969), pp. 622–3; Oliver Bainbridge, *John Strange Winter: A Volume of Personal Record* (London, 1916); and *Dictionary of National Biography* (Oxford, 1920), supplement, January 1901–December 1911, pp. 394–5.
4   Joseph McAleer, *Popular Reading and Publishing, 1914–1950* (Oxford, 1992), p. 34.
5   See Elaine Showalter, *A Literature of Their Own: British Women Novelists from Brontë to Lessing* (London, 1978, repr. 1979, 1984), pp. 58–9; Peter Keating, *The Haunted Study: A Social History of the English Novel 1875–1914* (London, 1989, repr. 1991), pp. 72–3, 340–1; Kate Flint, *The Woman Reader 1837–1914* (Oxford, 1993), pp. 222–3.
6   Keating, *The Haunted Study*, pp. 340–1.
7   See Janet Todd (ed.), *Dictionary of British Women Writers* (London, 1989, repr. 1991), pp. 726–7; Joanne Shattock, *The Oxford Guide to British Women Writers* (Oxford, 1993), pp. 467–8.
8   Bainbridge, *John Strange Winter*, p. 3.
9   Ibid., p. 4.
10  *Newcastle Weekly Chronicle*, 7 Sept. 1889, Literary Supplement. Article on John Strange Winter.
11  Ibid.
12  Bainbridge, *John Strange Winter*, pp. 5–6.
13  Todd, *Dictionary of British Women Writers*, p. 726.

14   Bainbridge, *John Strange Winter*, pp. 3–4.
15   *Newcastle Weekly Chronicle*, 7 Sept. 1889, Literary Supplement. The report states that 'she drew first blood from the *Yorkshire Chronicle*, her remuneration for a short story being ten shillings'. Two other literary ventures, according to Bainbridge, *John Strange Winter*, pp. 6–7 were 'Clotilde's vengeance' or 'The story of the French Revolution' and 'Wedding bells'; and reference to the *London Society* periodical is on p. 77.
16   *Newcastle Weekly Chronicle*, 7 Sept. 1889, Literary Supplement; see also Plarr, *Men and Women of the Time*, p. 1028.
17   Black, *Notable Women Authors of the Day*, p. 49.
18   *Dictionary of National Biography*, p. 395.
19   Todd, *Dictionary of British Women Writers*, p. 726.
20   Black, *Notable Women Authors of the Day*, p. 49.
21   Bainbridge, *John Strange Winter*, pp. 12–14, 89–90.
22   Ibid., p. 13.
23   *Dictionary of National Biography*, p. 395; Shattock, *The Oxford Guide to British Women Writers*, p. 468; and Todd, *Dictionary of British Women Writers*, p. 726.
24   Black, *Notable Women Authors of the Day*, p. 51. She states in 1893, 'there seems no intention of terminating its long run'.
25   Bainbridge, *John Strange Winter*, p. 14.
26   Plarr, *Men and Women of the Time*, p. 1028.
27   *Newcastle Weekly Chronicle*, 7 Sept. 1889, Literary Supplement. See also Adams, *Memoirs*, p. 622.
28   Plarr, *Men and Women of the Time*, p. 1028.
29   According to the *Dictionary of National Biography*, p. 395, 'there are 112 entries to her name in the British Museum Catalogue'. R.C. Alston, *A Checklist of Women Writers 1801–1900* (London, The British Library, 1990) pp. 410–11, lists seventy-three literary works by Stannard.
30   *Newcastle Weekly Chronicle*, 7 Sept. 1889, Literary Supplement for *Buttons: A Novel*, and *Newcastle Weekly Chronicle*, 6 Sept. 1890, Literary Supplement for *The Other Man's Wife*.
31   Owen R. Ashton, *W.E. Adams, Chartist, Radical and Journalist (1832–1906)* (Whitley Bay, Tyne and Wear, 1991), p. 112; and *Newcastle Weekly Chronicle*, 29 March 1893 and *Winter's Weekly*, 1 April 1893.
32   According to the University of Queensland, Australia, Victorian Fiction Research Guide no. 14, *A Fairy on Horseback* appeared in *Belgravia*, **92** (1897), 407–12, and VFRG no. 12, *A Pair of Young Things* in *Cassell's* **31** (1900/1), 488–8. VFRG no. 7 also reveals that Stannard had secured the serialization of *The Other Man's Wife* in *Tinsley's Journal*, **45** (1890) and **46** (1890/91).

33  This fact is cited in the bibliography of James Hepburn, *The Author's Empty Purse and the Rise of the Literary Agent* (London, 1968), p. 126.

34  *Newcastle Weekly Chronicle*, 7 Sept. 1889, Literary Supplement.

35  Ibid. See also Flint, *The Woman Reader*, p. 223.

36  Todd, *Dictionary of British Women Writers*, p. 726.

37  Black, *Notable Women Authors of the Day*, pp. 50–1.

38  *Newcastle Weekly Chronicle*, 7 Sept. 1889, Literary Supplement.

39  Black, *Notable Women Authors of the Day*, pp. 45–6.

40  Ibid., p. 51, and Plarr, *Men and Women of the Time*, p. 1028; *Winter's Weekly*, 18 March 1893, 'Answers to correspondents'.

41  Victor Bonham-Carter, *Authors by Profession: The Society of Authors* (London, 1978), Vol. 1, pp. 141, 158. The Society was established to help authors protect their literary property. According to Walter Besant, *Autobiography* (London, 1902), p. 220, when Stannard joined in 1888, there were 240 members including, for example amongst women, Charlotte Yonge, Eliza Lynn Linton and Mrs Humphry Ward.

42  Plarr, *Men and Women of the Time*, p. 1028. This Writers' Club was the 'first women's Press Club ever established'.

43  Ibid.

44  Bainbridge, *John Strange Winter*, pp. 106–7. Amongst her circle of actor friends were Sir Henry Irving and John Lawrence Toole.

45  Ibid., pp. 9–12, 15–19. See also Black, *Notable Women Authors of the Day*, pp. 54–5.

46  Bainbridge, *John Strange Winter*, pp. 15–17.

47  Ibid., pp. 17–19.

48  Ibid., p. 96 is accompanied by a black and white illustration of Eliot Stannard in the theatrical dress of Don Sylvio in a production of *Midshipman Easy*.

49  Black, *Notable Women Authors of the Day*, pp. 54–5; Bainbridge, *John Strange Winter*, pp. 17–18; and Shattock, *The Oxford Guide to British Women Writers*, p. 468.

50  Bainbridge, *John Strange Winter*, pp. 36–9.

51  David Rubinstein, *Before the Suffragettes: Women's Emancipation in the 1890s* (Brighton, 1986), pp. 69—89, 133–59, 214–28; and Barbara Caine, *Victorian Feminists* (Oxford, 1992), pp. 239–67.

52  See Cynthia L. White, 'An industry is born', *Women's Magazines 1693–1968* (London, 1970), Ch. 2, particularly pp. 58–91.

53  Black, *Notable Women Authors of the Day*, p. 56. See also *Golden Gates*, no. 40, 2 Jan. 1892, 'Answers to correspondents'. *Golden Gates* was kept as a subtitle.

54  Todd, *Dictionary of British Women Writers*, p. 726.

55  Black, *Notable Women Authors of the Day*, p. 56.

56  *Winter's Weekly*, 29 April 1893, 'Answers to correspondents'.

57   Ibid., 9 Jan. 1892, 'Editor's thoughts on membership of the Writers'
     Club'. See also Judith Rowbotham, *Good Girls Make Good Wives*
     (Oxford, 1989), pp. 251 and 264 for the opening up of the profes-
     sions to married women.

58   *Winter's Weekly*, 11 June 1892, 'Editor's thoughts: are soldiers
     drunkards?'

59   Ibid., 18 June 1892, 'Editor's thoughts on the imperial penny
     postage'.

60   See, for example, the Index to Vol. IV, *Winter's Weekly*, 1 Nov. 1892
     for a complete list of its content titles under various categories.

61   *Winter's Weekly*, 29 Sept. 1894, 'Editor's thoughts, farewell', and
     *Winter's Weekly*, 6 Oct. 1894, 'Editor's thoughts, greeting'.

62   Ibid., 29 Oct. 1892 and 17 Sept. 1892.

63   Ibid., 29 April 1893, 'Answers to correspondents'.

64   *Lady's Pictorial*, 5 May 1894.

65   *Winter's Weekly*, 27 Feb. 1892 contains all of these comments and
     many others printed within the confines of an eye-catching, half-
     page drawing of a large letter 'W'.

66   Ibid., 25 June 1892, 'Editor's thoughts'.

67   Ibid., 22 Sept. 1894, 'Editor's thoughts: shall women work?'

68   Ibid., 10 Nov. 1894, 'Editor's thoughts: women — the question of
     salaries'.

69   Ibid.

70   For the complete range of Stannard's involvements, see Bainbridge,
     'Mrs Stannard as an author', *John Strange Winter*, pp. 71–109, Ch V.

71   Ibid., pp. 104–5.

72   See, for example, *Winter's Weekly*, 9 Jan., 30 Jan., 17 June, 15 Oct.
     1892; 28 Jan. 1893. By October 1893 there were approximately 200
     members described as 'writing' women. Among its members were
     the novelists Mrs Linnaeus Banks, Miss Edna Lyall, Mrs Leith
     Adams, Mrs Kennard and Dora Russell; the poetess Mrs Augusta
     Webster; Miss Helen Blackburn, who succeeded the late Lydia
     Becker as head of the National Society for Women's Suffrage; Miss
     Lowe, the editor of the *Queen*; and Mrs Moberly Bell, wife of the
     editor of *The Times*.

73   Quoted from Emily Crawford, 'Journalism as a profession for women',
     *The Contemporary Review*, **64** (1893), 362–71, particularly 367.

74   *Winter's Weekly*, 9 June 1894, 'Editor's thoughts'.

75   Bainbridge, *John Strange Winter*, p. 105.

76   See, for example, Rubinstein, *Before the Suffragettes*, pp. 222–6; and
     Patricia Marks, *Bicycles, Bangs, and Bloomers: The New Woman in the
     Popular Press* (Lexington, 1990), particularly Ch. 4, pp. 117–46 on
     women's clubs.

77   Marks, *Bicycles, Bangs and Bloomers*, p. 117.

78  *Winter's Weekly*, 7 May 1892, 'Editor's thoughts: Mr. Gladstone's great mistake'. Stannard's lack of interest in politics was shared by some other women prominent in public life; see B. Harrison, *Separate Spheres: The Opposition to Women's Suffrage in Britain* (London, 1978), particularly pp. 111–25.

79  For the content, detail and reaction to Rollit's bill, see Rubinstein, *Before the Suffragettes*, pp. 143–5.

80  *Winter's Weekly*, 21 May 1892; *Sala's Journal*, 13 April 1892 contained his article on the Women's franchise.

81  *Winter's Weekly*, 26 Nov. 1892, 'Correspondence: post-card competition'.

82  Ibid., 23 June 1894, 'Indoors and out by "Mrs. Gadabout": women and the suffrage'.

83  See *Daily Chronicle*, 15 Dec. 1911, 'Death of John Strange Winter. Authoress who foiled attempt to revive the crinoline

84  Adams, *Memoirs*, p. 623.

85  See, for example, *Winter's Weekly*, 31 Dec. 1892, 'Indoors and out by "Mrs. Gadabout": the subject of tight-lacing'. For both contemporary and historical judgements on the controversy, see Valerie Steele, *Fashion and Eroticism: Ideals of Feminine Beauty from the Victorian Era to the Jazz Age* (Oxford, 1985), pp. 161–91; and Alison Lurie, *The Language of Clothes* (New York, 1981), pp. 220–5.

86  See, for example, *Winter's Weekly*, 9 Jan. 1892, 'Editor's thoughts'; 22 Oct. 1892, 'Editor's thoughts'; 4 March 1893.

87  Ibid., 26 Nov. 1892, 'Editor's thoughts'; 11 March 1893, 'Editor's thoughts'. For a critical evaluation of the impact of the new cycling craze on women's dress reform and emancipation, see Jihang Park, 'Sport, dress reform and the emancipation of women in Victorian England: a reappraisal', *International Journal of the History of Sport*, **6**, 1, May 1989, 10–30.

88  For the activities of the Rational Dress Society, see, for example, Stella Mary Newton, *Health, Art and Reason: Dress Reformers of the Nineteenth Century* (London, 1974), pp. 115–33; and Elizabeth Rouse, *Understanding Fashion* (Oxford, 1989). pp. 128–35.

89  Bainbridge, *John Strange Winter*, p. 114.

90  Ibid., pp. 114–15.

91  Ibid., pp. 117–18.

92  *Winter's Weekly*, 21 Jan. 1893, 'Death in our skirts' by John Strange Winter.

93  Bainbridge, *John Strange Winter*, the title of Ch. Vl, pp. 110–21.

94  *Winter's Weekly*, 21 Jan. 1893, 'Death in our skirts'. Winter had also sent two letters to the *Morning Post* and *Daily Graphic*, published 10 Jan. 1893, advertising the campaign.

95 *Daily Chronicle*, 15 Dec. 1911, 'Death of John Strange Winter'; and *Winter's Weekly*, 8 April 1893.
96 See *Winter's Weekly*, for example, 18 March 1893 and 8 April 1893, for the names of those enrolled in Italy, Switzerland, France, Dublin, India and the United States.
97 Ibid., 8 April 1893.
98 Ibid., 28 Jan. 1893, 'Crinolisation or Civilization?' by John Strange Winter.
99 See, for example, *Winter's Weekly*, 28 Jan. 1893 for the 'No-Crinoline' League supplement for both members' names and addresses, and the article cited in Note 98; *Winter's Weekly*, 4 March 1893, 'Answers to correspondents' on badges and brooches, and also drawing room meetings; and for poetry, see *Winter's Weekly*, 11 March 1893; for descriptions of the 'No-Crinoline' League paper and envelopes, see *Winter's Weekly*, 29 April 1893.
100 Ibid., 28 Jan. 1893, 'Crinolisation or Civilization?'
101 Ibid., 11 March 1893, 'Answers to correspondents'.
102 See John Saville's introduction to Adams, *Memoirs*, pp. 17–18.
103 See, for example, *Newcastle Weekly Chronicle*, 28 Jan. 1893, 'The ladies' corner, Geraldine's letter'.
104 Adams, *Memoirs*, pp. 631–2.
105 *Winter's Weekly*, 18 March 1893, 'Answers to correspondents'.
106 Ibid., 4 Aug. 1894.
107 Ibid., 18 March 1893.
108 Park, 'Sport, dress reform and the emancipation of women', pp. 14, 21.
109 *Winter's Weekly*, 28 Jan. 1893, 'Crinolisation or Civilization?'
110 G. Crossick (ed.), *The Lower Middle Class in Britain 1870–1914* (London, 1977), p. 11.
111 See, for example, *Winter's Weekly*, 4 June 1892, 'Editor's thoughts'; and *Winter's Weekly*, 13 Oct. 1894, 'Answers to correspondents'.
112 Todd, *Dictionary of British Women Writers*, p. 726.
113 Bainbridge, *John Strange Winter*, p. 33.
114 *Newcastle Weekly Chronicle*, 18 Oct. 1890, 'The children's corner'. For the impact of the Dicky Bird Society, see Ashton, *W.E. Adams*, pp. 136–8; and also N. McCord, *British History 1815–1906* (Oxford, 1991), p. 455.
115 *Newcastle Weekly Chronicle*, 18 Oct. 1890, 'The children's corner'.
116 McCord, *British History 1815–1906*, p. 455.
117 Rubinstein, *Before the Suffragettes*, pp. 222–3 for the activities of the Pioneer Club.
118 See *Winter's Weekly*, 19 May 1894, 'Is corporal punishment a mistake?'
119 See, for example, *Winter's Weekly*, 21 May 1892, 'Editor's thoughts'; and *Winter's Weekly*, 13 Oct. 1894, 'Answers to correspondents'.

120 Ibid., 30 April 1892. Stannard declared regarding Plaistow that 'my readers know how deeply interested in that parish I am'.

121 Black, *Notable Women Authors of the Day*, p. 56.

122 *Winter's Weekly*, 15 Sept. 1894.

123 Ibid., 22 April 1893, 'The Silver Cord League'.

124 Bainbridge, *John Strange Winter*, pp. 62–7.

125 *Dictionary of National Biography*, p. 395.

126 Plarr, *Men and Women of the Time*, p. 1028.

127 Bainbridge, *John Strange Winter*, pp. 132–3.

128 Ibid., p. 159.

129 For the changing attitude to cosmetics and beauty culture, see, for example, Aileen Ribeiro, *Dress and Morality* (London, 1986), pp. 135–6; and Penelope Byrd, *Nineteenth Century Fashion* (London, 1992), p. 87.

130 Bainbridge, *John Strange Winter*, p. 150.

131 *The Times*, 15 Dec. 1911, 'Obituary on John Strange Winter'.

132 Bainbridge, *John Strange Winter*, p. 159.

133 See obituaries in *Daily Chronicle*, 15 Dec. 1911 and *The Times*, 15 Dec. 1911.

134 For private–public role links, see the prosopographical study by Philippa Levine, *Feminist Lives in Victorian England: Private Roles and Public Commitment* (Oxford, 1990). As a publicly active married woman, Stannard provides an interesting foil to single, middle-class women discussed in Martha Vicinus, *Independent Women: Work and Community for Single Women, 1850–1920* (London, 1985).

135 Rubinstein, *Before the Suffragettes*, see Introduction, pp. xi–xii.

# 9

# Radical Reflections? Elizabeth Robins: The Making of Suffragette History and the Representation of Working-Class Women

ANGELA V. JOHN

During the first half of 1909 a 47-year-old suffragette toured Britain giving a lecture entitled 'Shall Women Work?' She spoke to audiences in rural Cheshire and in Manchester, at St James's Hall, London, Bradford's Mechanics' Institute and the Philosophical Hall in Leeds. After speaking at Brighton's Town Hall in June she was relieved to retreat to her Sussex home, admitting in her diary, 'Oh the rapture of being done with lecturing'.[1] She loathed public speaking but she was Elizabeth Robins (1862–1952), the actress who had helped introduce Ibsen to the London stage. She was too much of a draw for the Women's Social and Political Union (WSPU) to leave her alone for long.

Remembered by many as a great stage actress and now a very popular novelist (who could command the huge advance of £1000 for a book in 1907), she was currently more of a household name than suffragettes like Sylvia Pankhurst. Skilled in delivery and knowing how best to win over audiences, her first intervention at a women's meeting in Tunbridge Wells at the end of 1906 had immediately converted the writer Evelyn Sharp to the cause. Mrs Pankhurst personally assured Elizabeth Robins that she possessed 'the gift of personal magnetism in a far greater degree than I have by nature'.[2] 'Shall Women Work?' focused on married working-class women in particular. It was published in New York's *Metropolitan Magazine* and appeared in Britain in 1910 in the *Fortnightly Review*.

Yet why was this American-born ex-actress and writer, from an impoverished but genteel background, espousing the cause of the militant suffragettes? How did she contribute to the making of suffragette history and, more particularly, what did she—could she—know about the English working class? Born in 1862 in Kentucky, she had spent her childhood on Staten Island, New York, and then, after the break-up of her parents' marriage, moved to the home of her highly intelligent and influential grandmother in Ohio. By her mid-20s she had become a very experienced and much travelled actress in America and was already widowed. In 1888 she came to England where, despite frequent journeys home, she was to stay for the rest of her long life. In the early 1890s she was the first to play the parts of Hedda Gabler and Hilda Wangel in English and during that decade was a seminal figure in producing and publicizing Ibsen's prose dramas on the London stage. In a later novel, *The Convert*, the leading suffragette speaker is described as 'Hilda, harnessed to a purpose'.[3] Robins acknowledged that Ibsen was a vital force in transforming women's opportunities on the stage and argued that, through his plausible male and female characters, he helped to bring intelligent people back to the theatre.

Retiring from the stage in 1902 after a gruelling trip to Alaska to visit two brothers and expand her journalistic skills, she became a professional writer. From November 1905 she was cautiously naming herself a suffragist. The following year she began to write a play with a suffrage theme. Initially attracted by its topicality and drama, it became her first piece of writing inspired by strong moral convictions. In the process of researching material she had attended meetings and become converted. It was the discrepancy between her first-hand experiences and the 'extraordinary and flagrantly untrue' press accounts[4] of the same suffrage events that she saw her associates accepting unquestioningly that transformed her from an investigative writer into a committed participant. Soon she was recognizing that 'the women who work on constitutional lines cannot always reach out and stir the larger public'.[5] Police violence at the first Women's Parliament when she was almost trampled under horses' hooves helped the transition from suffragist to suffragette. By the autumn of 1907 she was persuaded by Mrs Pankhurst to join the committee of the WSPU, a position she held for five years.

Robins was, however, far better known for her popular fiction. *The Magnetic North* (1904), an allegorical adventure tale of the search for gold in the Yukon, had become a best-seller with glowing reviews comparing the author to Defoe. For admirers of such work Robins' new interest was an unwelcome intrusion. In 1912 *Every Woman's Cyclopaedia* noted with disapproval that Elizabeth Robins had, of late, devoted herself to women's suffrage rather than to literary pursuits. In fact the two co-existed, slightly uneasily, side by side. Although some elements of Robins' feminism can be read into all her works written during these years, 1907 saw not only the publication of *The Convert* but also the serialization in America of another Alaskan novel, *Come and Find Me* and publication of an early romantic novella.[6] The *Cyclopaedia* carefully praised *The Magnetic North* as a work of genius but added that:

Like Goldsmith, she has touched nothing which she has not adorned, if we except her book, 'The Convert' which was written with the avowed purpose of propagating the Women's Suffrage Cause, and like so much propaganda literature, cannot be estimated by the ordinary standards of criticism.[7]

*The Convert* was to be carefully distanced from serious literature in the same way that Chartist fiction and poetry had been pronounced by the establishment as politically subversive and so dubious art.

Today Robins is probably best remembered as the author of this book, a didactic yet engaging novel based on her Royal Court drama *Votes For Women!* Indeed, Robins' suffrage contribution is usually made synonymous with this drama and novel.[8] Yet these works were written before she joined the WSPU committee and although they ultimately transcend their own temporality, not least in the recognition that 'the personal is political', the play and novel are very much products of their own urgent political imperative at a particular historical moment and can only represent one stage, albeit an important one, in both Robins' thinking and in suffragette history. Indeed, had *The Convert* been written in, for example, 1912, whilst its lasting personal message would have been the same, the tactics and activities of the WSPU and reactions to them would have had to have been presented somewhat differently.

Robins' early suffrage literature needs to be set alongside her later speeches and essays. Many of these were published in pamphlets, newspapers and journals in Britain and the United States and twenty-one of her talks and articles (including 'Shall

Women Work?') appeared in March 1913 in a collection published by Hodder and Stoughton called *Way Stations*. This was
also published in America where it featured in *Hearst's* magazine as book of the month. Presenting the struggle for women's
suffrage as a railway journey with an important destination, it
had an American title signifying local stops or halts along the
line. Like travellers armed with their Bradshaw's *Way Stations*
(with its women's suffrage initials) was accompanied by prose
sections entitled 'Time Table' linking each piece. They detailed
Robins' understanding of the key events in WSPU history between October 1905 and June 1912, providing an accumulative
record of the distance the suffragettes (and the author) had travelled in these years. Robins' non-fiction appears at first sight to
camouflage the self, yet here and elsewhere there is a deceptive
occlusion. Whilst the WSPU seems to be centre stage, the careful choice of boarding and exit points demonstrates her own
political choices.[9]

*Way Stations* was the second history of the WSPU from within. The first had been Sylvia Pankhurst's *The Suffragette* published in May 1911. Originally suggested by Emmeline Pethick-
Lawrence of the WSPU, and less well known than Pankhurst's
later book *The Suffragette Movement* (1931), it developed out of a
serialized history published from 1907 in the Union's newspaper *Votes for Women*. *The Suffragette* only takes us to October
1911. In retrospect it appears pointedly premature. A story of
the militants prior to the full escalation of militancy—it ends
just before militant action was resumed and intensified—it was
written before Pankhurst's socialist feminist convictions resulted in a distancing from her family. More conventional in its
structure than Robins' book, it was nevertheless novel in other
ways, observing, as Kathryn Dodd has noted, the conventional
form of history writing through its focus on great leaders yet
actually substituting women, not least in her own family, for
great men.[10]

It was a valuable source for Elizabeth Robins' 'Time Table'.
*Way Stations* was billed as 'the only succinct account in existence
of the main line of the Militant Suffrage Movement'[11] (it was a
mere 352 pages compared to Pankhurst's 517!). Both inevitably
told a story without a known ending. These works anticipated,
as had Chartist poetry, a resolution of tension close at hand and
a much better future and both books therefore now appear

somewhat naïvely optimistic. Robins' 'Time Table' began with the Liberal Party meeting in the Manchester Free Trade Hall on 13 October 1905. Like Pankhurst, she viewed this as a transitional moment in the WSPU's own history. Here Christabel Pankhurst and Annie Kenney had audaciously interrupted Sir Edward Grey's appeal for the return of a Liberal government. For Robins, this was especially significant since she was a personal friend of the speaker and had been close to his late wife Lady Dorothy. The event had helped propel her into thinking through her emergent feminism. Her 'Time Table' ends somewhat abruptly in June 1912 even though Robins remained on the WSPU committee until the 'Peth–Pank' split that autumn. It was in the summer, however, that she confronted the implications of heightened militancy.

*Way Stations* takes us a stage further down the line than Pankhurst's history and Robins' own fiction. It also provides a valuable perspective outside the Pankhurst trinity which monopolizes so much writing on the suffragettes. At the same time it concerns a figure who was privy to important decisions made by the Union yet neither totally dominated nor obsessed by the WSPU or its leaders. Robins' fiction and documentary writings are also valuable as the views of an outsider, an American citizen (a position she retained throughout her life) intrinsically involved with the movement yet always seeing a wider international perspective. *Way Stations* is dedicated to Robins' sister-in-law Margaret Dreier Robins who was president of the Women's Trade Union League of America from 1907 to 1922 and was dubbed in the press the 'American Pankhurst'. Her husband Raymond Robins was, like his wife, a prominent human rights activist in the Chicago Settlement movement. The idea for a collection of essays had originated with Elizabeth Robins' American agent Paul Reynolds (in the summer of 1909) and the book was completed at the Robins' Florida home.

Three of the articles had already featured in American magazines before *Way Stations* appeared and the conclusion was published there as an article at the same time as the book. Robins' fiction and drama was already familiar to the American labour movement. After attending a reading of *Votes For Women!* for the Political Equality League in Chicago, Agnes Nestor, International Secretary of the Glove Workers' Union, aptly commented, 'It isn't only trade unions, and it isn't only votes, is it? It is just the whole question of woman'.[12] Robins' international approach was especially evident in her 1909 article named after Thomas Carlyle's essay of eighty years earlier, 'Signs of the Times'.[13] It opened with the latest election news from Denmark, briefly discussed Norwegian and Italian politics and reported on women's suffrage in Boston. Robins was also concerned to counter misinformation abroad about the British situation. She provided written introductions for Mrs Pankhurst on her American tours, arranging for her to meet Margaret Dreier Robins who formally welcomed her at Carnegie Hall in 1909 'on behalf of the working women'.

Although Robins had a difficult personal relationship with her sister-in-law, it is noticeable that during her years as a suffragettes the two women were far less antagonistic than they became later. There were, however, differences in their feminism. For example, Dreier Robins supported essentially separate roles for men and women, tended to see motherhood as a metaphor for female nature and, when forced to discriminate, her commitment to labour overrode her feminism.[14] Yet each admired the other's commitment and helped to bolster women's suffrage on a transatlantic basis. On her frequent trips home Robins met key figures in the women's and labour movements, for example Jane Addams and Frances Kellor, whilst Dreier Robins' own sister, Mary Dreier, was a Women's Trade Union League organizer in New York. Robins accompanied her relatives to gatherings such as a Woman's Labor League's meeting of shirtwaist strikers.

Was this extended to sympathy and support for the British labour movement and did Robins' writings provide a class-based analysis of women's wrongs and remedies? Although much of her fiction was concerned with the highly privileged, her representation of the ruling class was distinctly double-edged. As an American settled in England she could be a shrewd observer of the conventions of the English class system, freer than those constrained within it and, partly by virtue of her artistic fame, the beautiful ex-actress was able to socialize with different groups, including the very well connected who also became fodder and targets for her fiction. In *The Convert* the antediluvian Lord Borrodaile passes a tramp sitting on a municipal bench in Pimlico and fails to notice him, 'the only other person visible at that quiet hour—one of the "unemployed" like himself'.[15]

Most analyses of the suffragettes have stressed their upper-
and middle-class leanings, suggesting that they ignored or were
ignored by working-class women, especially from 1908 onwards.[16] Their increasingly hostile relationship with the organized labour movement has been stressed despite Mrs Pankhurst's
Independent Labour Party (ILP) background and the fact that
the first branch of the WSPU began operations in the dock
district of Canning Town. The WSPU's tactical adherence to
votes for women on the same terms as men, the 1907 split which
led to the founding of the Women's Freedom League, and
Sylvia Pankhurst's increasingly separatist organization of east
London women are cited as examples of the militants' problem-
atic relations with the labour movement. An analysis of the
potted biographies of just under 700 women activists in 1913
reveals that half of the WSPU women were from a 'middle-
middle-class' background, thus less privileged than the stereo-
typed image of titled ladies suggests, yet only three of this group
were definitely of working-class origin.[17]

R.S. Neale has argued that the WSPU's use of the former mill-
worker Annie Kenney was both instrumentalist and misleading
and concludes that working-class women were 'left behind unless they turned themselves into faithful Annie Kenneys'.[18] Yet
Kenney, like the Pankhursts, moved from Lancashire to London
and became part of the élite organizing group based there. She
cannot be made to stand as an exemplification of the WSPU's
attitudes towards working-class women generally, however
questionable the treatment of her may have been. Moreover,
Sandra Holton[19] has reminded us that WSPU branches seem to
have enjoyed some autonomy outside London whilst research
reveals, as do autobiographies, the involvement of working-
class women and not just in the early years. For example, Jane
Mackie Martin, daughter of a Glasgow shipwright and factory
worker, organized the WSPU in Penarth, South Wales, whilst
Catherine Griffiths, a young nurse and Labour supporter, daughter of a Welsh miner, put tin tacks on Lloyd George's seat in the
House of Commons in 1912 'to make him sit up'.[20] In 1908
Robins told her close friend Lady Bell that lectures at the Port-
man Rooms in London attracted 'the swarming of the well to
do' but 'At Homes' at the WSPU headquarters at Clements Inn
were attended by 'nearly all the poorest looking women'.[21]

*The Convert* reveals Robins' analysis of the situation in 1906–7. Although caution needs to be exercised in using such a source as evidence, it is worth noting that material for the suffrage meetings in the novel comes from twenty-six pages of typed notes of eight actual meetings held between July and October 1906 when Robins was gathering material for her play.[22] The book also adds some more recent developments (such as a reference to the 1907 legislation providing free school meals). Robins' fictional suffrage speakers are based on real people. Ernestine Blunt is modelled on Theresa Billington-Greig (though, as with the heroine Vida Levering, she also hints at Christabel Pankhurst) whilst Lothian Scott is Keir Hardie who spoke at the first Trafalgar Square demonstration in 1906.

Working-class women appear to be part of the WSPU's plans and practice. We are told that meetings are held at the pit brows, the mill gates and, more specifically, in south London for the Army and Navy clothing department workers and Woolwich Arsenal workers. Ernestine claims that their meetings at the docks are annoying socialists as they are poaching audiences. Robins' papers include descriptions of meetings at Victoria Park, Hackney and the 'purlieus' of Battersea where Christabel Pankhurst's speech provided the basis for the play's great Trafalgar Square scene. Annie Kenney's sister was there and a 'very cockney Mrs Cullow'. Pankhurst praised Robins' fictional account of a Battersea meeting for its verisimilitude and quoted from it.[23] *The Convert* depicts Vida 'prosecuting her acquaintance with cockney crowds', simultaneously fascinated and repelled.[24] Miss Claxton tells Vida that the *Labour Record* is 'the organ of our Party' and evokes the 'grey and squalid background of a Poor Women's Movement'.[25]

In addition to somewhat hackneyed comments about the working class made by middle-class speakers deploying and adapting well-known slogans of the labour movement, working-class women feature as speakers, spectators and servants. Robins has a working-class suffragette proclaim at Trafalgar Square: 'People 'ave been sayin' this is a Middle-Class Woman's Movement. It's a libel. I'm a workin' woman m'self, the wife of a workin' man'.[26] She is based on Lucy M. Baldock (Minnie), a Poor Law Guardian living in West Ham, who was imprisoned with Sylvia Pankhurst in 1906. Dressed in brown serge, she is also reminiscent of the Derbyshire-born suffragette Hannah

Mitchell who wore her brown costume to WSPU meetings and met Robins in 1906 at the Huddersfield by-election. According to Mitchell's autobiography, she told the writer 'one or two incidents' which were used in *The Convert*.[27]

By not naming this woman in her play, Robins laid herself open to the charge that she saw working-class women as undifferentiated, all facing the same problems,[28] though in *The Convert*, where there was scope for depicting a number of meetings, she was careful to insert other named working-class women such as Mrs Bewley, a stonemason's widow who, at Hyde Park, makes specific complaints about the lack of cheap lodging-houses for single women. Yet her 'rude eloquence' is diminished by her continual stress on 'Ackney, reducing her to a rather comic figure. Ultimately Robins' fictional representation of working-class characters turns on humour rather than argument, suggesting light relief in contrast to the serious messages conveyed by the likes of the carefully named Ernestine.

Long speeches are broken up by caustic interjections from working-class spectators, mainly men. Robins also introduces a woman 'apparently of the small shopkeeping class',[29] full of good sense and absorbed in her baby. She is revealed to Vida as the unlikely yet positive face of suffrage support. Robins presents Vida's maid as especially superior about suffrage gatherings and comments: 'no section of the modern community is so scornfully aristocratic as our servants.'[30] In a chapter invariably ignored by literary critics, Robins focuses on Vida's servant Wark, discusses the latter's personal life and reveals her mistress's dependence on her servant rather than vice versa. Robins encouraged her own servants to attend women's suffrage meetings. Her Danish housekeeper heard Mrs Pankhurst speak in Brighton in 1912. She went on to college, translated Robins' suffrage essays into Danish, eventually became principal of a Danish labour college and spent some time at Ruskin College, Oxford. She corresponded with her former employer for decades, maintaining that she was 'one of those who gets others growing'.[31]

Robins' most thorough fictional investigation of the working class was via domestic service. Indeed her fiction tended to situate working people primarily in relation to their employers. Her third book, *Below The Salt* (1896), had been a pseudonymous collection of short stories about servants.[32] One of these stories, 'Gustus Frederick', involves a lady bountiful who criticizes a working-class woman who chooses to have a child without any means of support yet cannot accept that her own sister is a childless spinster. Loosely based on a tale told her by Lady Bell, it used the working class to reveal the hypocrisy and inadequacies of those who thought they knew better and whom Robins understood best.

Robins' servant stories were broadly sympathetic to their subjects though the modern reader is struck by her use of phonetic spelling and malapropisms when recording their speech, a device which tends to patronize and humiliate. Yet unlike many from her background, Robins was critical of the 'charity-habit' and 'smug settlement workers' who 'plume themselves on leaving luxurious homes' to gain excitement and feel important.[33] She advocated eliminating the need for charity rather than boosting it. In *The Convert* she inverted the usual invasion by the wealthy into working-class space by having Vida intrude her experience of a tramp ward into the 'spacious quiet' of Ulland House gentility. Robins had discussed tramp wards with Beatrice Webb in 1906 and later sat on the council of the National Association of Women's Lodgings founded by the Congregationalist Mary Higgs whose experiences she utilized in *The Convert*.

In the early 1890s Robins' party political sympathies lay with Liberals of the ilk of Rosebery and Grey. She attended the inaugural meeting of the Liberal League. When Campbell-Bannerman was succeeded by H.H. Asquith in 1908, her disillusionment with Liberal promises concerning women's suffrage turned to alarm. She declared that the women's cause had lost 'a weak friend and gained a determined enemy'.[34] The 'Perfidy of Sympathisers' became an important plank in her speeches. Yet the controversial WSPU policy of opposing all Liberal candidates at by-elections regardless of their views posed serious consequences. Robins' eye-witness account of Mrs Pankhurst's speech to the Amalgamated Society of Engineers during the Newcastle-upon-Tyne by-election of 1908 romanticized the situation whilst her comment that 'The Government lost that by-election'[35] failed to mention that this involved the defeat of the sitting radical Liberal member (who had previously enjoyed a majority of over 6000), the failure of a socialist challenge and the election of a Conservative shipowner.

In 1906 Robins had read the revised edition of *Women and Socialism*,[36] an ILP penny tract by Isabella Ford, the middle-class

Quaker socialist and moderate suffragist. The two women were guest speakers at the suffragist Prisoners' Banquet that year. Robins declared Ford's ILP principles to be 'sound'. The pamphlet stressed the common interests and needs of the women's and labour movements, urging that they proceed in harmony and demanding political and hence economic freedom. Ford's use of history to make her point and quotations from the work of Robins' personal friend Mrs J. R. Green (Alice Stopford) would have won Robins' approval. In *Way Stations* Robins herself used history to show how, over time, changes once unthinkable and much opposed — for example, workmen's compensation — could become possible. She would have liked Ford's demonstration of a correlation between women gaining the vote in four western states in America and improved social and economic legislation in those states, such as the raising of the age of consent.

Ford's pamphlet was realistic about the everyday lives of working-class women but it did suggest that motherhood was woman's 'trade'. Robins was wary of such claims though she would have applauded Ford's earlier comments (in 1904) that motherhood was not always voluntary and that many mothers who were wage-earners were so because they were heading houses with dependents or were in families with very low incomes. Robins' own writings not only pointed out that those who accepted the responsibilities of motherhood might be a wider group than natural mothers — at this time she as middle aged and childless though helping her friend Flora Simmonds to raise a schoolboy David Scott — but she also stressed that every woman had children. Indeed, not every woman was cut out for motherhood so women must not be depicted solely as mothers or potential mothers. She argued that those who rightly valued motherhood would 'no more insist that *every* woman must be a mother than that every man must be a hunter or house-builder'.[37] Neither should the differing stages in family cycles be ignored. Since children grew up, women's position *vis-à-vis* the labour market did not remain static over time, yet mothers were almost invariably cast as forever burdened by young children. In an unpublished section of 'Shall Women Work?' Robins even added, 'few of us can honestly say that the best mothers we have known are those who never have time for anything or want to think of anything but their own children.

They are the mothers who are often of least advantage to their children'. Motherhood would be better served 'by the more complete human beings'.[38]

In the same year as 'Shall Women Work?' was published, another actress-turned-writer, Cicely Hamilton, published *Marriage as a Trade*. She chaired the Women Writer's Suffrage League founded in 1908 with Robins as president and the two women later collaborated on a drama about white slavery (banned by the Examiner of Plays) based on Robins' best-selling novel on that theme. Although daring in its depiction of romantic love and marriage as a form of calculated business, *Marriage as a Trade* nevertheless assumed that women must choose between marriage and employment. Moreover, unlike Hamilton, Robins' focus was not primarily on the middle class.

Robins' article sought to demolish the arguments of those advocating protective legislation. She stressed, as had the Fawcetts for many years drawing upon anti-statist traditions, that what women needed most was the protection of the vote. She did, however, recognize that women frequently worked excessive hours and that some restriction of hours might be desirable so long as this was not elided with a prohibition of labour on gendered lines. She seems to have ignored some of the complexities surrounding the thorny problem of protective legislation, issues such as the internal dynamics and degree of unionization of particular trades. Yet she was realistic enough to appreciate that women did not necessarily enjoy jobs such as mill work and that it was economic need that made them popular. She portrayed woman as 'the drudge of the world', providing another version of Ernestine Blunt's powerful speech in *The Convert* where her middle-class character's use of personal pronouns suggests a somewhat questionable notion of women as a class:

At the pit brows we sort coal. But a vote would soil our hands! You may wear out women's lives in factories, you may sweat them in the slums, you may drive them to the streets. You *do*. But a vote would unsex them.[39]

Although she could not resist including in her article a reference to the unremitting slog of the actress on tour, Robins was especially concerned here (and elsewhere) to counteract the threats to married women's employment made by John Burns, president of the Local Government Board. She argued, along with others, that what women really resented was not being consulted about what was best for them. Ray Strachey pointed out many years later in a chapter of *The Cause* entitled 'Women Must Work'[40] that, unlike the form of protection which men developed through trade unions, the legislative protection women faced was imposed on them without their consent and was legally binding. Robins stressed that women were the ones to decide between 'the great evil of semi-starvation and the lesser evil of confiding their young children to an older child'.[41] She added that there could in any case hardly be a real ban on women's work, only on their vital waged work. Adapting Kingsley's verse she commented, 'Men must work and women must work, or else both will have good cause for weeping'.[42] Elsewhere she argued that those seeking to ban married women's employment might better expend their energies abolishing 'the age-old legal abuses which any day may make a woman's home the worst place for her on the surface of the earth'.[43] Her emphasis on the lack of consultation ignored (perhaps deliberately to make her point?) the influence of organizations such as the Women's Labour League and of women in political families such as the MacDonalds.

In line with the 'social feminist'[44] Clementina Black, Robins supported the establishment of a legal minimum wage. Above all, she stressed the need for parliamentary representation to enable voters' pressure on the framing and enforcement of laws. Yet how the one would result in the other she never spelt out and her faith in the healing powers of the vote begged a lot of questions, taking somewhat literally Ford's stress on the links between political and economic freedom.

She sent a draft version of her long article 'Why?' to the Murrays in 1909. She had met Gilbert Murray, Oxford academic and translator of Greek tragedies, in her theatrical management days. Lady Mary Murray, daughter of the Women's Liberal Association president, the Countess of Carlisle, responded by questioning Robins' optimism about what the vote might achieve. Just as Chartists had been criticized for placing their faith in fundamental change occuring once the Charter became the law of the land without addressing how this social revolution might actually be implemented, so it was possible for critics like Lady Mary to probe Robins' tendency to believe that evils would cease once women-made laws were possible and in place. Describing herself as a 'keen suffragist' and a 'quasi-socialist radical' who retained faith in the Liberal party *and* cared more about labour questions 'than any man', Lady Mary also argued that Robins was taking Burns' comments too literally and that any proposal to ban married women's employment would simply not be practical politics.[45]

In response, Robins conceded that Lady Mary might have a point about Burns but added that she remained wary, particularly given the recent attempt to dislodge married women teachers. She also felt that should Burns' proposals be dropped, it would actually be largely because of women's pressure. She reminded Lady Murray that Eva Gore-Booth (author of the penny pamphlet *Women's Right to Work*) and others advocating trade unionism publicly quoted Burns' proposals as one of the strongest reasons for increased vigour in the struggle for women's suffrage. Both Robins and Lady Mary agreed that the endowment of motherhood should predate any restriction on labour.

For socialists such as Isabella Ford, the needs of working-class women were most immediately served by women's organization into trade unions. Not until the First World War could Robins be seen to be advocating this in print. In an article of 1917 entitled 'Conscription for Women' she discussed the vast increase in the female workforce, arguing that it was time that male trade unionists appreciated reality and worked with rather than against women workers. A cavalier use of women as docile and cheap labour placed them in a highly vulnerable position. She deplored the destruction of women's health in munitions work and praised Mary Macarthur who had founded the National Federation of Women Workers. Robins had taken out a subscription to Macarthur's paper, the *Woman Worker*, as early as 1908 when she had praised its 'strong and inspiring words' which she felt to be particularly effective in reaching out to the mass of women up and down the country.[46] In her 1917 article Robins warned that without a very organized, well-financed trade union backing, women would be defenceless. Yet her chief message remained fundamentally consistent. She could not endorse conscripting women into work since they lacked direct representation: 'There can be no palliation of the outrage of conscripting an entire sex which is forcibly prevented from having the smallest share in so momentous a decision.'

Unlike Ford who championed the Leeds tailoresses, Robins' acquaintances with the English working class was limited. Some working-class women attended her lectures but her fictional and documentary analyses of working-class women's lives were, in the main, culled from other people's observations. It was Sylvia Pankhurst, not Robins, who actually went to the pit brows of Wigan and the chainmakers of Cradley Heath where, despite her sympathies, Pankhurst was herself an outsider, commenting on another class and culture. Her six-month painting and writing tour of 1907 introduced her to women whose occupations were threatened by legislative bans and who were attacked for being 'unsexed' and frequently scrutinized and objectified by journalists, politicians and the simply curious. Pankhurst's accounts of these women appeared in *Votes For Women* and were carefully examined by Robins for her fictional speeches. Her notes also included an account of Pankhurst speaking at Hyde Park about the treatment of women at Peterloo and during the Chartist years.

Robins' research involved reading contemporary studies such as Cadbury, Matheson and Shann's *Women's Work and Wages* (1906). She joined other ladies at the misleadingly titled National Union of Women Workers annual conferences in 1906 and 1907. At the latter (in Manchester) she heard both Mrs Cadbury and Clementina Black speak. Her examples of women's employment were largely located in the industrial north. Ironically, the area of Britain outside London and her Sussex home which she knew best was the north east of England, one of the regions where the numbers of women in the formal waged economy was at its lowest. Here lived her close friend Florence (Lady) Bell who in 1907 published her investigations of a manufacturing town. *At the Works* was a study not just of her husband's ironworks and workers in that late but great industrial developer, Middlesbrough, but it was also an examination of the domestic habits of ironworkers' wives. Robins discussed Bell's work in detail with her and occasionally accompanied her to her pioneering scheme for 'Rational Recreation', the Winter Gardens in Middlesbrough. The case histories of working women elaborated in 'Why?' owe something to the style of *At the Works*. In 1893 the two women had co-written an anonymous, controversial play based on a Swedish story. Entitled *Alan's Wife* and performed on the London stage, it was a bold, sympathetic study of infanticide by a northern working-class woman.

'Why?' was published in 1909 in America and Britain (where it was serialized in *Votes for Women* and printed as a Women Writers' Suffrage League pamphlet). It appeared in 1913 as the longest essay in *Way Stations*. It accounts for women working together for the vote and why they had been brought to the point of revolt, providing authenticity via evidence in much the same way as Engels had done in his study *The Condition of the Working Class in England*. It is also suggestive of the Women's Industrial Council inquiry into the economic and hygienic effects of the industrial employment of married women and widows, instigated in 1908 and published in 1915 as *Married Women's Work*, edited by Clementina Black. Yet, unlike Black's anonymous numbered cases, Robins personalized many of her accounts and, being a consummate storyteller, her tales, such as that of the attempted suicide by Elizabeth O'Brien, tailoress, transcend the documentary form.

Robins' writings pay little attention to the newer, less dramatic forms of employment for working women such as shopwork, waitressing and clerical work, all of which were expanding very rapidly at this time.[47] She focused overwhelmingly on the manufacturing industry and/or on the most depressed and exploited, notably the sweated workers whose plight had been graphically revealed in the Sweated Trades Exhibition of 1906. Like many labour historians and others, she rather overlooked 'respectable' working-class women. Her zeal for women's suffrage and defence of militant tactics also made her somewhat dismissive of working-class men's struggles. Like Mrs Pankhurst, she pointed to miners with votes responsible for securing their eight-hour day yet nothing for women. She was cynical about governments' efforts to find compromises which would placate 'a great body of workmen armed with voting powers' and she protested that those who threw stones at windows in 1912 received harsher treatment than striking miners who attacked people. She even referred to the 'forbearance shown to malcontents in Ulster and at Tonypandy'[48] in contrast to the brutality facing women protesting against Lloyd George at Llanystumdwy.

In this year she was forced to confront a number of issues: privately she was increasingly uneasy about the escalation of militancy and its implications. Although she and Lady Bell had, as she put it, always seen life through 'separate windows', Robins' endorsement of militant action (in the press rather than in practice), combined with the national miners' strike, resulted in the non-suffragist ironmaster's wife Lady Bell deliberately distancing herself from her friend's utterances. In the process it revealed Robins at her most prescient. This outsider understood better than many just how deeply entrenched were 'feudal manifestations' in British society, how much needed to be changed and how it would be resisted. Robins wrote to her sister-in-law:

There is a bitter battle ahead — my suffrage friends don't altogether realize fortunately, what a flint of opposition they'll have to overthrow. The more we win friends, the fiercer are our foes . . . so much is involved in it besides 'votes'. It is really a pulling out of the chief cornerstones of privilege. Ibsen saw that years ago.[49]

Although she might fulminate in print against attacks on working women's rights, she was more familiar with the motives of those who ran the country's business and government and it is here that her understanding of class relations was at its sharpest. In 'Why?' she criticizes the tendencies of the poor towards servility and of the rich towards condescension. She also appreciated that herein might lie the key to Britain's lack of a political revolution. Nevertheless she became convinced that social change of a less dramatic sort was inevitable and indeed desirable.[50]

The writings of Elizabeth Robins deserve attention from historians as well as literary critics. Her suffrage play and novel suggest greater involvement with the working class amongst suffragettes than is sometimes acknowledged. Yet this needs to be accompanied by an examination of the years after 1907 when the militants' appeal to the working class and relations with the labour movement were less evident and much more fraught. As her 1909 writings in particular show, here was one militant (on paper, at least) who was interested in the problems facing women workers. These articles have tended to be neglected because it is her fiction which has been foregrounded and because by the time *Way Stations* was published in 1913, Robins had broken from the WSPU and was personally devoting far less time to suffrage politics. And even though they should not minimize the problems of the labour movement in dealing with Christabel Pankhurst in particular, or suggest that working-class women themselves found the structure and methods of the WSPU appealing, they do warn us against dismissing out of hand WSPU interest in working-class women or assuming that only Sylvia Pankhurst concerned herself with and wrote about them. Robins was contradictory: she could be patronizing and blinkered yet she was also capable of being perceptive and witty, particularly in her exposés of those whom she felt exploited others.

Up until the First World War she was wary of politics unconnected to suffrage. Yet she actually occupied a somewhat ambivalent position, socializing with Liberals such as Grey, making sympathetic noises about the problems facing the working class, yet subordinating all other political views to the primacy of women's suffrage. Her later years, however, reveal that, unlike many, her radical reflections became more pronounced and broader as she aged. She was a member of the feminist Six Point Group and wrote an anonymous study of sex antagonism in the 1920s, remaining a feminist for the rest of her life. At the same time her party political inclinations moved further left. Her sympathy lay with the miners in the General Strike. Her political friends were now Labour MPs and cabinet ministers, such as Margaret Bondfield, Ellen Wilkinson, Dr Thomas Jones and her old ally Frederick Pethick-Lawrence. The Labour victory of 1945 was one of the few changes she welcomed in her later years. A few weeks before her 85th birthday, at her own request, she attended the Miners' Gala in Morpeth where the highlight of her day was Aneurin Bevan's speech.[51]

Back in 1909 Lady Mary and Elizabeth Robins had differed in their sense of priorities, the former stressing that she cared more about labour questions than any other. For Robins, women's suffrage was itself 'the *chief* Labour Question'.[52] When women's suffrage was finally achieved she remained a feminist anxious for wider equality but she also now felt freer to support the labour movement.

## NOTES

I am grateful to the following individuals/institutions for permission to use material: Mr Alexander Murray; Dr Richard Pankhurst; Mrs Mabel Smith; the Bodleian Library (Oxford University); the Fales Library (New York University); the Harry Ransom Humanities Research Center (the University of Texas at Austin); Manchester Central

Reference Library; and the Smathers Library (University of Florida, Gainesville). Thanks also to Owen Ashton, June Hannam and members of the University of Greenwich Research Project on men and the women's suffrage movement.

1  Diary, 16 June 1909. Elizabeth Robins Papers, the Fales Library, New York University. For her life see Angela V. John, *Elizabeth Robins: Staging a Life* (London, 1995).

2  Emmeline Pankhurst to Elizabeth Robins, Harry Ransom Humanities Research Center (HRHRC), University of Texas at Austin, 23 Oct. 1908

3  Elizabeth Robins, *The Convert* (London, 1907), p. 299.

4  *The Times*, 6 Nov. 1906.

5  Elizabeth Robins to Mrs Fawcett, Millicent Fawcett Collection, Manchester Central Reference Library, M50/2/1/232.

6  For Robins' publications see Sue Thomas, 'Elizabeth Robins', *Victorian Fiction Research Guide*, **22** (1994). In 1909 Robins published her popular novel *The Florentine Frame* with a print run of over 10,000. *The Convert* was reprinted in Britain and America in 1980. *Votes for Women!* was published in 1908 and reprinted in Dale Spender and Carole Hayman, *How the Vote Was Won and Other Suffragette Plays* (London, 1985).

7  *Every Woman's Cyclopaedia*, **VI** (1912), 4401.

8  Though her pamphlet *Woman's Secret*, published the day before *The Convert*, is now receiving some attention. See Joanne E. Gates, *Elizabeth Robins, 1862–1952: Actress, Novelist, Feminist* (Tuscaloosa, 1994), pp. 166–8. See also Kate Flint, *The Woman Reader 1837–1914* (Oxford, 1993), pp. 313–14 for her appreciation of Robins' 1909 speech to the Women Writers' Suffrage League. This and 'Woman's Secret' were reprinted in *Way Stations* (London, 1913). Dale Spender and Janet Todd, *Anthology of British Women Writers* (London, 1989) include Robins' militant suffrage short story of 1912, 'Under his Roof' though, as with most summaries of Robins' life, the biographical details are inaccurate.

9  Claire Tylee has argued persuasively that *Way Stations* can be seen as a political autobiography in the tradition of a confession narrative. Paper given at the Women's Lives/Women's Times Conference, University of York, York, Jan. 1991. I am grateful to her for letting me read this.

10  E. Sylvia Pankhurst, *The Suffragette* (London, 1911); Kathryn Dodd (ed.), *A. Sylvia Pankhurst Reader* (London, 1993), p. 16.

11  Robins, *Way Stations*, Author's Note.

12  Robins Papers, Series 4, Box 2, Folder 9.

13  Robins, *Way Stations*, pp. 93–104, originally published in *Votes for Women!*

14 Elizabeth Ann Payne, *Reform, Labor and Feminism: Margaret Dreier Robins and the Women's Trade Union League* (Urbana and Chicago, 1988).

15 Robins, *The Convert*, p. 212.

16 For example, Les Garner, 'Suffragism and socialism: Sylvia Pankhurst 1903–14', in Ian Bullock and Richard Pankhurst (eds), *Sylvia Pankhurst: From Artist to Anti-Fascist* (Basingstoke, 1992), p. 63: 'By 1908 the WSPU had certainly deserted its working-class and northern origins.'

17 Jihang Park, 'The British suffrage activists of 1913: an analysis', *Past and Present*, **120**, (1988), 147–62.

18 R.S. Neale, *Class and Ideology in the Nineteenth Century* (London, 1972), p. 167.

19 Sandra Stanley Holton, *Feminism and Democracy* (Cambridge, 1986), p. 42.

20 Angela V. John, '"Run like blazes": The Suffragettes and Welsh-ness', *Llafur Journal of Welsh Labour History*, **6**, 3 (1994), 29–43.

21 Robins Papers, Series 5, Box 3, Folder 17.

22 Ibid., Series 7, Box 85, Folder 26.

23 Pankhurst, *The Suffragette*, pp. 99–100.

24 Robins, *The Convert*, pp. 198–9.

25 Ibid., pp. 158, 163.

26 Ibid., pp. 290.

27 Hannah Mitchell, *The Hard Way Up* (London, 1984 edn), p. 163.

28 Sheila Stowell, *A Stage of Their Own* (Manchester, 1992), p. 28.

29 Robins, *The Convert*, p. 112.

30 Ibid., p. 115.

31 Robins Papers, Series 2B, Box 6, Folder 1.

32 Published under the pseudonym of C.E. Raimond.

33 Robins, *The Convert*, p. 48.

34 Robins, *Way Stations*, p. 70.

35 Ibid., p. 162.

36 I.O. Ford, *Women and Socialism* (1904, 1906 2nd edn); June Hannam, *Isabella Ford* (London, 1989), Ch. 6.

37 Robins Papers, Series 7, Box 72, Folder 8.

38 Ibid.

39 Robins, *The Convert*, pp. 139–40, and *Way Stations*, p. 190.

40 Ray Strachey, *The Cause* (London, 1928, 1978 edn), p. 233. See Ch. 8 for Mrs Henrietta Stannard's defence in 1884 of middle-class widows' right to work in her 'Shall Women Work?' article.

41 Robins, *Way Stations*, p. 195.

42 Ibid., p. 201.

43 Ibid., p. 156.

44 See Ellen Mappen, 'Strategists for change: social feminist approaches to the problems of women's work', in Angela V. John (ed.), *Unequal*

*Opportunities: Women's Employment in England 1800–1918* (Oxford, 1986), pp. 235–59.

45  Correspondence between Robins and the Murrays, Gilbert Murray Papers, 16, The Bodleian Library, Oxford, ff. 43–4, 17 Aug. 1909; ff. 54–9, 9 Sept. 1909; 62–3, 13 Sept. 1909; Lady Mary Murray to Elizabeth Robins, HRHRC, 11 Sept. 1909. Compare Lady Murray's remark with Dorothy Thompson's comment on Victorian society's dependence on working-class women and their cheap labour: 'society would not have survived long had they been prevented from working.' 'Women and nineteenth century radical politics: a lost dimension' (reprinted) in Dorothy Thompson, *Outsiders: Class, Gender and Nation* (London, 1993), p. 77.

46  The *Woman Worker* printed on 26 June 1908 the letter of praise she had sent Macarthur. Elizabeth Robins, 'Conscription for women', *Contemporary Review*, **cxi** (April, 1917), 485.

47  Though she did mention one woman of the 'Strand Restaurant cashier class' in *The Convert*, p. 89.

48  Robins, *Way Stations*, pp. 298, 336.

49  Robins to Margaret Dreier Robins, Margaret Dreier Robins Papers, 3, University of Florida, Gainesville, FLA, 1 August 1908.

50  Robins, *Way Stations*, pp. 134–5.

51  See John, *Elizabeth Robins*, Chs 9 and 10 for her later life.

52  Gilbert Murray Papers, 16, ff. 62–3, 13 Sept. 1909.

# 10

# Poverty and the Poor Law in the First World War in Worcestershire

## GLEN MATTHEWS

### I

Attention still continues to be focused on the relationship between war and social change.[1] Much time and effort has been given to linking the participation of individuals and groups to the social, political and economic 'rewards' received in the aftermath of war. Further research has been undertaken on the condition of the civilian population during the period of war, and the extent to which their condition improved or deteriorated during the hostilities. It is the intention of this essay to examine the civilian population during the First World War in a local study of Worcestershire. In particular, attention will be focused on the assistance provided directly by the poor law for a range of social problems and other services closely connected to this administration while not directly under the supervision of the guardians. The main services to be examined under this criterion will be those provided for the mentally ill—the pauper lunatics and mental deficients.

There seems little doubt that much of the poor law administration in the several unions in Worcestershire was still conditioned by its nineteenth-century roots and remained undisturbed throughout the period of the war. A contrast is provided by other parts of the administration that were overwhelmed by the pressures or, owing to the lack of demand, became temporarily redundant. One important point needs to be made before commencing this examination. In studying social policy during a period of war there is some difficulty in distinguishing between problems that are created by the war and those that occur during the war, although independent of it. The condition of the county lunatic asylum falls into this category and will be discussed in more detail below.

212

Arthur Marwick's research on war and society in the twentieth century has done much to improve our understanding of
the events and their consequences in respect of the civilian
population. Marwick has identified four 'aspects' of war which
are relevant to social change. These may be briefly described as
the destructive and disruptive aspects of war; how war 'tests'
institutions; the gains and losses experienced by the participants; and the social–psychological effects of war. It is not the
intention in this essay to examine the four aspects, rather to
consider how the war 'tested' one institution—the poor law.

The recent work of Jay Winter has redressed earlier views
that the First World War had a totally negative effect on the
health of the civilian population of Britain.[2] Winter sees increased
earnings and nutritional levels bringing about an unanticipated
improvement in the civilian population's standard of health and
life expectancy during the war.[3] These improvements reached
even those at the 'bottom of the social scale'.[4] Marwick has also
stated that 'at no time during the first world war was there any
widespread privation in Britain'.[5]

It must be acknowledged that neither Winter nor Marwick
has directed his attention to the groups who will be examined
in this study, although their analyses have thrown much light
on the subject area. It seems that there still remains much, at a
local level, that could usefully be investigated in order to en-
hance our understanding of war and social change.

## II

Old age pensions and national insurance, introduced in 1908
and 1911, had reduced some of the demands on the poor law,
but this residual service still provided many with assistance.[6]
Poor Law infirmaries contained over 60 per cent of hospital
beds, the majority used by the old and infirm.[7] There was a
continued need to provide outdoor medical and financial relief,
care for mental defectives, protection for orphaned and deserted
children, and relief and control of vagrancy. The guardians at a
local level still enjoyed a large measure of responsibility. The
pauper lunatic asylum, although not directly under the control
of the guardians, was a further important aspect of this administration. Marwick was surely correct when he stated: 'In 1914 the
poor law, despite the adverse comments on it of both majority

and minority reports of the Royal Commission, remained the basis of British social security.'[8]

An examination of those who controlled the poor law and other parts of social provision in Worcestershire confirms that there was a nucleus of people, principally male, who formed what might be called an 'administrative élite'. Several of these can be traced back, by their families, into the nineteenth century. In the area examined few women or working-class men had managed to gain election to the boards of guardians by the outbreak of the war. The guardians elected in 1913 remained in office until the first post-war elections in 1919; the triennial elections due in 1916 and any further elections were postponed for the duration of the war.[9]

Vacancies on the boards, owing to the retirement or death of guardians, were filled by 'recommended' candidates.[10] The administration of the county pauper lunatic asylum was controlled by a visiting committee whose members were guardians, councillors and magistrates. The administration as a whole was safeguarded by the association of poor law unions and the local government board who remained alert to possible threats to their autonomy. We are safe in claiming that the framework of the administration remained little changed by the demands of war. Research on the administration of the poor law is curtailed to a degree by the loss of the records of the local government board, the central authority until the establishment of the ministry of health in 1919; the reduction in the number of administrators due to manpower demands of the war; the directives to reduce the written and statistical record-keeping; and less frequent meetings of the boards of guardians. One noticeable effect of the war is a marked reduction in the copious records normally available for research into the administration of the poor law.[11] Nevertheless at a local level, in Worcestershire, there were adequate sources available to complete this study.

## III

The evidence regarding the life expectancy and standard of health of one group, the over 65s, during the war contradicts the more optimistic claims that have been made. Their death rates followed an irregular but higher trend during the war.[12] This trend was recognized by Pat Thane who believes that deficiencies in civilian medical care may have contributed to it.[13] While Winter does not see medical care as being the most important issue, he does concede that the 'very elderly were not so fortunate because of an increase in their death rates due to respiratory tuberculosis and other respiratory disease'.[14]

Dealing with the slow decline and incapacity of old age, and the chronic sick, had become major tasks of the poor law administration well before the war. As one Kidderminster guardian had claimed, the workhouse had become a 'sort of infirmary' owing to the increasing numbers of inmates who were classed as 'non-able bodied'.[15] The financial demands on the poor rates had been reduced by the introduction of old age pensions in 1909, but there still remained much to be done for this group and for those below pensionable age who were incapacitated. The pension had reduced the numbers on outdoor relief within a year or so, while the demands for indoor relief declined more slowly. Few aged inmates could re-establish themselves outside the workhouse after losing their independence. Pensioners could, and did, receive medical treatment within the workhouse infirmaries while still retaining their pension, that is until it was taken to contribute towards their relief.

Death rates within these institutions were consistently high. Nevertheless during the war in one workhouse, where we have evidence, the death rates increased by 21 per cent over the period of the war.[16] This may be explained by the reduction and changes in the food provided within this institution. The evidence examined below points to diet in the institutions controlled by the poor law administrators as an important contributing factor to the increased death rates. One unrelated point that emerges from an examination of this part of the administration was the reduction in pauper funerals; an increasing number of relations paid the burial costs in order to prevent this stigma.

It was a difficult task for the poor law system to respond to the demands of war, but economies in food and manpower were achieved. There was a slow decline in the quality and quantity of food provided in both the workhouses and the pauper lunatic asylums. The continual increase in the price of foodstuffs could only be offset by an increase in rates or a decline in the quality and quantity of food—the latter appears to have been the normal response.[17] These institutions purchased in bulk at contracted prices; the pensioner and those on fixed allowances were faced with increased prices, and shortages. Examples of two commodities, milk and bread, confirm the problems facing the poor during the war. Milk increased from 11d. a gallon at the start of the war to a controlled price of 2s. 3d. at the war's end. Bread, while fluctuating in price, had nearly doubled in cost by the end of the war. Coal, important to the running of an institution as well as the home, increased in price from 15s. a ton to £1 14s. 6d., and by 1918 the guardians were prepared to pay the price for what coal could be supplied.[18] It is quite easy to to be misled by the dietary scales; a dietary scale is a gesture of intent, rather than what anyone actually gets to eat. Nevertheless there seems little doubt that the quality of life in terms of subsistence in these institutions declined during the war.[19]

Outdoor relief, that is relief provided outside the workhouse, while being continually monitored and criticized by the central authority, remained the most common and cheapest method of providing assistance. In the poor law unions examined in 1911, 2s. 6d. was the normal sum paid to adults, on relief; by 1914 this sum had been increased to 3s. 6d., with increased payments of 1s. for adults and 6d. for children in winter in order to buy extra coal. During the last winter of the war in the Worcester union each household on relief received, on average, 11s. 6d. per week; this included 1s. extra for coal.[20] Thane has calculated that individuals on outdoor relief were receiving at least 10s. a week, and perhaps as much as 15s., by 1918.[21] While the local figures are far from satisfactory for an accurate assessment, they are below these rates. What they do confirm is that outdoor relief lagged behind price increases for food and other commodities during the war.

For old age pensioners who had now been removed from poor law relief the war brought increased worries: while the cost of living increased, the value of the pension decreased.[22] The government was slow to react to the increasing financial problems of those who had only recently received their independence in old age. The pension had originally been set below a subsistence level, and it was not until 1916 that the government sanctioned a means-tested review of needs. A further 2s. 6d. was paid to those who could prove their needs. Even the lucky ones were still left short of the increased cost of necessities.[23]

The war had little noticeable effect on those parts of the administration designed to contain the cost of relief. The case

paper system, whereby a complete record of each family's income and expenditure was recorded and needs calculated, was
only partially observed. Some unions continued to use pay
stations whereby those in receipt of outdoor relief collected the
money from some central point. This system could sometimes
work to their benefit when the guardians, at their fortnightly
meetings, made arbitrary decisions on the level of relief to be
provided. Outdoor relief lists continued to be published in order
to keep the rate-payers informed and vigilant for economies;
and the relatives of those on relief continued to be approached
for financial contributions. The anachronistic settlement laws
were still applied in order to effect the removal of claimants
usually to their place of birth.

The outbreak of war in August 1914 had resulted in the sudden
departure to their units of husbands, fathers, and many unmarried men with family commitments. Allowances for depen-
dants of those in the forces did not commence until October,
some two months later. In the intermediate period local authorities were instructed to organize relief committees financed from
the Prince of Wales' relief fund 'to deal with any distress that
might arise in consequence of the War'.[24] It seems that depen-
dants had the choice of charity or the poor law: as the official
allowances began to be paid the local government board instructed guardians that 'all entries identifying recipients should
be erased from the records kept by the guardians'.[25] Here again
the relief paid by the guardians was reimbursed from the Prince
of Wales' fund.

The English-born wives and children of interned aliens were
other unfortunates to come into contact with the poor law as a
result of the war.[26] A brief glimpse into their treatment is provided in the sources examined. The financial support was even
more stringent, until the guardians were informed that the cost
of their relief could be reclaimed from the Prince of Wales' fund.
It was then brought into line with the standard payments.[27]

The local evidence examined confirms that this part of the
poor law administration was little changed by the pressures of
war. Parsimony continued to be practised, with the added support of economy because of the war. The government was also
reluctant to provide financial assistance, preferring charitable
aid to meet the needs.

## IV

The scale and range of medical services provided by the poor law authorities, both indoor and outdoor, increased in importance throughout the nineteenth century—we still have much evidence of this within our present health system. This was a service that many guardians viewed with concern; it was usually costly and the guardians were cautious when dealing with the professionals—the medical officers. An examination of the records confirms the hostile relationship between the guardians and the medical officers, and this was exacerbated by the continual search for economy. Nineteenth-century procedures to control expenditure remained tightly in place: the relieving officers were expected to see all outdoor cases before the medical officer was called; and the medical officers were retained on restrictive contracts which penalized them financially if they were too 'generous' with indoor or outdoor treatment.

As the war dragged on, frequent demands were made for the release of all doctors who could be spared for military service, and in excess of 50 per cent of the profession eventually joined the services.[28] All civilian provision was curtailed by these events, and none more so than the poor law medical services where all doctors who were suitably fit and under 45 years of age had enlisted. At the same time the flood of war casualties increased the pressure on all institutional accommodation. Asylums and workhouses were forced to take inmates from other institutions or to take wounded service men.

The institutional problems were aggravated by a shortage of nurses. There had been an inadequate number of nurses in the poor law infirmaries before the war. Few boards were prepared to offer salaries that would attract competent nurses, and the workhouse infirmaries were no more attractive to staff than they were to patients. Pre-war shortages had been offset by the poor law unions training their own nurses, but the guardians in the area examined had for many years refused to comply with the local government board orders on the ratio of nurses to patients.[29] These directives had recommended a ratio of one nurse to ten patients, with a maximum of one nurse to fifteen patients; in the infirmaries examined, the ratio was in excess of one nurse to twenty-four patients.[30] The shortages were overcome by using pauper nurses, as inmates who attended the sick in workhouse infirmaries were described, even though this practice had long been condemned by the local government board.

The medical facilities in the workhouse infirmaries, with one or two exceptions, were not only limited by the number of staff and their expertise, but also by the equipment and the general facilities required to attend to the sick. Each poor law union moved the responsibility for the treatment of 'complex' cases over to the local charity hospitals. The cost of this treatment was covered by the practice that had developed in the nineteenth century of purchasing 'tickets' of admission to these hospitals.

The cautious use of the nursing associations that had developed in the latter decades of the nineteenth century for the outdoor poor continued throughout the war, and beyond. As the local government board had stressed in 1892 this service was only to be used under 'exceptional circumstances'.[31] The guardians were receptive to services that could reduce potential indoor relief costs, and the distinction between the provision of indoor or outdoor medical relief seems to have been determined whenever possible on a cost basis. There was a general reluctance to expand the medical services beyond a necessary minimum. There was little evidence of the 'rapidly improving poor law medical facilities', that Bentley Gilbert identified in this area.[32] A further financial constraint was placed on these services when the annual grant from the county council for the salaries of poor law staff and the care of lunatics was frozen at the March 1916 level. The evidence examined suggests that the war reinforced the guardians' determination to control their medical services.

## V

One part of poor law administration that can easily be overlooked dealt with mental disorders. The legislation of the 1840s had forced the counties to provide suitable provision for pauper lunatics.[33] By the early 1850s a system of pauper lunatic asylums was in place providing the necessary secure accommodation. The County and City of Worcester Pauper Lunatic asylum opened in August 1852, and received its first patients, who had previously been kept in their homes, public and private asylums, and union workhouses. The 1845 Lunacy Act had initially established the committal procedures for pauper lunatics, a procedure that was controlled by the union relieving officers, medical officers and magistrates, many of whom were guardians. It was quite usual for the person awaiting committal to be placed in the workhouse while these procedures took place. The major part of each pauper lunatic's maintenance costs was paid by the unions from the poor rate. From 1874 central government made a contribution to these costs, although this contribution was transferred to the county councils in 1888. The annual visits of representatives from the boards of guardians to examine their pauper lunatics were a further source of contact between the poor law and the asylum. These visits usually terminated with an examination of the financial circumstances of each inmate, and their relations and friends, in order to determine if any financial support could be obtained. The normal parsimonious response of the guardians to relief matters flowed over into the administration of the county pauper lunatic asylum. These policies were to contribute to the problems that emerged during the war.

The movement of lunatics from overcrowded asylums, or 'transfers' as they were described, had been a popular practice throughout the second half of the nineteenth century and continued up to the outbreak of the war. The increasing number of persons committed had outstripped the asylum accommodation and counties were virtually locked into permanent building programmes to meet these demands. The transfer of inmates to asylums in other counties provided a temporary breathing space and at times was viewed as a substitute for increased expenditure on accommodation. The county magistrates and city councillors forming the visiting committee, and later the county council, had continually been forced to increase the accommodation of the Worcester asylum, but further extensions were eventually refused by the central authority, the lunacy commissioners. The commissioners criticized the infrastructure of the asylum where an inadequate and often contaminated water supply resulted in endemic typhoid and dysentery attacks. Overcrowding continued to be a problem even after a second asylum was opened in the county in 1907.

One or two other points need to be considered regarding the old asylum at the outbreak of the war. As the anticipated cures for lunacy had failed to materialize in the nineteenth century, the food provided for the inmates had deteriorated in both quality and quantity; parallel to this had been a decline in the quality of accommodation, with new blocks similar in design and comfort to workhouse buildings.[34]

The incidence of phthisis, pulmonary tuberculosis, in the old asylum had been noted in the last years of the nineteenth century, when both the medical superintendent and lunacy commissioners had recommended isolating inmates suffering from the disease.[35] The visiting committee, after obtaining estimates for extending the isolation ward decided—on cost alone—to leave matters in abeyance.[36] This inertia continued until the local authorities were informed that 'no less than 35 per cent of the male cases coming to autopsy presented evidence of active tuberculosis'.[37] In an era of strict separation of the sexes, the limited response was a veranda built on to one of the female wards, while the needs of the male side of the asylum were ignored. This was the situation at the old asylum in 1914.

In order to provide hospital accommodation for the military, nine of the ninety-seven asylums in England and Wales were cleared of their civilian patients who were placed in other asylums. The Worcestershire asylums, ever ready to accommodate 'out-county' patients, and charge accordingly, responded to the demands of war. In 1915 some four hundred patients were transferred to the old asylum.[38] The scene was set well before the war, with overcrowding, inadequate water supply, and the constant drive for economy, for some sort of catastrophe to strike the inmates at this asylum.

Economies continued after the outbreak of war. By 1916 the average amount spent on food per inmate each week had been reduced to 2s. $4\frac{1}{2}d.$ — one of the lowest levels in the country.[39] In 1918 the board of control's inspector commented on the reduced rations and the loss of weight of the patients.[40] It was inevitable that some inmates would pay the price of such policies.

The consequences became apparent during the war. In the first year of the war, 81 patients died in the asylum, followed by 99 in 1915, 148 in 1916, 277 in 1917, 318 in 1918, falling back to 108 in 1919, and 48 in 1920.[41] Of the 703 deaths during the period 1917–19, no less than 294, 42 per cent, were attributed to pulmonary tuberculosis.[42] Deaths on this scale did not pass unnoticed at that time, or since. The board of control's inspector, in his 1918 report, commented on the fact that patients suffering from tuberculosis were accommodated in twelve wards in the asylum, seven wards on the female side and five on the male side.[43] A further two years elapsed before these contagious patients were isolated when the deaths from tuberculosis were reduced to a modest level of nine.[44]

There are several reasons that can be put forward for this great loss of life. The most obvious one is the deterioration of the conditions in the asylum brought about by the decline in the food scales and the overcrowding. The role of the asylum management in this period — their indifference to the conditions or possible incompetence—requires further examination. A comparison of the number of deaths at the Worcester asylum with those of other asylums should throw some light on these issues. The details are provided in the board of control's annual reports. From these reports we can see that in 1918 the Worcester asylum recorded the highest number of deaths from tuberculosis in the country, and overall the third-highest number of deaths from all causes in these institutions.[45] J.L. Crammer, in his research on the Buckingham County asylum, another institution with very high death rates during the war, particularly on account of tuberculosis, claims that this was 'consistent with food deprivation'.[46] Crammer has also examined the death rates in prisons over the period of the war and confirmed that these showed little change.[47] There seems little doubt that poor diets were a contributing factor at the Worcester asylum, which became the cheapest mental hospital, in respect of patient costs, in the country.[48] Yet death rates from tuberculosis declined without an appreciable increase in subsistence when these patients were isolated. This evidence suggests that the asylum authorities' failure to provide separate accommodation for these patients was due to carelessness, indifference or intent. The war, it seems, had made some material difference to a situation that already existed, albeit on a smaller scale prior to 1914.

Crammer claims that the board of control failed in its duty to safeguard the patients, but the war had provided the asylums with a ready-made excuse to disregard central directives.[49] The evidence presented tends to support the claim that the authorities at the Worcestershire asylum, particularly the visiting committee, made a calculated decision to do nothing about the increasing death rate. The lunacy commissioners, and their successors the board of control, had tried for twenty years to get the visiting committee to make appropriate arrangements for patients with pulmonary tuberculosis—and failed. Local autonomy prevailed. The war made some impact on the lives of those in the asylum, but the policies pursued by those in charge appear to have been more significant.

In 1920 when a typhoid outbreak took place at the asylum the directive to the medical staff was to inoculate all patients against the disease—except the 'feeble and senile'.[50] It is difficult not to link these two events: both demonstrate indifference to the life prospects of those incarcerated in the asylum.

## VI

The royal commission on the care and control of the feeble-minded, 1904–8, had drawn attention to the plight of the feeble-minded and harmless epileptics, and the Mental Deficiency Act 1913 appears to be the product of their deliberations.[51] The question of institutional care for these unfortunates, and what type of institution, had been the subject of a long debate in Worcestershire. The asylum authorities had made frequent requests for the guardians to commit acute cases as soon as possible, and at the same time to take back to the workhouses chronic, harmless incurables. The asylum and the workhouses over the latter decades of the nineteenth century were constantly in need of more accommodation, the workhouses primarily to deal with the old and sick. Building extensions and a new asylum had been the active response to increasing numbers requiring institutional care, but the feeble-minded were deposited in any place of convenience, many still retained in their homes or with 'friends'. The returns provided by poor law authorities suggest that well in excess of two hundred feeble-minded persons were resident in the area examined.[52]

The introduction of old age pensions in 1909 had contributed to the gradual reduction in the number of aged inmates in the workhouses, and it was in the wake of this that the Worcestershire guardians acted, and made separate provision for 'mental defectives'.[53] The Stourbridge workhouse was selected as most suitable for these 'mental boarders'. This was very much a cost-saving exercise as workhouse provision was considerably cheaper than asylum provision. A programme of committing these unfortunates commenced, although a few feeble-minded were still retained in the workhouses as cheap labour in order to assist with cleaning and other domestic duties.

The 1913 Mental Deficiency Act placed new responsibilities on county and borough councils. This was an all-encompassing piece of legislation that extended the criteria for institutional confinement from mental defectives to habitual drunkards, criminals, and pregnant single women in receipt of poor relief. As far as the Worcestershire authorities were concerned they had already fulfilled the requirements of this legislation by using spare capacity in the workhouses. The board of control had anticipated that special institutions would be provided—particularly for children—but these were not forthcoming. The outbreak of war saw the military take-over of the Stourbridge workhouse and the mental boarders shunted around the county, the majority being placed in the Kidderminster workhouse. Complaints from local people about the inconvenience of this, and from the board of control regarding the inappropriate accommodation, continued throughout the war.

Once more we see the administration quickly respond to the changing conditions with very little disturbance, and find a cheap solution. The war, if anything, strengthened their position and allowed them to limit their obligations under the Mental Deficiency Act, and provide relief to the ratepayers.[54] This extension of institutional care became even cost-effective following the 1913 Act, when the county or borough councils and the board of control assumed financial responsibility for this part of the administration. The workhouses had the necessary space, and while the number of staff had declined as a result of the war, these institutions were still capable of offering, according to the guardians' criteria, an appropriate service.

## VII

Hugh Owen, the permanent secretary of the local government board in 1887, commented 'that there is no class of persons whom boards of guardians generally regard with so much disfavour as vagrants'.[55] In 1910, the local government board inspector for the district examined, claimed that 'How to deal with vagrants still remains one of the most difficult problems of the poor law'.[56]

The term vagrant is used together with 'casual pauper' in poor law sources. Other names given to these persons included tramp, beggar, loafer and vagabond; the 1882 Casual Poor Act had defined a casual pauper as any 'destitute wayfarer or wanderer', while a modern euphemism is 'persons without a settled way of living'. The poor law authorities, and historians, have been frustrated in their attempts to quantify the problem of vagrancy: official workhouse returns give the total number of persons relieved each day, but over a given period the same person could be counted any number of times. Large numbers slept rough so that official returns underestimate those on the tramp.[57] Even so, in 1905, which was viewed as the worst year in respect of numbers relieved in the vagrancy wards prior to the war, the Worcestershire unions dealt with no less than 82,610 vagrants.[58]

We have little more information regarding the identity of those who tramped the roads of Britain in the pre-war period, or awareness of their physical or mental condition. The departmental committee on vagrancy, 1904–6, claimed that there were four distinct categories among the casuals: bona fide work-seekers, men willing to undertake casual labour for a short time, habitual vagrants, and old and infirm persons.[59] Local evidence suggests that a large percentage of those on the tramp were genuine work-seekers.[60]

A local initiative, started in 1882 and organized by the Worcestershire wayfarers' relief society attempted to co-ordinate the work of the police and the guardians in order to 'satisfy the public that sufficient food, as well as lodgings, is supplied from public and organised sources to the vagrant class, and thus check alms-giving which is the principle introduced by professional vagrancy'.[61] Casuals had to keep to a strict timetable and route; tickets prescribing the breadstations and workhouses were provided by the police. This scheme, quite often described as the 'wayticket' system, only enjoyed limited success. It was under-capitalized and the police and workhouse officials failed to keep strictly to the system; it seems the police viewed this as an inconvenience and an extra duty, while the guardians were reluctant to incur increased costs and detain vagrants. The departmental committee's report had recommended that the workhouse casual wards should be taken over by the police, that labour colonies should be established for vagrants, and that more lenient and constructive assistance should be provided for genuine workmen.[62] The majority and minority reports of the Royal Commission on the Poor Laws, 1909, confirm a degree of similarity to the departmental committee's recommendations to combat vagrancy, both reports recommending special centres where vagrants could be detained.

The local government board, while not responding directly to the recommendations of the departmental committee or the Royal Commission, issued a vagrancy order in 1913 endorsing the wayticket system. Once again several poor law unions failed to respond, and even before a partial scheme in the West Midlands was under way the war intervened.

In April 1916, the guardians were instructed to 'detain all single men of military age who may have relief in casual wards until the nearest recruiting officer could be appraised of their admission'.[63] This instruction was repeated the following year, and some idea of the success of these policies is demonstrated by the claim of the Worcester workhouse master that he had handed four hundred tramps over to the recruiting officer.[64] The numbers on the tramp during the war dwindled quite significantly and for a period vagrancy no longer troubled the poor law authorities. Enhanced employment opportunities and the threat of military service obviously had their effects, although the guardians were also instrumental in further reducing the numbers who claimed relief in the workhouses.

In 1917, following encouragement from the local government board, a uniform system of relief was introduced in the counties of Staffordshire, Warwickshire, and Worcestershire. Several vagrancy wards were closed. It seems the guardians believed that the provision of accommodation created the demand. As in previous attempts, some guardians would not co-operate, once more confirming the degree of autonomy that guardians enjoyed even in the face of constant attempts by the central authority to impose a uniform system of relief.

The war only brought temporary relief for the poor law authorities when the local inspector confirmed that, 'As to be expected, the number of vagrants has increased considerably since the Armistice'.[65] The return of vagrancy immediately after the war may well confirm that there was a more direct relationship between the labour market and those on the tramp than has been admitted. The poor law authorities, or the local relief societies gave little attention to this. Being obsessed with the symptoms of vagrancy rather than the causes, they responded with deterrence and harsh treatment to this problem. Perhaps the view expressed by the Webbs that vagrancy was 'inevitable and unconquerable' epitomizes a problem that is still with us today.[66]

## VIII

While the recommendations of the minority and majority reports of the Royal Commission, 1909, had been evaded by both the local government board and the guardians, a fresh assault on the whole poor law system developed in July 1917. A local government committee was set up to re-examine the evidence of the royal commission. Dr Christopher Addison, the minister of reconstruction, later to become the first minister of health, wanted to bring together all departments 'concerned in matters affecting the health of the people'.[67] News of this threat brought a unified response from the guardians and demands for representation on the committee.[68] The eventual report of this committee in January 1918 recommended that the boards of guardians should lose their powers and that the poor law unions should be abolished. The reaction of the guardians is fully recorded by Gilbert, but needless to say they managed to repulse the threats, the only casualty being the local government board which was replaced by the ministry of health in July 1919.[69]

Not only the many elements, but also the whole edifice of poor law administration had remained intact and to a degree had been impervious to the effects of the war. The evidence presented in this brief survey of the operation of the poor law during the period of the First World War confirms just how important this administration was, and its ability to withstand the pressures of war. Each area of the administration that has been examined emerged from the war basically unchanged. In this area of Britain the poor law withstood the 'test' of war.

The intransigence of the system is confirmed by its operation in the inter-war period, when Gilbert, perhaps slightly exaggerating, claims the guardians were the 'defenders of the nation against revolution'.[70] The guardians' duties were handed over to the county councils and county boroughs in 1929, when a series of changes closely matching the recommendations of the minority report of the Royal Commission were introduced. The main elements of the poor law, however, remained in operation until 1948.

## NOTES

I wish to thank John Bourne for his advice during the preparation of this essay. Thanks also to Hereford and Worcester County Record Office for permission to quote from material in their possession.

1  R. Pope, *War and Society 1899–1948* (London, 1991). This short study provides a synopsis of the debates on war and social change.
2  On the negative effects of the war on the civilian population see, for example: M. Greenwood, 'British loss of life in the wars of 1794–1815 and 1914–1918', *Journal of the Royal Statistical Society*, **CV** (1942); S. Dumas and P. Vedel-Peterson, *Losses of Life Caused by the War* (Oxford, 1923); R. Ellis, 'Social change and child health, *Paediatrics*, **XX** (1955); B. Abel-Smith, *The Hospitals 1850–1948* (London, 1964); J. Drummond and A. Wilbraham, *The Englishman's Food* (London, 1957).
3  See especially J. Winter, *The Great War and the British People* (London, 1986), *passim*; and also 'The impact of the First World War on the civilian health in Britain', *Economic History Review*, 2nd ser., **XXX** (1977); 'Aspects of the First World War on infant mortality in Britain', *Journal of European Economic History*, **XI** (1982).
4  Winter, *The Great War*, p. 280.
5  A. Marwick, *The Deluge: British Society and the First World War* (London, 1965), p. 191.
6  G. Matthews, 'The public response to poverty vagrancy and lunacy: a study of the Worcestershire experience, 1870–1920' (unpublished Ph.D. thesis, University of Birmingham, 1984).
7  This figure refers to hospital beds for the physically ill: R. Pinker, *English Hospital Statistics 1861–1938* (London, 1964), p. 62. Workhouses were retitled institutions in 1913, Poor Law Institutions Order, 1913; in this study I shall continue to use the title of workhouse.
8  A. Marwick, *Britain in the Century of Total War* (London, 1968, Pelican edn, 1970), p. 34.
9  Local Government Board (LGB) Circular, 10 Aug. 1915; Elections and Registration Act, 5 & 6 Geo. 5, c. 76, 1915.
10  Worcester Guardians Minutes Book (MB), 8 Mar. 1917, County of Hereford and Worcester Record Office (CHWRO).
11  LGB circulars, 28 June, 17 Dec. 1915.
12  *Registrar General's Annual Reports for England and Wales*, 1914, 1915, 1916, 1917, 1918.
13  P. Thane, *The Foundations of the Welfare State* (New York, 1982), p. 133.
14  Winter, *The Great War*, p. 123.

15   *Kidderminster Shuttle*, 15 Feb. 1890.
16   CHWRO, Kidderminster Union Register of Deaths, 31 Mar. 1907–26 Mar. 1919, BA 8481.
17   CHWRO, Droitwich Guardians MB, May 1914–Sept. 1918, BA 401; J.L. Crammer, 'Extraordinary deaths of asylum inpatients during the 1914–1918 War', *Medical History*, **36** (Oct. 1992), 433–5.
18   Ibid.
19   Crammer, 'Extraordinary deaths', 433.
20   CHWRO, Worcester Guardians MB, 17 Oct. 1917, 6 Mar. 1918, 20 Mar. 1918, BA 8165.
21   Thane, *Welfare State*, p. 142.
22   H. Jones, *Health and Society in the Twentieth Century* (London, 1994), p. 53.
23   CHWRO, Worcester Pensions Committee MB., 25 Oct., 1, 15 Nov., 6 Dec. 1916, BA 11 241.
24   LGB Circular, 10 Aug. 1914.
25   CHWRO, Bromsgrove Guardians MB, 8 Sept., BA 400.
26   Jones, *Health*, pp. 49–50.
27   CHWRO, Droitwich Guardians MB, 19 Jan., 2 Feb., 16 Feb., 7 June 1916, 21 Sept. 1917, BA 401.
28   Thane, *Welfare State*, p. 129.
29   Nursing of the Sick in Workhouses Order, 6 Aug. 1897.
30   Memorandum on Nursing in Workhouse Sick Wards, 29 Jan. 1895, *Worcestershire Chronicle*, 14 Apr. 1900.
31   Appointment of District Nurses by Boards of Guardians Order, 27 Jan. 1892; Circular Letter, 1 Feb. 1892.
32   B.B. Gilbert, *British Social Policy, 1914–1939* (London, 1970), pp. 205, 207.
33   Lunatic Asylums and Pauper Lunatics Act, 1845, 8 & 9 Vict., c. 126.
34   CHWRO, Commissioners in Lunacy (CL) Report in the County and City of Worcester Pauper Lunatic Asylum (WLA) Visitors' Book, 14 Nov. 1889, BA 8343. Many of the asylum's records are deposited at the CHWRO; the remainder that are still extant are deposited at Newtown Hospital, Worcester.
35   47 Annual Report (AR) of the WLA, 1889, 26.
36   CHWRO, WLA Visitors Book, 20 July 1903, BA 8343.
37   CHWRO, CL Report in the WLA Vistor's Book, 15 June 1912, BA 8343.
38   63 AR of the WLA, 1915–16, 8.
39   4 AR of the Board of Control (BC), 1917, part 2, p. 49. The Com - missioners in Lunacy were replaced as the central authority by the Board of Control in 1913.
40   Ibid., 12 Dec. 1918.
41   68 AR of the WLA, 1920–21, 33.

42  67 AR of the WLA, 1919–20, 18–19.

43  CHWRO, BC inspector's report in the WLA Visitors Book, 12 Dec. 1918, BA 8343.

44  68 AR of the WLA, 1920–21, 24.

45  5 AR of the BC, 1918, 21–2.

46  Crammer, 'Extraordinary deaths', 435.

47  Ibid.

48  P. Hall, 'The history of Powick Hospital', P. Hall and I. F. Brockington (eds), *The Closure of Mental Hospitals* (London, 1991), p. 47.

49  Crammer, 'Extraordinary deaths', 441.

50  68 AR of the WLA, 1920–21, 26.

51  There is a question of semantics here: the term 'lunatic' was used in a very imprecise manner during the whole of the nineteenth century and later to cover a whole range of behavioural and mental problems; there is no more precision with the terms 'imbecile' and 'idiot', even the 1913 Mental Deficiency Act fails to provide this, but usually the terms refer to those defective from birth or an early age, and not dangerous.

52  ARs of the WLA, 1853–1916.

53  Conference of Worcestershire Guardians, in *Berrow's Worcester Journal*, 21 Aug. 1909.

54  BC circular, 18 July 1919.

55  Public Record Office, Memo, 26 Mar. 1887, MH32 52.

56  39 AR of the LGB, 1909–10, 65.

57  See G. Matthews, 'The search for a cure for vagrancy in Worcestershire, 1870–1920', *Midland History*, XI (1986), 101–3; 35 AR of the LGB, 1906.

58  35 AR of the LGB, 1905–6.

59  Report of the Departmental Committee on the Vagrancy Question, 1906, Cd. 2852, 24–5.

60  Matthews, 'Vagrancy', 103–5, 109.

61  *Berrow's Worcester Journal*, 21 Oct. 1882, 16 Dec. 1882. This system came to be known as the 'Berkshire System'.

62  Departmental Committee, 118–19.

63  LGB Circular, 10 Apr. 1916.

64  CHWRO, Worcester Guardians MB, 7 Feb. 1917, BA 8165.

65  1 AR of the Ministry of Health, 1919–20, 95.

66  S. and B. Webb, *History of English Local Government: English Poor Law History Part 2: The Last Hundred Years* (London, 1929, repr. 1963), p. 414.

67  Marwick, *The Deluge*, p. 242; Gilbert, *Social Policy*, p. 6.

68  CHWRO Bromsgrove Guardians MB, 4 Dec. 1917, BA 400; Droitwich Guardians MB, 19 Dec. 1917, BA 401

69  Gilbert, *Social Policy*, pp. 118–34.

70  Ibid., p. 136.

# 11

# The Immigrant Alternative: Ethnic and Sectarian Mutuality among the Liverpool Irish during the Nineteenth Century

## JOHN BELCHEM

The Irish in nineteenth-century Britain, Dorothy Thompson has observed, have generally been categorized (and caricatured) as a single out-group. Historians have paid insufficient attention to the divisions and complexities of their political and associational life.[1] Recent work has at last acknowledged the pronounced heterogeneity of the migrant influx, but in contesting the image of the Irish as 'outsiders', historians and historical geographers have also insisted on 'ethnic fade'. Distinctive 'Irish' cultural and associational forms were of rapidly diminishing significance as migrants readily identified, affiliated and integrated with host members of their particular class.[2] For those who settled in Liverpool and north-west England, Pooley contends, residential location, employment structure and living conditions 'were determined more by structural constraints of the labour and housing markets than by their Irishness'.[3] While acknowledging the materialist logic of such analysis, I want to highlight areas where ethnicity was accentuated by migration and remained at a premium. Through ethnic affiliation the Liverpool Irish were able to develop welfare and associational networks which extended beyond the reach of conventional labour movements and working-class voluntarism.

Liverpool demands attention because of the size and nature of its Irish population (although it is dismissed on these grounds from the latest study of Irish Catholics in England!).[4]

The Irish were located firmly at the bottom of the local occupational and social hierarchy, a pattern established before the Famine influx rendered Liverpool 'the hospital and cemetary [*sic*] of Ireland'.[5] Factor analysis of the 1841 census—by which time there were already 49,639 Irish-born in Liverpool, some 17.3 per cent of the population—has highlighted three main clusters of interrelated variables, a three-class model with an Irish/unskilled/lodging/industrial service/court-house cluster at the base. Predominantly unskilled, the Irish tended to congregate around 'core streets' in the city's two major working-class areas, close to the docks and the casual labour market: the 'instant slum' of the north end with its purpose-built court housing, and the failed middle-class suburb of the south end, hastily 'made down' into overcrowded and cellared street housing. Strictly speaking, these were not Irish ghettos. Outside the 'scale trap' of the core streets the index of segregation was not significantly high, while the persistence rate was remarkably low as the Irish, lacking attachment to particular jobs or buildings, favoured short-distance movements within familiar territory. As in Boston, however, few moved outwards and upwards.[6]

While the Irish in Britain were to distribute and integrate themselves throughout the urban hierarchy, taking up a number of occupational and residential opportunities, the large numbers who remained in Liverpool, the main port of entry, were a case apart. Father Nugent was to describe them as 'the dregs', the *caput mortuum*, unable, unsuited or unwilling to take advantage of opportunities elsewhere.[7] Confronted by their immovable presence, the Catholic Church in Liverpool was soon compelled to redefine its mission, to 'hibernicize' its philanthropic and associational provision. Along with the Irish pub, court and core street, the Catholic parish duly became another focus for collective mutuality, adding to the infrastructure of 'ethnic' solidarity and social security which made the Irish reluctant to leave Liverpool. Seen in these terms, continued residence in Liverpool, the 'black spot on the Mersey', was quite as rational as the peripatetic quest for 'success' elsewhere.

I

In Liverpool's courts, where housing conditions were among the worst in the country, women relied on each other for mutual aid. Those who gave expected to become recipients themselves when the wheel of fortune—or the family cycle—took a turn for the worse.[8] Newcomers were quickly welcomed and enlisted into the network, as an interviewee reported to Hugh Shimmin:

Why, before my wife had got her furniture put into any sort of order, she had been visited by half the women in the court—in a friendly way, of course. One and all wished her good luck; some wanted to borrow pans and mugs, some wished her to join them in a subscription to bury a child that was dead in the top house; others that had joined for a little sup of drink, wished her to taste with them; some wanted her to subscribe to a raffle for a fat pig, which had been fed in the cellar where it now was, and that was right opposite to the house in which I lived.[9]

While primarily instrumental in balancing the family budget, such female networks were by no means devoid of conviviality, good cheer and personal indulgence, as evinced by the Monday 'tea party' following the obligatory weekly visit to the pawn-shop to pledge the Sunday best:

On these occasions there appeared to be no lack of meat or drink, and immediately after the arrival of each visitor a little girl would be sent off to the grog shop for spirits.... There was generally a great bustle to get all indications of the tea party cleared off before the time at which the husbands might be expected home — that is supposing them to be at work—and the women separated with very loud protestations of friendship for each other.[10]

The Irish inflexion of such street-based networks is currently under investigation as part of a wider research project examining the various means by which Irish women coped with the economics and politics of poverty in nineteenth-century Liverpool.[11]

At least in part, the complementary pattern of male-dominated, pub-based secret societies offering welfare and protection, has already been reconstructed. In Irish–Liverpool ethnic consciousness was fostered first in the pub, later by the parish. Liverpool was notorious for its numerous pubs: Abraham Hume's survey noted nearly 1500 in the borough in 1858.[12] Competition for custom was intense, particularly in Irish areas where publicans encouraged various forms of convivial and bibulous associational culture, extending from legally approved Hibernian burial and friendly societies — founded in 1834, the Liverpool Hibernian Benevolent Burial Society provided the model for the expansion of Catholic collective mutuality throughout the Irish diaspora[13]—to secret Ribbon branches linked to networks across the Irish Sea. As in Ireland, Ribbonism in Liverpool was multi-functional and morally ambiguous. Its secrecy and ritual served *inter alia* to promote republican revolution, organized crime, sectarian protection and collective mutuality.[14] On the Liverpool waterfront, Ribbonism functioned as a form of primitive trade unionism, as Irish dock-labourers sought to corner a niche of the labour market by threats and violence against outsiders. Newly arrived migrants unaware of the 'goods', the latest secret Ribbon grips and passwords, often found themselves at painful disadvantage within dock-labour gangs.[15] Here, too, were a number of lucrative business opportunities for members of the 'friendship'. Ribbonmen, it was reported in 1840, were 'straining at a monopoly in the shipment of Irish emigrants. One man, from nothing, has realised a large fortune and has several Delegates on both sides in his employ as agents'.[16] Others sought financial gain at the movement's expense, selling their services within the shady intelligence network. Having failed in trade, E. Rorke moved in with his Liverpool mistress to exploit his old mercantile contacts with Irish connections, eliciting information which he then sold to the authorities. His main informant, P.H. McGloin, a respectable young businessman, employed by wool merchants on a salary of £100 per annum, later claimed that until approached by Rorke, he had 'taken very little part in the thing, because being in a respectable situation and having business to attend to, it was against his interest to spend his nights in attending meetings and *"boozing"*, which the Officers of the Society must do'.[17] McGloin's reports provide a useful insight into the operation of the Northern Union (also known as Hibernians or Widgeons) in Liverpool in the late 1830s. They should be read in conjunction with the vast amount of Liverpool material in the papers seized at the Dublin house of Richard Jones, national secretary of the rival Ribbonite network, the Irish Sons of Freedom, following his arrest in the major round-up of Ribbon leaders in October 1839.[18]

As the main port of entry, Liverpool was the pivotal point for both Ribbon networks as they extended their cover among migrant workers. Ribbonism, indeed, provided an important complement to the normal mechanisms of chain migration, serving as reception and assistance centre for migrant Irish Catholic workers.[19] Working through family networks, social connections and regional solidarities, chain migration involved social arrangements with people already at destination, who characteristically helped newcomers to find jobs and housing, thereby protecting them from disorientation, dislocation and anomic behaviour. This functional analysis, however, should not be pushed too far. Information was shared by kin, friends and acquaintances, but there was considerable discrepancy in the knowledge and assistance—the 'personal information field'—available to individual migrants.[20] As the pace of Irish emigration increased dramatically from the 1820s, Ribbonism, with its extensive secret organizational structure, served both to fill the gaps in these informal networks and to provide cheap, flexible and mobile benefits for those unable to gain employment at the chosen destination. The secret network which provided 'political' sanctuary for members in flight from the Irish authorities also offered 'tramping' benefits to itinerant migrant workers.

Radiating from Liverpool, the two networks provided cover and benefits for migrant workers in 'unskilled' and mobile sectors of the labour market, often excluded from organized forms of working-class collective mutuality. In artisan networks, tramping was a means of control in the interests of local closed shop: in Ribbon networks, by contrast, tramping facilitated mobility in pursuit of whatever work was available, while offering 'political' sanctuary for members in flight from the Irish authorities.[21] Railway navvies and building labourers appreciated the advantages of membership, and were increasingly prominent in both networks.

The essential qualification for membership was Catholicism, a point scrupulously checked before new arrivals were admitted to the Liverpool lodges:

Much precaution is used in the introduction of members, none but Roman Catholics being admissible; and a *report list*, with the name, age and residence, the parish and county where each candidate comes from, must be read out in each *body*, and afterwards in the General Committee of the Town . . . each must be passed in two or more bodies and afterwards approved by the General Committee.[22]

In the Northern Union, basic cover was provided at modest cost, normally 1s. for admission and a quarterly payment of either 3d. or 6d. Sickness and death benefits were left to the discretion of the local branch or lodge: tramp relief, however, was distributed out of the 'box' (held at local headquarters—in Liverpool, the Grapes Inn, Grayson Street) through the highest local officer, the 'county delegate', and charged quarterly upon each branch—tramps holding 'regular certificates' were generally given a bed for the night and a payment of 1s. 6d. Elected by the branch officers at the quarterly meeting of the general committee, the 'delegate' was entrusted to attend the quarterly General Board of Erin or 'market' in Ireland to receive the 'goods', the latest signs and passwords, the correct version of which had to appear on the card or certificate presented by tramps seeking relief. The delegate's expenses in attending the General Board had the first call on funds, followed by relief and assistance for arrested or fugitive members in Ireland, leaving the remainder for benefit payments. On occasion, there was misunderstanding of this order of priority, although such matters were generally dealt with internally by the 'select', a gathering of the parish masters, sitting above the general committee to assist and advise the county delegate and act, if required, as arbitration tribunal.[23] There was considerable embarrassment in 1842 when Patrick O'Neill brought an action before the Liverpool magistrates against John McArdle, president of the Second Hibernians. Having joined the Provident Friendly Society, a society accorded legal recognition and approval by Tidd Pratt, the Registrar of Friendly Societies, O'Neill had fallen ill—and apparently into arrears—when the society was subsumed into the Second Hibernians, which then denied him sickness benefit. Under cross-examination, Patrick Doyle, president of the Provident Friendly Society, admitted that he had spent £6 of the funds of the society on a trip to Ireland to help raise bail for someone charged with Ribbonism.[24]

Smaller in scale, the Liverpool branch of the Irish Sons of Freedom operated from headquarters in George Carrick's Hibernian Tavern in Newton Hill Street, where much of the administration was left to the local 'president'. Within a few months of his election in 1838, William Wilson, a painter and decorator, complained of the disproportionate burdens of office, for which he received no expenses. On top of his onerous responsibilities for tramp relief, he had to attend the general meeting, take reports, read letters, in effect do the whole work of the society . . . Every Sunday night either 3 or 4 of our bodies meet, they require my attendance every Monday night. I have to attend at Mr Carrick see the money forthcoming, receipt the Stewards books, see the sick money paid.[25]

One of his main initiatives during his term as president, an attempt to introduce a properly funded and administered system of tramp relief, left him so disillusioned that he decided to tender his resignation:

Any good rules I propose I cannot get them carried into effect to meet the wants of distressed tramps. I proposed that each member should pay 1d. per month that it be lodged in the hands of Mr Carrick and according as any distressed friend would come and apply to me for assistance for me to give a note to Carrick for the price of his bed and supper. Carrick to keep all these dockets and get credit for nothing at the quarterly settlement but what he could provide a docket for . . . all we could get to pay was 22 men . . . all my labour was in vain in introducing good discipline among them, they are all generals and no privates.[26]

In 1842, by which time the movement was past its peak, Head Constable Whitty calculated that there were still thirteen Ribbon pubs in Liverpool.[27] Dublin Castle asked the Liverpool police to keep a close watch on Jack Langan, a former Irish champion boxer, who ran the most famous 'Irish' pub, strategically positioned opposite Clarence Dock, the disembarkation point for Irish passenger traffic—it was immediately recognizable by the effigy of St Patrick, shamrock in hand, high on its walls. Langan enjoyed considerable fame and fortune in Liverpool—his estate was valued at over £20,000 on his death in 1846—appearing on the platform when his hero Daniel O'Connell visited the town. After close surveillance, the police concluded that the former pugilist was 'too wealthy and too prudent' to engage in secret Ribbon activity.[28] Lacking such celebrity, other Irish publicans undertook Ribbonite office, concealing the secret operations behind their promotion of legally approved forms of associational culture. Hugh McAnulty, a Grayson Street publican and one of the founders of the Hibernian Benevolent Society, was 'by far the best-known man in Ireland', regularly representing Liverpool at the Board of Erin until his death in the mid-1830s. His various responsibilities were assumed by George

Hamill, who married his widow, took over the pub, and attended the Board three or four times before his own death a couple of years later. Undaunted, the twice-widowed Mrs Hamill proved a jealous guardian of the Ribbon tradition, one of several female licensees who provided important services for a male-based, pub-centred culture of secrecy.[29] Under cover of the legally approved Provident Friendly Society, the Grapes Inn remained the most important Ribbonite venue in Liverpool. Some publicans, however, proved reluctant to commit themselves beyond the provision of premises. John McArdle, an Ulster Catholic by birth, hosted a number of societies at his Crosbie Street pub—including the Second Hibernian Friendly Society, the Third Hibernian Mechanical Society, and one of the earliest lodges of the Ancient Order of Hibernians—some of which, as the action brought against him in 1842 revealed, were undoubtedly a cover for Ribbon activities. According to informers, however, McArdle was 'a decent and honourable man who always opposed the continuation of Secret Communication with Ireland'. Having the misfortune to be appointed Liverpool delegate at the time of the arrests and trials of 1840, he chose not to fulfil his duties.[30]

Given its nodal location, Liverpool figured prominently in the unity discussions of the two Ribbon networks, providing a 'neutral' venue away from regional rivalry, and offering a ready-made communications network: 'as all persons going on tramp to England would have to call in Liverpool, they would be able to send word to all parts of Ireland.'[31] The discussions proved abortive, further evidence of the intense regional and local loyalties within Ireland itself. Emigrants were no less prone to factional feuding. In Liverpool, however, such 'private battles' soon gave way to 'sectarian violence', conflicts based on a wider sense of ethnic identity.[32] Ribbonism was the proactive force in this sectarian implantation. Extending beyond the familial and regional affiliations through which chain migration typically operated, Ribbonism was to subsume lesser rivalries as it widened its constituency among other Catholic migrants. At this stage, Orangeism lacked such a capacity for growth. Yet to be appropriated by the local Tory establishment, it lacked resonance beyond the limited ranks of immigrant Ulster Protestants, probably no more than one in five of the Liverpool Irish.[33] In terms of paid-up membership, Ribbonism remained a minority movement in Liverpool, strongest among migrants from Ulster and adjoining counties, but its sectarian mentality helped to construct a wider sense of national identity and affiliation in which Catholic and Irish became synonymous.

## II

As this sense of Irishness developed, the focus of associational culture and collective mutuality shifted from pub to parish. Previously, the Catholic Church had tried to eradicate Ribbonism by proscription. 'The clergy here this several years past,' the Liverpool president of the Irish Sons of Freedom reported to Dublin, 'were violently opposed against Irishmen on this side of the Channel holding a communication with Ireland. These Hibernians or Widgeons had recourse to every open artifice to deceive the clergy but God help them they were deceiving themselves when they would go to confession.' Under threat of denial of the sacraments, some members of the Northern Union withdrew altogether; others alternated in attendance, according to conscience and need, between church and lodge; and certain sections of the leadership contemplated a range of exculpatory options, even severance of the offending link with Ireland. There was much internal dissension (and increased friction between the rival networks) when the Hibernians gave serious consideration to 'dropping Ireland . . . of complying with the Bishops declaration and setting up shop for themselves confining their system, *as they say*, to England alone'.[34]

Having left Ireland before its 'devotional revolution', the migrants presented considerable problems for the Catholic Church in north-west England. Unacquainted with the discipline of Tridentine conformism the Irish posed an unwelcome challenge, detracting from the high standard of practice among the small indigenous Catholic community.[35] In the human entrepôt of Liverpool, impoverished transients imposed a disproportionate burden on confessional welfare resources. The extent of destitution, the local Catholic Benefit Society stressed, was compounded by 'the arrival from Ireland of many persons who intended to emigrate, but who were stricken down by sickness and want, and were thus compelled to remain'.[36] Confronted by the full force of the Famine influx, the Catholic Church in Liverpool underwent a process of 'hibernicization' more rapid and thorough than elsewhere in England,[37] an adaptation which contributed much to the city's subsequent exceptionalism in political and labour history.

There were early indications of the new approach in St Patrick's Day processions in the early 1840s. Hibernian Societies and the Ribbonmen, exclusively Catholic but in the hands of the laity, were joined by various associations under clerical control. These included the Liverpool District of the Grand United Order of the Catholic Brethren of the Blackburn Unity. From its Blackburn base, the United Catholic Brethren, as J.H. Treble has shown, 'sought to supersede all those secret societies which had hitherto ensnared innocent Catholics'. To match Ribbonism, however, it needed to construct a national framework, to offer not merely sickness and death benefits but also tramping relief. The necessary growth beyond the regional base, however, was impeded by the episcopate, who gave their blessing instead to local 'guilds' on the Bradford model, benefit societies strictly under the control of the local clergy and integrated into the spiritual life of the parish. Outside of Liverpool, however, the northern guilds quickly collapsed, victims of cyclical depression in the early 1840s. Catholic workers, Treble contends, turned back to trade unionism, towards which the clergy duly abandoned much of its former hostility.[38] In Liverpool, however, a different pattern prevailed. Catholic social welfare continued to expand.

From the early days of sectarian rivalry in Liverpool, the Catholics proudly asserted their supremacy in welfare provision. Protestant charity, the *Catholic Institute Magazine* critically observed, 'proceeds with a fixity of system, a calm calculation of practical results, a rigid economy of good works, which utterly destroy to Catholic eyes all that in Charity is most beautiful and most holy'.[39] Certainly, there were important differences in cultural style and strategy between what might be termed Protestant 'scientific charity' and Catholic 'alms-giving'. While the Liverpool Domestic Mission, founded by members of the Methodist Chapel on Renshaw Street, saw itself as an agency for moral reform rather than of relief distribution, the St Vincent de Paul Society served—in Catholic Glaswegian fashion—as a 'General Purposes Society', granting generous relief in case of need and where there was proof of minimal religious observance.[40] The best-documented study of the Society relates to

St Mary's, Highfield Street, a parish established in the eighteenth century close to the business quarter to serve the small Catholic population, but then overwhelmed by the famine influx of poor Irish immigrants into what became the 'most squalid part' of town.[41]

Instead of moral condemnation, Catholic philanthropists displayed a materialist understanding, taking an inverse pride, as it were, in the destitution of Irish immigrants, 'the thousands of homeless, moneyless, raimentless, foodless creatures that call the Catholic Church their mother in Liverpool'. In this 'sinkhole of sinfulness and depravity',[42] environmentalism extended to immigrants seemingly lost to the faith:

The best of the labouring classes do not emigrate. Those who do, are not treated on their coming, with kindness and considerateness—very much the reverse. They must descend to the worst work, and accept the worst pay ... they are on all sides treated with disrespect, and in many cases, unfortunately, they fail to respect themselves. Their new circumstances suggest brutal habits, and equally brutal enjoyments ... Those men of course are not Catholic, but they are not Protestant, and they are Irish.[43]

Claiming the depraved Irish as their particular concern—as their special mission for spiritual salvation and welfare protection—Father Nugent and the Catholics sought to outmatch Protestant achievements.

In this competitive provision, particular attention was accorded to the growing number of street children—'Save the Boy!' was Nugent's motto.[44] The mid-Victorians, Gertrude Himmelfarb has observed, associated the streets with licence and abandon, as the place where conventional distinctions of what was legal and illegal, moral and immoral, proper and improper, permissible and impermissible, did not prevail. Hence their attraction, as Mayhew's London survey had shown, to a particular 'tribe' or 'race', 'street-folk' who could not bear the physical and psychic confinements of civilized Victorian life, who could not live indoors, within the closed walls of home and workshop, bound by the constraints of time, place and convention.[45] Street poverty, however, was not simply a form of social pathology. In Liverpool, the streets were the site of a boisterous 'secondary economy', the domain of hawkers and costermongers, common lodging-house keepers, bookies, pawnbrokers, prostitutes, petty criminals and others, constantly moved on by the police from respectable areas. Catering for the needs of the city's poorest inhabitants and its least wary visitors, this street economy was the point of consumption and/or income for many immigrants, including single and deserted women, children and orphans.[46] A double imperative prompted the local Catholic Church to take action to 'rescue' children from this corrupting environment. First there was the need to counteract the baleful influence of the local authorities, to stem 'the fearful leakage of Catholic children under Poor Law management'. 'Necessitous' children taken in care by the authorities were denied proper Catholic religious instruction in the workhouse, one of many instances of Protestant bigotry (and deficiency) in civic social policy subsequently chronicled by Thomas Burke.[47] Then there was Nugent's personal mission, his determination to set the lead in social policy by placing the Catholic Church at the forefront of the reformatory movement:

... of late years the circumstances of Ireland have flung into the vortex of Liverpool low-life, innumerable creatures, without father, mother or friend. These are indeed, beings, whom to know, is to pity, and whom no Christian can desire to leave exposed to the temptations of the world. In their course of life, their normal condition is one of crime — and it is only in Reformatories they can, without the intervention of a special providence, become Christian. It is only thus these Arabs of society can be brought under the civilizing influences of citizenship.[48]

By enlisting the funds and support of the Catholic Club and of members of the professional and business classes associated with his Catholic Institute in Hope Street, Nugent established the Association of Providence. This provided the finance for a number of schemes, including the Night Shelter and Refuge in Soho Street, an attempt 'to deal more effectively with his street arabs'.[49]

Although criticized for his showmanship by his co-religionist M.J. Whitty, editor of the *Liverpool Daily Post*, Nugent was the inspirational figure in a remarkable extension of philanthropic endeavour. The inscription on his statue in St John's Gardens chronicles his achievements: 'Apostle of Temperance, Protector of the Orphan Child, Consoler of the Prisoner, Reformer of the Criminal, Saviour of Fallen Womanhood, Friend of All in Poverty and Affliction, an Eye to the Blind, a Foot to the Lame, the

Father of the Poor'.[50] Nugent's personal drive aside, sectarian rivalry was the crucial spur to such welfare efforts. Excluded from the British 'master narrative' of Protestant constitutional liberty, Catholics propounded an alternative concept of citizenship in which charitable provision held pride of place. Here Catholic Europe with its charitable institutions set the example, offering the solution to the 'Condition of England' question:

> ... England receives another lesson, that while in the Science of Government her knowledge is supreme, there are many social questions upon which her neighbours' knowledge is superior . . . if we have triumphed through Representative Government, other countries who know not its advantages, have had their triumphs also; and have not neglected the interests of the poor. Again, it is a wholesome lesson that England should be taught, amid her pride of power and place, that she must draw the remedy for her social evils, and learn the means of reforming her seething population, from the wisdom and beneficence of that Church, which repudiating, she has never ceased to persecute.[51]

Catholic charity flourished in Liverpool, the *Catholic Institute Magazine* proclaimed, notwithstanding 'the restraints and confinements of countless obstacles to its natural development':

> The great bulk of the Catholic population is hopelessly poor, the number of our priests and religious is miserably disproportionate to the amount of labour they are obliged to undertake, and the watchful jealousy of our non-Catholic fellow-countrymen, excited by the incredible misrepresentations of a certain portion of their so-called pastors, clogs and impedes our every action . . . in spite of the necessity under which we lay of expending a very great portion of our means in building churches to supply the stately edifices of which the ruthless injustice of a tyrant had unscrupulously deprived us, England is already giving abundant proof that no persecution can stifle the Church of God, no pressure of poverty can destroy the Charity of her children.[52]

By the late nineteenth century there was a flourishing local 'vereinskatholizismus', to use the German term for the multiplication of organizations designed to meet the special needs—spiritual, economic and recreational—of every identifiable group within the Catholic population.[53] The *Catholic Family Annual and Almanac for the Diocese of Liverpool* (1884) accorded pride of place to the local orphanages, industrial schools and reformatories (by this time, the Liverpool Reformatory Association was responsible for the reformatory ship 'Clarence', a farm school at

Ainsdale and a girls' reformatory in Old Swan), along with other charitable institutions, including the Brotherhood of St Vincent of Paul; the Catholic School for the Blind; the Convent of the Good Shepherd where penitent women were occupied in laundry work; the Convent of Mercy which in administering to 'the corporal and spiritual wants of the poor' also admitted young women who were 'trained up to habits of virtue and industry'; the Home for the Aged Poor; the Liverpool Catholic Benevolent Society which provided the clergy with alms to relieve the sick poor; the Sisters of Bon Secours de Troyes who nursed the sick of all ages; and the Liverpool Catholic Children's Protection Society which found homes in Canada for 'Catholic children destitute or neglected, and in circumstances of danger and loss of their Religion'.

While primarily concerned with spiritual salvation, Catholic welfare provision sought to prepare the poor for citizenship by conformity to dominant notions of respectability. However, by imparting these 'respectable' values within a self-enclosed network of charity and collective mutuality, Catholic social policy served to underline Catholic apartness. Indeed, it may well have engendered a dependency culture as the inverse pride in poverty and destitution, the initial register of Catholic middle-class social consciousness, was embraced by impoverished Irish immigrants, by the poor recipients themselves. In Liverpool, as in Dundee, poverty was rationalized by the conflation of religious adherence and ethnic affiliation.[54] Sanctified by Catholicism, poverty became the proud hallmark of being genuinely Irish. Unlike the Liverpool Liberal élite which preserved its distance from the crude conviviality of working-class culture, Catholic priests and Irish nationalist politicians displayed a willingness to compromise with the street and the pub. Their efforts to develop a 'respectable' framework of associational culture were punctuated by intervention in such matters as fighting and drinking, regular exhortations which carried no expectation of permanent moral reform.[55] In the absence of a patronizing improvement ethic, the Irish constructed their own 'culture of poverty', a pattern replicated throughout the Irish diaspora. Some Irish–Australians chose to eschew the Australian ethic of individual material advancement in favour of the communality and solidarity—and welfare benefits?—available only at the bottom of the social, but not the spiritual, scale.[56]

## III

Having failed to eradicate pub-based Ribbonism by proscription, the Catholic Church in Liverpool developed a rival, parish-based framework of associational culture, offering cradle-to-grave sustenance and support for Irish immigrants, male and female. In the second half of the nineteenth century, Liverpool's north end emerged as a distinctively Irish—and Catholic—community in which new churches with Irish priests became the centre of associational life, encouraging the tendency to residential propinquity.[57] In these dockland parishes, the benefits reached down to casual labourers and their families, bad risks excluded from new model forms of work-based collective mutuality whose actuarial calculations precluded what Dutch social historians have called 'moral hazards' and 'adverse selection'—the increased likelihood of the risk occurring once cover is granted, and the expectation of gaining benefits in excess of contributions.[58]

Taken together, the pub and the parish provided the infrastructure for an effective 'pillarized' form (to adopt another useful term from Dutch social history) of welfare politics. Mobilized through these dual networks of ethnic and sectarian associational culture, the Irish national political machine enjoyed considerable local success. A counterweight to the dominant Tory–Democratic electoral machine, it catered for second-generation (i.e. Liverpool-born) Irish, for whom the fate of Ireland was of less account than the immediate housing and employment needs of local Catholics.[59] Its long-term viability, however, depended upon the continued estrangement of the Liverpool Irish from other (class-based) political formations.[60]

This essay has drawn attention to alternative immigrant forms of collective mutuality and welfare agency, but the extent (and influence) of such ethnic/nationalist/sectarian provision should not be exaggerated. The workhouse and other official institutions loom large in Pat O'Mara's autobiography of a 'Liverpool Irish Slummy'. Accepting the Catholic Church's teachings on marriage, his much-abused mother was unable to turn to the priest and the parish at times of greatest need, when compelled to leave her drunken and violent husband.[61] Seen from the perspective of an Irish nationalist in the early years of the twentieth century, there was much to be done in the 'Irish Colony' in

Liverpool. While friendly society membership of the Irish National Foresters should be encouraged among 'all people of Irish birth or descent' in the city, the most pressing need was the establishment of 'a non-political and non-sectarian Irish society of social workers in Liverpool to improve the conditions of slum life'. No less urgent than welfare, however, was the need to recover and project a sense of 'Irishness'. Here other forms of associational and political culture were recommended: the Gaelic Athletic Association, the Gaelic League, the Liverpool Irish Society, the Liverpool Irish Literary Society, and the prompt formation of a Liverpool branch of Sinn Fein.[62]

# NOTES

1  Dorothy Thompson, *Outsiders: Class, Gender and Nation* (London, 1993), p.18.
2  See the essays by Colin Pooley, David Fitzpatrick and Graham Davis in R. Swift and S. Gilley (eds), *The Irish in Britain 1815–1939* (London, 1989). See also Graham Davis, *The Irish in Britain 1815–1914* (Dublin, 1991).
3  Colin Pooley, 'Irish settlement in North West England in the mid-nineteenth century: a geographical critique', *North West Labour History*, **19** (1991–2), 32.
4  Steven Fielding's study of *Class and Ethnicity: Irish Catholics in England, 1880–1939* (Buckingham, 1993), p. 5, dismisses Liverpool as a sectarian redoubt, 'marginal to the cultural and political life of the nation'.
5  Quarterly returns of the Registrar General, Third Quarter, 1847, quoted in I.C. Taylor, 'Black spot on the Mersey: a study of environment and society in 18th and 19th century Liverpool' (unpublished Ph.D. dissertation, University of Liverpool, 1976), p. 163.
6  J.D. Papworth, 'The Irish in Liverpool, 1835–71: segregation and dispersal' (unpublished Ph.D. dissertation, University of Liverpool, 1982), Ch. X.
7  Quoted in Taylor, 'Black spot', p. 101.
8  M. Anderson, *Family Structure in Nineteenth-Century Lancashire* (Cambridge, 1971). J. Winter, 'Widowed mothers and mutual aid in early Victorian Britain', *Journal of Social History*, **XVII** (1983–4), 115–16.
9  Quoted in H. Shimmin, 'The courts at Christmas time', in J. Walton and A. Wilcox (eds), *Low Life and Moral Improvement in Mid-Victorian England: Liverpool through the Journalism of Hugh Shimmin* (Leicester, 1991), p. 156.

10   Shimmin, 'The social condition of the people', p. 111.

11   Martha Kanya-Forstner's unpublished paper, 'Gender, ethnicity and the politics of poverty: Irish women in mid-Victorian Liverpool', gives an indication of the important findings of her eagerly awaited Ph.D. thesis.

12   A. Hume, *Condition of Liverpool, Religious and Social, Including Notices of the State of Education, Morals, Pauperism and Crime* (Liverpool, 1858), p. 28.

13   T.F. McGrath, *History of the Ancient Order of Hibernians* (Cleveland, Ohio, 1898), pp. 51–5; Wayne G. Broehl, Jr, *The Molly Maguires* (Cambridge, MA, 1964), pp. 32–3.

14   Tom Garvin, 'Defenders, Ribbonmen and others: underground political networks in pre-Famine Ireland', *Past and Present*, **96** (1982), 133–55; M.R. Beames, 'The Ribbon societies; lower-class nationalism in pre-Famine Ireland', *Past and Present*, **97** (1982), 128–43.

15   John Denvir, *The Irish in Britain* (London, 1892), pp. 127–31.

16   Public Record Office, Kew: Colonial Office Papers (hereafter CO) 904/8, ff. 82–9.

17   Matheson's report to Drummond on his interview with McGloin in Dublin, CO 904/7, ff. 465–70.

18   The transcription of these papers proved difficult and contentious, see Co 904/7 ff. 313–28; hence only a small selection was produced at the trial: see M.J. Martyn, *An authentic report of the trial of Richard Jones ... with an appendix, containing the letters and correspondence of the secret society read in evidence at trial* (Dublin, 1840). However, transcriptions of all items can be found in the papers of Messrs Kemmis, Crown Solicitors, in National Archives, Dublin: Frazer MSS 43, Transcript of the books written in short hand found on the person of Richard Jones on the 1st October 1839 (hereafter Jones transcript). A near complete copy is available at the Public Record Office, Kew: Home Office Papers (hereafter HO) 100/263.

19   John Belchem, '"Freedom and friendship to Ireland": Ribbonism in early nineteenth-century Liverpool', *International Review of Social History*, **39** (1994), 33–56.

20   For a useful comparative and 'systemic' perspective on migration, see Leslie Page Moch, *Moving Europeans: Migration in Western Europe since 1650* (Bloomington, 1992), in particular pp. 16–18 and 103–60.

21   E.J. Hobsbawm, 'The tramping artisan', in his *Labouring Men* (London, 1968), p. 38.

22   Extracts from communications from the informant A.B., CO 904/8, ff. 309–10.

23   Ibid., ff. 309–17. Statement of John O'Brien, 3 Nov. 1841, HO 45/184.

24   *Liverpool Mercury*, 29 Apr. 1842.

25   Jones transcript, no. 80, Wilson, 22 Aug. 1838.

26 Ibid.

27 Whitty's report, 2 April 1842, CO 904/9, ff. 210–15.

28 Liverpool Police Office, 27 May 1839, CO 904/7, f. 192; *Liverpool Mercury*, 19 June 1846; John Denvir, *The Life Story of an Old Rebel* (Dublin, 1910), pp. 3–4, 52.

29 Widow McNamara provided similar services at her jerry shop in Union Street, Preston: see Gilgun's statement, 5 Dec. 1840, HO 100/263 ff. 346–50. Women also provided the premises for clerically approved societies, such as the St Anthony's Society at Ellen Wood's, Cockspur Street, and the Roman Catholic Teetotal Association at Mrs Mountain's, Flood Street, Liverpool.

30 'Delegates in Liverpool since 1830', CO 904/8, ff. 79–80. McArdle's public readings from the *Nation* became a regular Sunday night attraction at Crosbie Street: see Denvir, *Life Story*, pp. 15–16.

31 Jones transcript, no. 75, Jones, 6 Aug. 1838.

32 See the useful distinctions drawn by Anne Bryson in her study of 'Riotous Liverpool, 1815–1860', in John Belchem (ed.), *Popular Politics, Riot and Labour: Essays in Liverpool History 1790–1940* (Liverpool, 1992), pp. 98–134.

33 On the origins of Orangeism in Liverpool, see Frank Neal, *Sectarian Violence: The Liverpool Experience 1819–1914* (Manchester, 1988), pp. 17–32.

34 Jones transcript, no. 42, Wilson, Liverpool, 4 May 1838. Ribbonism was the main target, but clerical proscription applied to all forms of oath-bound societies: see J.H. Treble, 'The attitude of the Roman Catholic Church towards trade unionism in the North of England', *Northern History*, V (1970), 93–113; G.P. Connolly, 'The Catholic Church and the first Manchester and Salford trade unions in the age of the Industrial Revolution', *Transactions of the Lancashire and Cheshire Antiquarian Society*, **135** (1985), 125–39.

35 G. Connolly, 'Irish and Catholic: myth or reality? Another sort of Irish and the renewal of the clerical profession among Catholics in England, 1791–1818', in R. Swift and S. Gilley (eds), *The Irish in the Victorian City* (London, 1985).

36 Liverpool Record Office, 361 CAT: Liverpool Catholic Benefit Society Minute Book, 1850–58, press cutting from *Liverpool Mercury*, 23 Dec. 1851.

37 David Fitzpatrick, '"A peculiar tramping people": the Irish in Britain, 1801–70', in W.E. Vaughan (ed.), *A New History of Ireland, V: Ireland under the Union* (Oxford, 1989), pp. 650–4.

38 Treble, 'The attitude of the Roman Catholic Church', 104–13.

39 'Liverpool Catholic Charities: No. 1', *Catholic Institute Magazine*, Jan. 1856.

40  Martha Kanya-Forstner, 'Coping with poverty: the experience of Irish women in mid-Victorian Liverpool', unpublished seminar paper, Institute of Irish Studies, University of Liverpool (1994). Bernard Aspinwall, 'The welfare state within the state: the Saint Vincent de Paul Society in Glasgow, 1848–1920', in W.J. Sheils and D. Wood (eds), *Studies in Church History: Voluntary Religion* (Oxford, 1986) pp. 445–59.

41  John Davies, 'Parish charity: the work of the Society of St Vincent de Paul, St Mary's, Highfield Street, Liverpool, 1867–68', *North West Catholic History*, **XVII** (1990), 37–46.

42  'Church-going in Liverpool', *Catholic Institute Magazine*, Nov. 1855.

43  'Reformatories: their nature, origin and tendency', *Catholic Institute Magazine*, Sept. 1856.

44  Canon Bennett, *Father Nugent of Liverpool* (Liverpool, 1949), Ch. III

45  Gertrude Himmelfarb, *The Idea of Poverty* (London, 1984), pp. 366–8.

46  M. Brogden, *The Police: Autonomy and Consent* (London, 1982), pp. 43–73. See also the series of twenty weekly letters on 'Labour and the poor: Liverpool' which began in the *Morning Chronicle*, 20 May 1850.

47  T.N. Burke, *Catholic History of Liverpool* (Liverpool, 1910), p. 165 and *passim*.

48  'Reformatories', *Catholic Institute Magazine*, Sept. 1856.

49  Bennett, *Father Nugent*, pp. 40–1.

50  Ibid., pp. 11, 74–5.

51  'Reformatories', *Catholic Institute Magazine*, Sept. 1856.

52  'Liverpool's Catholic Charities: No. 1', *Catholic Institute Magazine*, Jan. 1856.

53  H. McLeod, 'Building the "Catholic ghetto": Catholic organizations 1870–1914', in Sheils and Wood (eds), *Voluntary Religion*, pp. 411–44.

54  W.M. Walker, 'Irish immigrants in Scotland: their priests, politics and parochial life', *Historical Journal*, **15** (1972), 649–67.

55  John Belchem, 'The Irish in Britain, United States and Australia: some comparative reflections on labour history', in John Belchem and Patrick Buckland (eds), *The Irish in British Labour History* (Liverpool, 1993), p. 20.

56  Patrick O'Farrell, *The Irish in Australia* (Kensington, NSW, 1986), p. 299.

57  Papworth, 'The Irish in Liverpool 1835–71', Ch. V. See also Frank Boyce, 'Irish Catholicism in Liverpool: the 1920s and 1930s', in Belchem and Buckland (eds), *The Irish in British Labour History*, pp. 86–101.

58  Marco van Leeuwen, 'Trade union welfare in the Netherlands 1910–1960', paper presented to the Ninth British–Dutch Conference on

Labour History, Social Policy and the Labour Movement, Bergen, 2–4 September 1994.

59 Bernard O'Connell, 'Irish nationalism in Liverpool, 1873–1923', *Eire-Ireland*, **10** (1975), 24–37; A. Shallice, 'Orange and Green and militancy: sectarianism and working-class politics in Liverpool, 1900–1914', *Bulletin of the Northwest Labour History Society*, **6** (1979–80), 15–32; L.W. Brady, *T.P. O'Connor and the Liverpool Irish* (London, 1983). See also P.J. Waller, *Democracy and Sectarianism: A Political and Social History of Liverpool, 1868–1939* (Liverpool, 1981).

60 Joan Smith, 'Labour tradition in Glasgow and Liverpool', *History Workshop Journal*, **17** (1984), 32–56.

61 Pat O'Mara, *The Autobiography of a Liverpool Irish Slummy* (London, 1934).

62 Anon., *The Liverpool Irishman, or Annals of the Irish Colony in Liverpool* (Liverpool, 1909).

# 12

## 'We All Come from Round Sora': Italians in Birmingham, c.1821–1919

### CARL CHINN

### I

Today, Birmingham is a multi-cultural city. Newcomers walking along its main shopping thoroughfares are bewildered and impressed by the medley of languages and accents which strain to catch their attention: the broad cries of English butchers, market traders and newspaper sellers; the rapidly spoken patois of Afro-Caribbean entrepreneurs; the Greek of Cypriot fish and chip shop owners; the variety of Irish intonations, from the country lilt of Roscommon-born building contractors to the city-speak of Dublin-bred publicans; the Cantonese of Chinese restaurateurs; and the South Asian languages of Punjabi and Kashmiri balti-house keepers, Gujarati jewellers and sweet-shop proprietors, Bangladeshi curry-house owners, and Sikh builders' merchants.

This ethnic and linguistic diversity is a recent phenomenon. As late as 1951, 89.1 per cent of Birmingham's inhabitants were English. Indeed, a massive 71 per cent of its people came from one county—Warwickshire.[1] The intimate connection of the city to the surrounding district was long-standing. W.H.B. Court examined the certificates of settlement which exist for the years 1686–1726. These gave the origins of 695 migrants to Birmingham. They indicated that 539 of these people had moved in from the adjoining counties of Warwickshire, Staffordshire and Worcestershire.[2] Autobiographies and oral evidence emphasize the continuing importance of migration from nearby villages.[3] So do the Brummie accent and dialect, both of which are derived from the speech of the people of the city's rural hinterland.[4] But whilst local migrants remained dominant, members of ethnic minorities did become more noticeable during the eighteenth and nineteenth centuries. The Welsh, especially, were important in Birmingham. Many of them came from the counties of Brecon

251

and Radnor, whilst the first Lloyds bank was founded in the city's High Street in 1765 by descendants of incomers from Montgomeryshire.[5]

The Welsh did not gather in a distinct part of Birmingham. Nor did the smaller number of Scots, whose presence was indicated not only by well-known names like William Murdock and the industrialist George Kynoch but also by the opening of a 'Scotch Church' in Islington in 1824.[6] Similarly, German manufacturers were scattered throughout the city, as were German-born Jewish businesspeople. Unlike them, from the 1870s poorer Jews from the Russian Empire gathered in Ellis Street, near to the Singers Hill synagogue.[7] Compared to London, Manchester, Leeds and Glasgow, the number of Jews in Birmingham was small. By contrast, according to the 1851 census the city was amongst 'the twenty largest Irish settlements in Britain'.[8] Ten years later, its Irish-born population peaked at 11,322.[9] Though large numerically, these people did not make up more than 3.8 per cent of Birmingham's 296,000 citizens.[10]

It would be a mistake to assume that all of the city's Irish were poor and unskilled. They were not. The *Birmingham Daily Post* was founded in 1857 by an Irishman, John Frederick Feeney. He became one of the leading benefactors of the city's art gallery; whilst another of his countrymen, Sir Charles Haughton Rafter, was a distinguished Chief Constable of the Birmingham Police Force.[11] Still, many Irish migrants did lack manufacturing skills.[12] They had no choice but to work in low-paid and precarious occupations such as labouring or street trading. Their poverty meant that they had to settle in the cheapest and worst housing in the most insanitary neighbourhoods. Before its decrepit tenements were cleared in the mid-century, the Inkleys was regarded as an 'Irish Quarter'; but from the 1860s this name was given to the area 'in and about Park Street'. This was part of St Bartholomew's Ward, and in 1883 its population was estimated at 26,225. Of this number, only 680 people were Irish-born and another 759 were of Irish descent. Most of them were concentrated in a number of very poor streets, Park Street amongst them.[13] Yet even here they represented a low proportion of the local residents. This makes it clear that Birmingham's 'Irish Quarter' was not comparable to the large Irish presence in places like Scotland Road, Liverpool and the Gorbals in Glasgow.

Situated to the south east of the city centre, St Bartholomew's was close to Birmingham's main central market in the Bull Ring — the focal point for street traders and musicians. It was a low-lying site in the valley of the River Rea, and was criss-crossed by the high-level viaduct of the Great Western Railway, by the line of the North-Western Railway and by the Birmingham to Warwick Canal. A large number of works and warehouses were located in the district, as were canal docks. This meant that the atmosphere locally was smoky, gloomy and comparatively sunless. Back-to-backs were the dominant form of housing. These tiny three-roomed structures were jerry-built in terraces, usually facing a courtyard. They had few facilities of their own. Water was drawn from a communal pump in the yard, lavatories were shared between two or more families, and the brew'us (washhouse) was used by all the inhabitants of a terrace.

Reports from Birmingham's Medical Officers of Health emphasized the link between back-to-back housing and illnesses.[14] One of them focused on the Floodgate Street area, into which Park Street fell. Carried out in 1904, it revealed that measles, scarlet fever, diphtheria, diarrhoea, enteritis, tuberculosis, bronchitis, pneumonia and pleurisy were 'decidedly more fatal' here than they were in Birmingham overall. Tragically, the mean death rate was '60 per cent higher than that in the City as a whole', whilst it was a massive 90 per cent greater than that for 'the more or less artisan district of All Saints Ward'. Yet even within the Floodgate Street locality there were marked differences in the statistics of life and death. The mortality rate in Fazeley Street was 21.8 per 1,000. In Park Street it was a horrendous 63.5. Over the district as a whole, one in five people died in the workhouse; in Park Street, it was twice that proportion.[15] These discrepancies can be accounted for by the preponderance of lodging houses in Park Street, as the journalist J. Cuming Walters noticed in 1901.[16] This kind of accommodation was one step away from the hated workhouse, and it was home to the poorest people. Some of them were mentally ill, physically disabled, chronically sick, friendless and forlorn. Others were able-bodied, young and single. Many of these were migrants from across Great Britain and Ireland and immigrants from Italy.

As Lucio Sponza has shown, a few 'Italian strolling artists, acrobats and street musicians had appeared in Britain since at least the beginning of the eighteenth century'. Their numbers increased noticeably in the early 1800s, when agricultural depression and famine affected much of Italy and forced many peasants off the land.[17] In 1820, *The Times* commented on the presence of Italian organ grinders in London, adding that 'the public have of late been exceedingly annoyed by the appearance of a number of Italian boys with monkeys and mice, wandering about the streets, exciting the compassion of the benevolent'.[18] By the mid-nineteenth century, most Italian street musicians were settled in the Saffron Hill part of Holborn, which was similar to the Park Street district of Birmingham. Sponza observed that it was 'one of the poorest localities in London, full of overcrowded and dilapidated common lodgings'. It had such an infamous reputation as a rookery that it was chosen by Dickens as the site of the thieves' den in *Oliver Twist*.[19] But within Holborn there were also skilled Italians who made barometers, looking glasses and picture frames. As David Green has noticed, these people 'inhabited better quality housing in the wealthier streets such as Hatton Garden and Charles Street'.[20] Most of these artisans were from Como in Lombardy, with some originating in Piedmont and Liguria. The majority of the street musicians came from the valley of the Upper Valtaro, near to Parma in the north of Italy; and from the southern province of Campania, which formerly had been in the Kingdom of the Two Sicilies.[21]

The first Italian to be mentioned in Birmingham was a man called Carlotti. At the end of the eighteenth century, he and an Englishman called George Western were involved in the manufacture of barometers and thermometers.[22] There is no further indication of Carlotti—although a century later a connection was re-established with Italian barometer makers. In 1918 the firm of Thomas Fattorini started a factory in Birmingham. Previously this family was established as watchmakers and jewellers in Skipton, North Yorkshire. Like the artisans of Holborn, the Fattorinis originated in the Como area and they had relationships with barometer makers. It is probable that they moved to Birmingham because of the importance of the city's Jewellery Quarter, where their firm remains an important manufacturer of medals, badges and insignia.[23]

There is no definite mention of Italian street musicians in Birmingham until the 1841 census. This showed their presence in two places: the very poor quarter of Lichfield Street, which was cleared in the 1870s; and Park Street, where a John Spinetto was a lodging-house keeper. He lived with his wife and two sons and he provided accommodation for thirty lodgers, twenty-three of whom were Italians. Apart from a married couple with a baby, all of them were teenaged boys. Those whose occupations were recorded were employed as street musicians or looking-glass makers.[24] These latter workers suggest the presence of northern Italians, whilst the preponderance of youths hints that Spinetto was a *padrone*. This was a man who had established himself in England and who returned to Italy regularly to find parents who would sell him the labour of their son for a specified time. In 1863 a Birmingham journalist reported that such lads gave all their earnings to their *padrone*, who gave them their board, lodging and just four shillings a month. Their tasks depended upon their age. Each young boy was given 'a little wax image of the Madonna', with which he paraded the streets and which 'he exhibits for coppers, but this depends a great deal upon his good looks'. Slightly older lads gained their money by carrying a box in which was kept a couple of white mice or guinea pigs. These were shown to other children for a halfpenny. The oldest boys walked about with hurdy-gurdies (barrel organs), whilst youths played street pianos. Their incomes were estimated at a pound a week.[25]

Many British and Italian commentators saw the *padrone* system as a form of child slavery, and they agitated for action to eradicate it. They had some success. In 1873 the Italian government passed laws against the operations of the *padroni*, and it asked for their extradition from Britain.[26] This request was refused, but four years later the British Home Secretary did issue directives to the police urging the prosecution of *padroni* for procuring children to beg.[27] Yet as Green noted, further legislation was needed to limit the operation of the system. This came with the 1889 Act for the Better Protection of Children.[28] Contemporaries felt that such actions were helpful in stopping the exploitation of children, although Sponza has argued differently.[29] He stated that 'the issue of "Italian Begging Boys" was not solved by any of the measures taken either by private individuals and institutions; or by Italian and British authorities'. In his opinion, the number of children employed as street musicians had peaked before the mid century 'and then consistently diminished until it virtually disappeared at the beginning of the twentieth century'.[30]

Sponza was too optimistic in this assertion that the *padrone* system almost died out. As late as the early 1900s, there were two well-known men in Birmingham's Italian Quarter who were bringing across a significant number of boys from Italy.[31] Despite this qualification, the general thrust of Sponza's argument was sound and it is supported by evidence from the 1881 census in Birmingham. This recorded an Antonio Cassara as operating a lodging-house at 38, Bartholomew Street, close to Park Street. This was to become the focus of Birmingham's Italian Quarter. Spinetto rented accommodation to ten Italian image makers, ranging in age from 23 to 36 years. Next door was another lodging-house kept by John Spinetto's son. With him lived his wife, Elizabeth, an ice-cream dealer; his daughter and his son, a looking-glass frame maker; and six unnamed lodgers, who were street musicians.[32] Ten years later, Spinetto had as his lodgers a Scottish looking-glass maker and his two children; two adult ice-cream vendors, one of whom had an Italian name but was born in Birmingham; three middle-aged English street musicians, one of whom was a woman; one English bricklayer; and three adult Italian image makers, two of whom were elderly.[33]

After this entry for 1891, there is no further trace of the Spinetto family in Birmingham. Apart from them, there is little evidence of Italians residing permanently in Birmingham before the end of the nineteenth century. An exception is that of the Bacciochis. In 1856 the baptismal registers of St Michael's Catholic Church recorded a Catherina Bacciochi. Her mother had the Welsh surname of Rogers.[34] Five years later, a Giovanni Bacciochi was living at 30, Bartholomew Street. He was a lodging-house keeper who was born in northern Italy, whilst his wife Elizabeth came from Swansea.[35] The 1891 census indicated that his son, John Bacciochi, was still living in Bartholomew Street. His wife was called Jane, and their five children also had English forenames. John himself was a brass caster aged 44, and he had been born in Birmingham.[36] The Bacciochis remained in this area, intermarrying with later Italian immigrants. They are still in the city, operating the firm of B. and D. Public Works.[37]

Emmanuel Divo's investigations have emphasized the distinctiveness of this family. In 1871 there were eighty-nine people in St Bartholomew's who were of 'Italian birth and origin'. Sixty-four of them were men and twenty-five were women. Most were single persons living in lodging-houses, 'and above all they were represented in the 20 to 40 years age group'. Ten years later most of these people had disappeared from Birmingham. They had been replaced by other young and single people, and more of them were women.[38] In this period, it seems that most street musicians returned to Italy, died in England, or became *padroni* themselves and moved elsewhere in Britain.[39]

### III

The measures against the *padroni* came at a time when a growing number of southern Italians had begun to emigrate. According to Colin Holmes, the catalyst for their movement was the collapse of their region's economic system following the unification of Italy 'and changes in the international economy in the late nineteenth century'.[40] Most of these emigrants went to the United States of America, but some came to Britain. In Glasgow and Edinburgh there were large numbers from the commune of Picinisco, in the province of Caserta.[41] This was part of Campania and belonged to the region of Naples.[42] It lay in the mountains above the River Liri, south of the larger town of Sora and north of Montecassino. Nearby were the communes of Atina and Gallinaro, and closer to Sora was the village of Carnello. These were the places of origin of the majority of Birmingham's settled Italians.[43]

There is little doubt that poverty and hardships caused the mass emigration from Campania and the rest of the south. Winifred Mullane's mother came from Carnello and her father from S. Vincenzo, to the north of Sora. They recalled that the land was owned by *padroni*, who employed whole families 'forming small villages'. Work on the farms and in the vineyards started 'about 4-0 a.m. until noon because of the heat'. The life of women was especially arduous. The younger ones toiled with the men, and 'many babies were born in the fields and some mothers worked right away' after the birth of their children. Older women went to church each morning and then did the washing in local streams as 'bed sheets were dried and replaced *everyday'*. After the siesta, at about four o'clock in the afternoon, all the women prepared the evening meal, 'killing 2–3 chickens running around the farm, making spaghetti and bread, cooking among fire stones'.[44] For Beattie Eastment's grandmother, bread itself symbolized the difference between Italy and England.

Granny Volante used to say about her mother-in-law about how hard she was and she used to say 'Oo, the bread, we used to have to eat black bread'. And do you know don't matter how much money she'd got she used to get a piece of bread, dry bread and eat it. And I used to say, 'Gran, what are y'doing that for?', and dip it in her tea. I used to say, 'Gran, what are y'having?' and her used to say, 'Oh', in her way of talking, used to say in broken English, 'It's marvellous bread compared to what we used to eat, black bread'.[45]

Documentary material suggests that members of a family called Delicata were important in the initial stages of the emigration of people from Atina and Gallinaro. In 1881 a Giuseppe Delicatto was recorded as a street musician living at the back of 33, Bartholomew Street.[46] His wife, Maiscatta, was aged 19, and their 15-month-old son had been born in Birmingham. They had fifteen street musicians lodging with them. These ranged in age from 17 to 58, although the majority were in their late teens and 20s. Only one of them was English and the rest were Italian. Amongst them was an Antonia Frezza, whose family remain in Birmingham. Four other lodgers had the surname of Delicato, one of whom was called Domenico.[47] In 1885 a Lucia Capocci married Gerarde Abrezese, a musician, at St Michael's Catholic Church. Their granddaughter, Lucy Ryethorpe, recalled that Lucia was from around Sora, whilst Gerarde was from Venezia in the north of Italy. Both of them made their mark on their marriage certificate, as did one of their witnesses, Veronica Bello. However, their second witness, Domenico Delicata, signed his name.[48]

A further indication of this family's presence is given in the 1891 census. This recorded a man called Delicata as the head of a lodging-house at 37, Bartholomew Street. His first name is difficult to read, but it seems to be Giuseppe. He was married and aged 41. It is likely that he is the same person as the 28-year-old Giuseppe Delicatto mentioned in the 1881 census.[49] The evidence is highly suggestive that this man was a type of *padrone*. However, it seems that his operations differed significantly from those of his predecessors who had caused such an outcry. It is likely that he was similar to the *padroni* of Holborn in the 1870s and described by Green. These were men who 'probably acted as recruiting agencies bringing over migrants from their own home area in Italy or as a point of reception for those with the same regional background as themselves'.[50]

In 1891 all of the people who lodged with Delicata were adults, and some of them were connected to him strongly by communal and kinship loyalties. He rented accommodation to twenty-two organ grinders and other street musicians, three of whom were from one family — Anne, Maria and Filamina Volante.[51] Significantly, the baptismal registers for Gallinaro indicate that the Volantes intermarried with the Delicatas in the 1850s and 1860s.[52] At 33, Bartholomew Street lived Tomas and Mary Volante. They had a 7-year-old boy who was born in Birmingham; and they gave accommodation to two lodgers, Mary and Pasqua Delicata — the latter was 30 and worked as a hawker. In the courtyard behind this address lived Antonio and Antonia Tavolier, in the house occupied in 1881 by Giuseppe Delicatto and his lodgers.[53] Antonio was born in 1863 in the commune of Atina. His birth had been registered by another Giuseppe Delicata, a farmer.[54]

One other family from around Sora also established themselves in Birmingham during the 1880s. Giuseppe and Maria Saracine lived at 109, Coleshill Street.

This was a double-fronted café with a long counter similar to those seen in old cowboy films. At the back was a large living room, big enough to seat about 50 people. There was a private sitting room and a kitchen. Outside was a big private yard with an old-fashioned brewhouse with a large coal fired boiler. This is where all the washing was done. They also had a couple of dozen chickens in the yard. Upstairs there were 7 bedrooms and an outside fire escape which led to a workshop. Giuseppe earned a living doing odd joinery and grinding jobs. Maria took in lodgers, with the help of two girls and one man servant. Opened up the cafe. Giuseppe then started up in ice cream.

Maria and Giuseppe had eloped, and 'due to the way they left Italy' they did not maintain contact with their family.[55] This meant that they were not influential in the chain migration from Caserta, unlike the Delicatas.

Interestingly, there is no memory of this family amongst the Brummies of Italian descent with whom I have had contact, although as late as 1916 the Birmingham Aliens Register gives an Anerella Delicata as a lodging-house keeper at 6, Bartholomew Street.[56] Indeed, the Tavoliers claimed that they were pre-eminent in the movement from Gallinaro and Atina, asserting that 'if it weren't for us, half of em'd still be up the mountains'. This was an exaggeration, but there is little doubt that the family's residence in Birmingham encouraged the emigration of some of their relatives. Antonia Tavolier was a Bove by birth, and by the turn of the century she had been joined by her brother Peter and other members of their family.[57] Similarly, in 1892 the family of Vincente Volante arrived in Birmingham. As his granddaughter remembered, 'our grandad went to America first 'cus his brother was there, Peter Paul. But he didn't like it. So he came here where his other brother was. Cecedio. And settled nearly next door'.[58]

These pioneering families were followed by others from their district: Pasquale and Angela Verechia; the Reccis; the Farinas; the Secondinis; and Martino Changretta, who was thought to have 'come with a Volante'.[59] In a strange land, the Delicatas, Tavoliers and Volantes provided a support system for these newcomers. Importantly, they also established Birmingham's Italian Quarter as a place which was dominated by *Nobladans*—speakers of the Neapolitan dialect. This made the place distinctive from London's 'Little Italy', with its large numbers of northern Italians.[60] As a result, Birmingham was an attractive destination to all southern Italians. Thus the emigrants from Gallinaro were joined by families from other communes in Caserta. The Bianchis came from Peschosolido, north east of Sora; the Grecos and Iafrattis both originated in Carnello; and Vincent Pontone and Enrico Facchino both stated they came from Sora itself.[61] Other southern Italian immigrants were the Polsinellis, the Taronis, now well-known scrap metal merchants in Birmingham; and Pip Mattiello, from Naples itself.[62] He came to Birmingham as a 16-year-old in 1898. His son Joe recalled visiting his father's home city.

Yes, we traced our roots, with my missus and me daughter. Really tough. And I can understand why the old man left there. Must a been poverty what drove 'em here. We was poor here, but they'd got a be better off than they was. I went in the sixties, and don't forget he left at the turn of the century, so how bad could it a been then? . . . Chap come out and he was a dead ringer for our Mick. Exactly the same, and I knew he was one of us. Straight away . . . His mom was me dad's sister. And that was the house me dad was born in, a bit of a hovel . . . From the main street, the Via Roma, up this side street we went, and it was just like walking up Cannon Street, but it was all little houses. And the people I spoke to, asking me way, they spoke in a lingo that I could understand. Like an accent. Cus the old man spoke *Noblidan*, as you'd say, Neapolitan . . .[63]

It appears that Bristol was the port of entry for some of these southern Italian immigrants, as Jackie Tamburro brought to mind. His father was from Atina, as were his wife and her brothers, the Fiondas. In the early 1900s they settled in Bristol as an extended family group, 'and they used to go around the city playing the mandolins and the organs and my one uncle had a big brown bear, used to go round with the bear and the bear used to dance on his hind legs, you know, with his paw'. If the audience was appreciative, 'the people used to drop the money in the cup and they used to keep this bear down the cellar'. From Bristol, Jackie's parents moved to Preston. This was the base from which Felipo Tamburro 'would go to different towns playing his accordion, you see. Busking as we call it. And he used to come every now and again and bring the money, you see'. During the mid-1920s, the family moved to Birmingham where Felipo's brother and mother were settled. Here he continued to busk until he opened a shop, where he repaired accordions and gave lessons in their playing.[64] Jackie carried on in this business, achieving fame in Birmingham as a first-rate accordionist. He died in 1994.

Salvatore Miele's family followed a similar pattern. He was born in Cassino in 1891, and 'was brought over to England with his family about 1897–98'. The Mieles 'first lived in Barnstaple', from where they 'went busking around Devon and Cornwall as work was unattainable'; and later they moved to Birmingham.[65] But not all of the southern Italians in Birmingham arrived as members of family groups, or came to join relatives. It seems that two men continued to operate in a manner reminiscent of the *padroni* of the early and mid-nineteenth century. One of them brought over a number of teenaged boys from his own district of Sora. Amongst them were the 15-year-olds Giovanni

Paolucci and Anthony Lombardi, whose job was 'to take out Potatoes Chestnuts Machines and the Barrel Organs'.[66] It is likely that the same *padrone* was also responsible for the emigration of Giuseppe Panacci. He was born in 1892 in S. Vincenzo, by Sora. After his mother died and his father remarried, he and some friends 'were brought to England aged about 12 years'. If Giuseppe 'didn't earn two bob a day with the barrel organ he didn't get any supper'. Unable to speak English, he was totally dependent on his *padrone*. Eventually Giuseppe and some other boys rebelled against their treatment and ran away from Birmingham. They 'got to North Wales'. Here they lived in a cave at Bangor, 'working by day at local farms'. Giuseppe later returned to Birmingham, where he married.[67]

## IV

According to Green, by the late 1860s and early 1870s the Italian community in Holborn 'had begun to take on a more permanent and settled role, characterised by an increasing proportion of both older Italians and women'.[68] This process did not become obvious amongst their fellows in Birmingham until the end of the nineteenth century and the beginning of the twentieth century. During these years the number of Italians in Birmingham rose significantly, in line with national trends.[69] In 1871, there were only fifty-six of them in the whole of St Bartholomew's Ward. Twenty years later they had increased to 102, forty-six of whom lived in Bartholomew Street itself.[70] By 1915, it was estimated that there were between 600 and 700 members of 'the Italian colony' in Birmingham, of which some may have been the English-born children of Italian parents.[71] Still, the researches of Doreen Hopwood have confirmed that by this date there were hundreds of Italians in the city. She examined a sample of 2,371 entries in the Birmingham Aliens Register for 1916. It contained 322 Italians, of whom 143 had their addresses in Bartholomew Street and Duddeston Row.[72]

This growth in numbers was associated with a changing profile. According to Divo, in 1891 the age structure of the Italians in St Bartholomew's 'resembled a pyramid of immigration (like that of 1871)'. There were more men than women; 'the preponderance of young men is clear'; and most Italians still lived in lodging-houses. However, at the base of the age pyramid there was a significant number of children under ten. This suggested an increase in Italian families.[73] As the oral evidence and other material have shown, this phenomenon became more apparent in the rest of the 1890s and in the early 1900s. Unsurprisingly, this trend was accompanied by a decline in the number of Italians living in lodging-houses and by an increase in those in family households. This is indicated by Hopwood's examination of the rate books for Birmingham. In 1901 these indicated twenty-two Italian householders in Bartholomew Street and Duddeston Row, most of whom lived in back-to-backs. Fourteen years later, their number had risen to fifty-two. By this date, the majority of their properties were larger, fronted on to the street and had higher status.[74]

The Tavoliers exemplified this type of move. In 1891 they were ice-cream vendors, living at number one, back of 33, Bartholomew Street. By the turn of the century they were renting 39, Duddeston Row. This was a confectionery shop as well as their home, as was noted in 1916 in *Kelly's Directory for Birmingham*.[75] The publication also recorded an N. Barlone as a greengrocer in the same street. In Bartholomew Street it mentioned Lewis Saracine, ice-cream vendor; Mrs Maria Facchino, shopkeeper; and Antonio Farina, lodging-house keeper.[76] Unlike these people, some other local businesses were not noted in the directory. They included the boot repairer Catullo, the Frezzas who hired out barrel organs and ice-cream carts, the Secondinis who did the same, and Pip Mattiello the tinsmith.[77] Nearby in Banbury Street, Clement Alberici had a small factory, where he 'made barrel organs for the Italians and also retuned them and remarked them'; whilst Frank Iommi made ice cream and sold it from his house in Buck Street.[78] Outside the Italian Quarter, there was also the well-known knife-grinding firm of Maturis, which still trades in Birmingham. This family came from Venezia in the north of Italy and its members tended to keep themselves apart from the *Nobladans*.[79]

From Hopwood's sample of the Aliens Register in 1916, twenty-seven Italians were self-employed. Another fifty-six were housewives; eleven had no specified occupation; and forty-eight were employed in a variety of occupations. The latter group included labourers, factory workers and those engaged in mosaic work. Of the self-employed, only four were street musicians.[80] This was a major difference to the situation in 1861.

In that year in Bartholomew Street, there were fifty-four Italians who earned their livings in this way. This compared to three who were lodging-house keepers, one who was a shoemaker and another who was a piano tuner.[81] As late as 1891 there were twenty-five Italian street musicians in Bartholomew Street. This occupation remained the most popular for Italian immigrants; nine others were ice-cream vendors; four were hawkers; three were image vendors; two were lodging-house keepers; and one was a labourer.[82]

By 1919, Birmingham's Italian community was concentrated in two streets. Its members were settled in family groups. Most of them came from a defined part of southern Italy. A sizeable proportion of them were self-employed, and the rest were engaged in various occupations. No longer were they transient or bound to street trades. Though small in numbers, these Italians made a significant contribution to the social and economic life of Birmingham and its people. Still, they were distinguished by their names, by their looks, by their language, by their Catholicism, by their dominance of the ice-cream trade, and by their concentration in one part of the city. Once their settlement was established, historical research needs to address these issues. Did their ethnicity separate the Italians from their English and Irish neighbours; or were they all brought together by neighbourhood and class loyalties?

## NOTES

A number of people have helped me greatly in my research for this article, and I thank them for their support, interest and generous sharing of knowledge. They are Peter Leather of the *Metronews*, who publicized my appeal for information about Birmingham's Italians; Doreen Hopwood, Genealogist, Birmingham Library Services; Richard Albutt, Community History Development Officer, Birmingham Library Services; Micky Volante, who has led me to many contacts with Brummies of Italian descent; Carol Eggington, another of the Volantes; and all the Brummies of Italian descent who have shared their memories with me. Most of all I acknowledge the assistance and influence of Dorothy Thompson, whose urgings led me to become a historian.

1 Anthony Sutcliffe, *History of Birmingham, Volume III: Birmingham 1939–1970* (London, 1974), pp. 202–3.

2   W.H.B. Court, *The Rise of the Midland Industries 1600–1838* (London, 1938), pp. 45–50.
3   Carl Chinn, *Birmingham: The Great Working City* (Birmingham, 1994), pp. 90–4.
4   Carl Chinn, *Poverty Amidst Prosperity: The Urban Poor in England, 1834–1914* (Manchester, 1995), pp. 130–1.
5   Chinn, *Birmingham*, pp. 87–9.
6   Ibid., pp. 89–90.
7   Moritz Stern, 'Wisdom and folly' (unpublished manuscript, 1920), thanks to Lily Gompertz; Chinn, *Birmingham*, pp. 85–6.
8   Roger Swift, *The Irish in Britain 1815–1914: Perspectives and Sources* (London, 1990), p. 13.
9   Emmanuel Divo, 'Irlandais et Italiens dans le quartier de Saint Bartholomew à Birmingham à la fin du XIX$^e$ siècle' (unpublished Mémoire de Mâitrise d'Histoire, Université de Franche-Comté, 1993), p. 29.
10  W. B. Stephens (ed.), *A History of the County of Warwick, Vol VII: The City of Birmingham* (London, 1964), p. 14; see also Marie B. Rowlands, *The West Midlands from AD1000* (London, 1987), pp. 256–7.
11  Chinn, *Birmingham*, pp. 81–3.
12  Robert Rawlinson, *Report into the Sanitary Condition of the Borough of Birmingham* (1848) in John Thackray Bunce, *History of the Corporation of Birmingham: With a Sketch of the Earlier Government of the Town* (2 vols, Birmingham, 1878), Vol. I, p. 324; David R. Green and Alan G. Parton, 'Slums and slum life in Victorian England: London and Birmingham at mid-century', in S. Martin Gaskell, (ed.), *Slums* (Leicester, 1990), pp. 51–2; John Thackray Bunce, *History of the Corporation of Birmingham: With as Sketch of the Earlier Government of the Town* (2 vols, Birmingham, 1885), Vol. II, p. 292, and Kaja Ziesler, 'The Irish in Birmingham 1830–1970' (unpublished Ph.D., thesis, University of Birmingham, 1989), p. 28.
13  Bunce, *History*, Vol. II, p. 503; Divo, 'Irlandais et Italiens', pp. 36, 53–4.
14  See Carl Chinn, *Homes for People: 100 Years of Council Housing in Birmingham* (Birmingham, 1991), pp. 8, 12, 15, 19–21.
15  Medical Officer of Health of Birmingham, 'The Floodgate Street area', in *Annual Report* (Birmingham, 1904), pp. 7–9.
16  J. Cuming Walters, *Further Scenes in Slumland: Pen Pictures of the Black Spots in Birmingham*, articles reprinted from the *Birmingham Daily Gazette*, 'No. 9. The case for an official inquiry' and 'No. 10. The city of the dreadful night' (Birmingham, 1901); see also, Chinn, *Poverty*, pp. 79–81.

17    Lucio Sponza, *Italian Immigrants in Nineteenth-Century Britain: Realities and Images* (Leicester, 1988), pp. 23–9.

18    *The Times*, 20 Mar. 1820, cited in Sponza, *Italian Immigrants*, p. 24.

19    Ibid., pp. 21–2.

20    David Green, 'Little Italy in Victorian London: Holborn's Italian community', *Camden History Review*, **15** (1988), 3.

21    Ibid., 4–5; Sponza, *Italian Immigrants*, pp. 31–6.

22    'Optical and mathematical instruments', in Samuel Timmins (ed.), *Birmingham and the Midland Hardware District* (first published 1866, London, 1967 edn), p. 524.

23    Information supplied by Thomas Fattorini Junior, Thomas Fattorini Ltd., Regent Street, Birmingham.

24    Census Enumerators Books (CEB), St Bartholomew's Ward, Birmingham 1841; see also *Local Reports on the Sanitary Condition of the Labouring Population of Great Britain* (Parliamentary Papers, 1842, XXVII), pp. 197–8.

25    'The nightside of Birmingham — No. 5. Organ boys and their owners', *Birmingham Sketches*, 3 Dec. 1863, thanks to Doreen Hopwood.

26    Sponza, *Italian Immigrants*, pp. 149–53.

27    'Italian beggar children in Birmingham', *Aris's Birmingham Gazette*, 13 Sept. 1877, thanks to Doreen Hopwood.

28    Green, 'Little Italy', 5.

29    'Italian Beggar Children'.

30    Sponza, *Italian Immigrants*, p. 159. Both he and Green believe that the issue of Italian child labour was exaggerated.

31    See pp. 261–2

32    CEB, St Bartholomew's Ward, Birmingham, 1881.

33    Ibid., 1891.

34    St Michael's Catholic Church, Moor Street, Birmingham, 'Baptismal Registers', 21 July 1856, thanks to Carol Eggington.

35    CEB, St Bartholomew's Ward, Birmingham, 1861.

36    Ibid., 1891.

37    Chinn, *Birmingham*, p. 79.

38    Divo, 'Irlandais et Italiens', pp. 63–4.

39    'The nightside'.

40    Colin Holmes, *John Bull's Island Immigration and British Society, 1871–1971* (Basingstoke, 1988), p. 30.

41    Sponza, *Italian Immigrants*, p. 33. As Sponza notes, a commune was the smallest unit of local government in Italy, consisting 'of either a big city, or a small town, with its surrounding territory', p. 276, n. 3.

42  In 1926, this area was transferred from Campania to the province of Frosinone. This was in Latium and came under Rome's region: Sponza, *Italian Immigrants*, p. 276, n. 2.

43  Italians from Caserta also settled in Ancoats, Manchester: see Anthony Rea, *Manchester's Little Italy* (Manchester, 1988), pp. 7–8.

44  Carl Chinn Letters, Winifred Mullane, 1994, p. 3.

45  Carl Chinn Interviews, Beattie Eastment (daughter of Ernest Volante), Les and Micky Volante, and Albert Alberici, 1992, p. 6.

46  One of the greatest difficulties in tracing Italian families in Birmingham is caused by the mis-spelling of their names by English people. For example, the Grecos had their name changed to Grego when their arrival was registered in England in 1896: Interviews; Pat Houghton (Grego), 1992, pp. 6, 8–9. Similarly the surname of Martino Changretta can be spelt as Cianretta: Charles Alberici, 'A book of sorts' (unpublished MS, c.1980), p. 8, thanks to Madeline Dickson, daughter of Charles; and Letters, Pam Overthrow (Martino's great-granddaughter), 1994. Given the difficulties associated with the spelling of Italian names in England, I am confident that Giuseppe Delicatta and the Delicatos who lodged with him were all part of the Delicata family who came from Gallinaro. Indeed their name is given as Delicato in the baptismal registers for this commune, whilst it is written as Delicata on other official documents; see n. 51 and n. 53.

47  CEB, St Bartholomew's Ward, Birmingham, 1881; Letters, Mr R. Phillips, 1992.

48  Interviews, Lucy Ryecroft, Tommy and Leslie Green and Madeline Mitchell, 1994; St Michael's Catholic Church, Moor Street, Certificate of Marriage, Gerarde Abrezese and Lucia Capocci, 2 June 1885. The baptismal registers for the commune of the Gallinaro, Provincia di Terra di Lavora, Province di Caserta indicate that members of the Capocci family lived in Gallinaro.

49  CEB, St Bartholomew's Ward, Birmingham, 1891.

50  Green, 'Little Italy', 6.

51  CEB, St Bartholomew's Ward, Birmingham, 1891.

52  Baptismal registers for the commune of Gallinaro, Provincia di Terra di Lavora, Province di Caserta, 22 Dec. 1858, baptism of Luigi Volante son of Giuseppe Volante and Palma Delicato; thanks to Beattie Eastment.

53  CEB, St Bartholomew's Ward, Birmingham, 1891.

54  Uficio Dello Stato Civile, Estrato dal Registro, Atti di Nascita, Antonio Tavolier, 1863, Num. 106; thanks to Johnny Sartori and Maria Giansante, the grandchildren of Antonio Tavolier.

55  Letters, Lyn di Mascio-Walton, One and Two, 1992.

56 Birmingham Aliens Register, 1916, Police Museum (PM), Sparkhill Police Station, Birmingham.

57 Interviews, Johnny Sartori and Maria Giansante, 1992, pp. 3 and 5; Eileen Kenny (daughter of Ernestro Bove), 1994, pp. 1 and 7; and Sante and Maria Reggio (daughter of Johnny Bove), p. 1.

58 Interviews, Beattie Eastment, Micky and Les Volante, and Albert Alberici, 1992, pp. 1–2; see also Letters, Mrs P. Alberici, 1992.

59 Letters, Ronald Watt (whose wife's mother, Beatrice, was the daughter of Pasquale and Angela), 1992; Interviews, Peter Recci, 1992, p. 1; Letters, Mrs P. Arnold (daughter of Marcus Farina), One and Two, 1992, and Three 1994; Interviews, Edward Secondini, 1992, p. 1; and Beattie Eastment, Micky and Les Volante, and Albert Alberici (grandson of Martino Changretta), 1992, p. 2. In the baptismal registers for Gallinaro the Verechias are mentioned regularly, as are the Riccis (Reccis), Farinis (Farinas) and Secondinos (Secondinis).

60 Sponza, *Italian Immigrants*, pp. 32–51.

61 Interviews, Beattie Eastment, Micky and Les Volante, and Albert Alberici (grandson of Martino Changretta), 1992, p. 5; Interviews, Pat Houghton, 1992 pp. 5–6, 8–9, and the British Passport of her father, Francesco Grego; Letters, Winifred Mullane, 1994, p. 1, whose mother was Emelia Iafrati; and PM, Aliens Register. These two men may not have come from Sora itself. As this was the largest town in the district, many immigrants named it as their place of origin even if they came from a nearby commune.

62 Letters, Peter Peters (formerly Polsinelli), 1992; and Chinn, *Birmingham*, p. 123.

63 Discussion on the people of Birmingham, Anderson Country, BBC Radio 4, 24 June 1994; for more on the dialect of the Nobladans, see Interviews, Jackie Tamburro, 1992, p. 3. After the Second World War, Sante Mizzoni left Sora to work in Birmingham. He had no family here, and unlike the earlier immigrants he does not regard himself as a *Nobladan*, but as belonging to Rome: Interviews, Sante Mizzoni, 1992, p. 2. This change in loyalties can be accounted for by the transfer of the Liri Valley to Frosinone in Latium, n. 42.

64 Interviews, Jackie Tamburro, 1992, pp. 1–2, 4.

65 Letters, Mrs V. Miele, One and Two, 1992. It is possible that the Mieles are the part of the Mele family indicated in the baptismal registers for Gallinaro.

66 Letters, Mrs Hughes (daughter of Giovanni Paolucci), 1992; and Mrs J.N. Evans (daughter of Anthony Lombardi), 1992. I have not named the *padrone* as his family still live in Birmingham. The other *padrone* had a lodging-house in the Italian Quarter and also sent boys out with barrel organs.

67  Letters, Winifred Mullane, 1994, pp. 1, 4.
68  Green, 'Little Italy', 6.
69  Holmes, *John Bull's Island*, p. 30; Sponza, *Italian Immigrants*, p. 57.
70  Divo, 'Irlandais et Italiens', pp. 36, 50. Part of the enumerator's returns for Bartholomew Street are missing for 1871. This may mean that the Italian population in St Bartholomew's is underestimated. CEB, St Bartholomew's Ward, Birmingham, 1891. In this year the size of the Italian community in St Bartholomew's could be increased to 144 with the inclusion of the English-born children of Italian parents.
71  *Birmingham Daily Mail*, 2 June 1915.
72  PM, Aliens Register.
73  Divo, 'Irlandais et Italiens', pp. 63–5. His figures include children born of Italian parents.
74  Birmingham Rate Books, Bartholomew Street and Duddeston Row, 1901 and 1915.
75  CEB, St Bartholomew's Ward, 1881 and *Kelly's Directory of Birmingham* (Kingston-upon-Thames, 1916), p. 128; see also Interviews, Johnny Sartori and Maria Giansante, 1992, pp. 1–2.
76  *Kelly's*, pp. 57, 128, For Saracine's see Letters, Lyn di Mascio-Walton, One and Two, 1992; and for Farina's lodging-house see Letters, Mrs P. Arnold, One and Two, 1992 and Three, 1994.
77  Alberici, *Book of Sorts*, pp. 4–5.
78  Letters, Clement Alberici, 1992; and Interviews, Beattie Eastment, Micky and Les Volante, and Albert Alberici, 1992, p. 1; and Letters, Jean Thompson, 1992.
79  Chinn, *Birmingham*, p. 79.
80  PM, Aliens Register.
81  CEB, St Bartholomew's Ward, Birmingham, 1861.
82  CEB, St Bartholomew's Ward, 1891.

# Dorothy Thompson: A Select Bibliography

1   (As Dorothy Towers) 'The Chartist poets', *Our Time* (April 1948).
2   'Chartism in industrial areas', *Amateur Historian*, **III** (1956).
3   'Letters from Ernest Jones to Karl Marx, 1865–1868', *Bulletin of the Society for the Study of Labour History*, **4** (Spring 1962).
4   'La Presse de la classe ouvrière anglaise, 1836–1848', in Jacques Godechot (ed.), *La Presse ouvrière 1819–1850* (Paris, 1966).
5   'Notes on aspects of Chartist leadership', *Bulletin of the Society for the Study of Labour History*, **15** (Autumn 1967).
6   *The British People, 1760–1902* (London, Heinemann, 1969). (School textbook.)
7   'Chartism as a historical subject', *Bulletin of the Society for the Study of Labour History*, **20** (Spring 1970).
8   *The Early Chartists* (London, Macmillan and University of South Carolina Press, 1971). (Collection of documents with introduction.)
9   'Chartism, success or failure?', in David Rubinstein (ed.), *People for the People* (London, Ithaca Press and New York, Humanities Press, 1973).
10  'Women and nineteenth-century radical politics: a lost dimension', in Juliet Mitchell and Ann Oakley (eds), *The Rights and Wrongs of Women* (Harmondsworth, Penguin Books, 1976).
11  (With J.F.C. Harrison), *Bibliography of the Chartist Movement, 1837–1976* (Sussex, Harvester Press and New Jersey, Humanities Press, 1978).
12  *Il Cartismo, 1838–1858* (collection of documents with introduction) (Milan, La Pietra,1978).
13  (Edited with James Epstein), *The Chartist Experience: Studies in Working-Class Radicalism and Culture, 1830–1860*, including her essay 'Ireland and the Irish in English radicalism before 1850' (London, Macmillan, 1982).
14  (Edited) *Over Our Dead Bodies: Women Against the Bomb*, to which she contributed two chapters: 'Defend us against our defenders:

democracy and security' and 'Building on the positives: the U.S.A.' (London, Virago Press, 1983).

15 *The Chartists* (London, Maurice Temple Smith and New York, Pantheon Books, 1984; Japanese edn, 1988).

16 (Edited) *Chartism: Working Class Politics in the Industrial Revolution* (New York, Garland, 1986). A twenty-two-volume facsimile series reproducing Chartist journals, pamphlets, autobiographies and other contemporary documents of the Chartist movement.

17 'The languages of class', *Bulletin of the Society for the Study of Labour History*, **52**, 1 (1987). (Essay reviewing Gareth Stedman Jones' *Languages of Class*, Cambridge, 1983.)

18 *British Women in the Nineteenth Century* (London, The Historical Association, 1989). (Pamphlet.)

19 *Queen Victoria, Gender and Power* (London, Virago Press, 1990).

20 'Gender, work and the family', *Labour History Review*, **56**, 3 (1991). (Paper given at the Spring 1991 Conference of the Society for the Study of Labour History.)

21 'Il Movimento Cartista', in Marco Guidi and Nadia Torcellan (eds), *Europa 1700–1992: Il trionfo della borghesia*, Vol. 3 (Milan, Electa, 1992).

22 *Outsiders: Class, Gender and Nation* (London and New York, Verso, 1993). A collection of essays, including introduction to item 8, item 10, her essay from item 13, and three new essays: 'Chartism and the historians'; 'Seceding from the seceders: the decline of the Jacobin tradition in Ireland, 1790–1850'; and 'Queen Victoria, the monarchy and gender'. There is also an autobiographical introduction.

23 'The personal and the political', interview with Sheila Rowbotham, *New Left Review*, **200** (July–August 1993).

24 'Queen Victoria: the monarchy and gender', Institute for Advanced Research in Humanities, University of Birmingham, 1994. A reprint of the essay in item 22.

25 Introduction to Owen Ashton, Robert Fyson and Stephen Roberts (eds), *The Chartist Movement: A New Annotated Bibliography* (London, Mansell, 1995).

26 'Who were the "people" in 1842?', in Malcolm Chase and Ian Dyck (eds), *Living and Learning: Essays in Honour of J.F.C. Harrison* (Aldershot, Scolar Press, 1995).

# Index